Social work with adults

Social work with adults

Edited by Georgina Koubel

McGraw Hill Education Open University Press

Open University Press
McGraw-Hill Education
McGraw-Hill House
Shoppenhangers Road
Maidenhead
Berkshire
England
SL6 2QL

email: enquiries@openup.co.uk
world wide web: www.openup.co.uk

and Two Penn Plaza, New York, NY 10121-2289, USA

First published 2013

A catalogue record of this book is available from the British Library

ISBN-13: 978-0-335-24542-0
ISBN-10: 0-335-24542-0
eISBN: 978-0-335-24543-7

Library of Congress Cataloging-in-Publication Data
CIP data applied for

Typeset by Aptara Inc.

Praise for this book

Contents

Contributors

Ian Devereux was a Director and Partner in two successful businesses. One week after marrying his second wife, Denise, Ian contracted a virus which resulted in Denise having to drive him to A&E. Twenty-four hours later he was in a coma, resulting in his becoming paralysed from the neck down and spending most of 2007 in hospital trying to recover. Three years later, Ian still needs the support of PAs to get out and about and carers to help with his personal care, and he uses Direct Payments to manage his own support. Having become extremely frustrated while in hospital, following his discharge he jumped at the opportunity to join the TREND project as a co-sessional trainer. Using Direct Payments has meant Denise is Ian's wife, not his carer, and they have even been able to organize family holidays together with the support Ian needs.

Felicity Elvidge, RGN, BA (Hons) Social Work Studies, KAPT, Advanced Certificate SW&CM, Post Graduate Diploma Interprofessional Health and Social Care, practised as a Registered Nurse in a variety of settings before going into care management. She was one of the first appointments in the country to the dedicated post of Adult Protection Coordinator (now Safeguarding Co-ordinator) over 12 years ago. Felicity is a contributor to the *Journal of Adult Protection* and the *Kent Journal of Practice Research* with a particular interest in the prevention of institutional abuse arising as a consequence of poor quality accommodation-based care provision.

Donna Francis has been a service user for two and half years. She employs her own Personal Assistant. Donna has a form of dwarfism that means that she needs extra support to live independently. Donna is now a self-employed co-trainer for her local council, giving social services staff a perspective of what it is like to be a disabled person and receive services. Having been to university, had a paper published and been travelling, Donna does not let her dwarfism stop her living a full life. Donna also works for a small charity promoting independent living for disabled people.

Keith French is a social work practitioner who works as a care manager with people with sensory disabilities. Keith is himself profoundly deaf. He is currently studying for the post-qualifying award in specialist social work at Canterbury Christ Church University. Keith has a wealth of knowledge and experience of the Deaf community and Deaf culture and is most interested in seeking the rights of and redress for this oppressed linguistic cultural minority group. He has a deep interest in the psychological perspectives of D/deaf people and of their social welfare and in whether society has been or is enabling or disabling them.

Yolaine Jacquelin, MA Women's Studies, is a Training Consultant within a local authority Learning and Development team. She leads on adult services care management training and is interested in making user participation a meaningful reality. Her professional background includes over 15 years working in service provision for adults with a learning disability.

Georgina Koubel, CQSW and MSc Interprofessional Health & Community Studies, currently working as a senior lecturer in social work at Canterbury Christ Church University (CCCU), qualified as a social worker in the mid-1970s and spent many years as a generic statutory social worker in London. Moving to Kent Social Services in 1993 she developed a specialist interest in adult services, first as a care manager and then as a training consultant and training manager. An appointment to the social work team at CCCU followed in 2003, which involves teaching on social work and interprofessional learning programmes. This post has enabled the development of particular interests in the areas of rights and risks, adult safeguarding, disability discourses, reflective practice and person-centred approaches to working with vulnerable adults. Publications include two books co-edited with Hilary Bungay, *The Challenge of Person-Centred Care: Interprofessional Perspectives* (Palgrave Macmillan 2009) and *Rights, Risks and Responsibilities: Interprofessional Working in Health and Social Care* (Palgrave Macmillan 2012).

Edith Lewis is a Senior Lecturer in Social Work at Canterbury Christ Church University who was born and brought up in Zimbabwe. She completed an MSc in Social Policy and Planning at the London School of Economics in the late 1990s and has 16 years' experience of working in health and social services in different roles. Her areas of interest and expertise include issues of identity, equality and diversity, globalization, improving access to services for people with learning disabilities, social policy issues related to social work practice and managing change in human services.

Charley Melville-Wiseman is a Senior Social Work Practitioner in an integrated Health and Social Care Community Mental Health Team. She has worked in mental health services for over ten years and has a particular interest in the holistic mental health needs of women. She also works as an Approved Mental Health Professional and was awarded an Outstanding Professional Practice Award by Kent Police for a piece of work in this role. She has experience of teaching in both the UK and Finland and hopes to pursue her research interests into the relational needs of women with acute mental health difficulties in the future.

Julie Potten is a Care Manager in an Integrated Health and Social Care Community Learning Disability Team. She has extensive experience and expertise in working as a practitioner in both health and social care services and in January 2011 completed the BSc in Health and Social Care.

Marilyn Russell is a senior social work practitioner based in a hospice where she works with people facing life-threatening conditions, and their networks and families. Marilyn has previously worked extensively with domestic abuse and is particularly interested in all areas of safeguarding, and also in working with couples where a partner is coping with a life-threatening condition or receiving end-of-life care. While working at the hospice she has qualified as a couples counsellor with Relate. She is in the process of undertaking studies on the post-qualifying social work programme at Canterbury Christ Church University.

Louise Watch, BSc, MA Disability Studies, has 15 years of experience working with local authorities and organizations of disabled people. Her work has focused on establishing and managing Direct Payment support services and in the provision of training around self-directed support, independent living, rights and citizenship.

Through her company, Louise has also provided disability equality training, consultancy and independent living support for individual disabled people and those working within social care. Louise utilizes personal assistance and is actively involved in campaigns that seek to improve the quality of day-to-day life for disabled people.

Mark Wiles is a social worker who has been working as a case manager within an adult coordination team for the past five years. Many of the people who use services are older adults who come to the service as a result of the effects of long-term health conditions, including many living with dementia. He has developed a particular interest in this area of work, and has recently completed his studies for the post-qualifying award in specialist social work at Canterbury Christ Church University.

Introduction

Georgina Koubel

Social work with adults could cover a vast range of people who need to use social work services at some stages in their lives. It is not possible for one book to do justice to the complexities of work with everyone who may need to make use of such services. As the majority of people who work with adults in Social Services Departments are most likely to engage with older people or people with physical disabilities or learning disabilities, these are the main areas on which the book concentrates. Not all practitioners who carry out social work with adults are qualified social workers. Some may have developed their interest and expertise through other personal or professional pathways. Nevertheless, throughout this book the application of social work knowledge, skills and values will be highlighted.

> Social services for adults are right at the heart of the welfare state. They carry out essential tasks working with a wide range of people – home care services, day centres, residential care schemes, rehabilitation of blind or partially-sighted people, provision of equipment to aid independent living, help to parents with disabilities to carry out their parenting tasks, support for families who have caring responsibilities, work with people with mental health problems and support to learning disabled people and their families.
>
> (DH 1998: Chapter 1)

The history of social work with adults can sound like an unremitting tale of woe. Adults who use services including social work services can be reasonably considered as individuals or groups who have been, at various times, ignored, pitied, abused, institutionalized, exploited, patronized or marginalized by services and society.

This book certainly does not ignore or reject the many limitations and hardships people have had to face because of the attitudes and actions of others. However, in addition to rigorous analysis of the disadvantages and deprivations experienced by many adults who use services, what the reader will also find in this book are examples of challenges met, opportunities embraced, lives enhanced rather than restricted, and consideration of the role and significance of social workers and various other social care practitioners in promoting positive and person-centred practice.

However, social work practice does not take place in a vacuum. Legislation, social policy, political ideologies and global movements of peoples all interact to form a network within which social work with adults can operate and the social and political contexts that frame social work permeate and underpin the personal and professional accounts in this book. There are some fields where social work perspectives occupy a particular place within, for example, more medicalized or specialized areas of practice such as hospice services, multidisciplinary mental health teams and social work with people with sensory impairments and these will also be addressed. Although the book will focus mainly on statutory services, these areas of practice will also be covered.

Contributors to this book have been carefully chosen because of the personal or professional experience or perspective that each can offer to enhance our understanding of what is meant by social work with adults. This is an academic textbook with reference to a raft of books and papers which students, practitioners and hopefully some people who have used services, i.e. those who have become 'experts by experience', will find interesting, enlightening and possibly challenging. One of the challenges that will be explored within this book, and indeed in the context of the future of social work with adults, is the validity and power of the personal within the professional sphere. A particular focus within the concept of this book is to capture the voices of practitioners and service users as well as academics. To assume that academics are somehow uniquely removed from the impact of personal experience would be as erroneous as to assume that the personal testimonies of service users have no wider significance than their own lives.

To develop a hierarchy of validity without carefully assessing the diverse perspectives offered in this book would be premature. The idea of professionals learning from the accounts offered by people who use services is not new but it is still emerging. Notions of partnership and power-sharing do challenge traditional notions of who is the helper and who is the person being helped (Shakespeare 2000). However, I believe that the establishment of common aims and causes, as discussed in several of the chapters in this book, could be an important aspect of the future for social work with adults, and that working together in a variety of ways can embrace the common humanity that connects all those whose lives interconnect through the medium of social work and social care.

The first part of the book, *The Context of Social Work with Adults*, will introduce readers to a range of underpinning and fundamental features that frame social work with adults. These will include the evolution and development of social work from its historical twin bases in casework/charity and social justice until it was established as a profession in the 1970s.

In Part II of the book, which highlights the challenges and complexities involved in *Working with Different Service User Groups in Adult Services*, individual chapters will concentrate on working with particular individuals and groups who comprise many of the service users that practitioners within social work with adults are likely to encounter. These include people with physical disabilities, people with learning disabilities, older people and people with dementia, people facing life-threatening illnesses and people with sensory disabilities. Mental health is a key consideration within social work with adults, and although it is not explicitly the remit of this book, a number of chapters also recognize the challenges that face practitioners working with adults who additionally experience mental health issues. Other areas such as interprofessional working, the changing role of service users and carers, culturally aware practice, modernization and personalization will be discussed throughout the book; some will form the focus for a particular chapter.

This is not specifically a book about social work theory, although social work knowledge, skills and values provide a basic underpinning for every element of the book. Each chapter contains a number of different theories as well as the legislation and policies that inform and frame social work practice with adults. However, rather than address each of these as separate issues, the following chapters aim to show what practitioners actually do, i.e. how within practice they apply and integrate social work knowledge, skills and values. At the end of this Introduction there are some suggestions for books to read if you want to explore these aspects further.

The first two chapters are written by Georgina Koubel who has been in social work almost since the inception of statutory Social Services Departments, which were set up in 1970. The intention of these first two chapters is to set the framework for thinking critically about the changing role of social work and social care with adults. Looking back at the treatment of, for example, disabled people and people with mental health difficulties over the centuries provides an opportunity to understand how notions of poverty, disability, risk, choice, vulnerability, dangerousness and dependence are constructed within the context of the social strategies and beliefs of the times. Once it has been accepted that elements (such as our views about people with disabilities) within society are constructed by the views and ideologies prevalent at the time rather than that they have always been the same and are natural and inherent, the stage is set for a critical interrogation of what in each age may have been 'taken for granted'.

The second chapter will examine the modernization of social work with adults from the end of the 1970s to the present day and the implications for social work practice. These chapters will establish the framework within which readers can enhance their understanding of the changing and contextual nature of social work with adults, evaluate their own values and attitudes, and develop a critically analytical perspective of their own experience of practice.

The next two chapters take the current context of social work and social care and look at two essential aspects of the work: safeguarding and user involvement. In Chapter 3 Felicity Elvidge, a very experienced Safeguarding Coordinator, provides an introduction and overview of the challenges and complexities involved in safeguarding vulnerable adults. Exploring the history and development of adult protection and safeguarding, the chapter explores the importance of person-centred safeguarding as a core value of good practice in the multi-agency context and not solely as a procedural response to abuse. This will be linked to relevant theoretical models of practice within social work and social care. Issues of risks, choice, capacity and vulnerability will inform the analysis and case scenarios will include consideration of the relationship between adult safeguarding and domestic violence.

Chapter 4 offers a very different perspective, and hopefully one that will engage and invite readers who think they understand the delicacies of involving service users in consultation and partnership to review and reflect upon any prior assumptions about the complexities and challenges involved. This chapter examines the process of partnership working through exploring the co-provision of training. It asks questions about whether authentic partnership between trainers and service users can really be possible, and highlights the need to analyse how such collaborations can be used to enhance practitioners' awareness of the need to look beyond the label and see – really see – the person behind the reductive and marginalizing categories reserved for people in society who need different levels of support. The main author for this chapter is Yolaine Jacquelin who has been involved in social care and training in Adult Services for many years. She has worked closely with Donna Francis and Ian Devereux as co-trainers on the TREND programme, and their comments and stories are very much part of the chapter to ensure their views as service users and as participants in delivering training are clearly heard.

Most communities and work places are now multi-ethnic and multicultural and this requires practitioners to be sensitive and be knowledgeable about how other people may think and act. It is also crucial to realize the role migration takes in constructing situations and the patterns of ethnic relations and how attitudes to those considered different are formed. It therefore becomes a prerequisite in social work practice to respond appropriately and meet the needs of those accessing social services regardless of their background. In Chapter 5, Edith Lewis, who was born and brought up in Africa, explores the need for practitioners in social work and social care who are self-aware, knowledgeable about other cultures' perspectives and who have the relevant skills required to respond effectively to the challenge of globalization as it affects social work with adults. She critically examines issues of difference/sameness; the nature of identity and the concept of Britishness as articulated by politicians and by those who may (or may not) see themselves as different from mainstream society. The chapter explores the growing need for well-qualified and competent social work professionals who are able to respond sensitively to an increasing level of intercultural interactions. Social workers need empathy and interpersonal skills as well as cultural awareness and knowledge of what it means to be or feel 'different' and to understand the importance of individual identity for those who have settled or are settling in British society today by continuously challenging their own personal beliefs, values, assumptions, stereotypes and prejudices (Laird 2008).

Having set the scene and looked in some depth at the historical and political context of social work, the second part of the book addresses the challenges and complexities of the integration (and sometimes dissonance) between contemporary policy and practice. Each of these chapters is written by an expert in the field, a practitioner (who may also have experience as a user of services) who contributes the benefits of his or her many years of personal and practice wisdom. Practice examples (all fully anonymized) are considered in the context of relevant research, theory and policy drivers, and reflective exercises encourage readers to think more deeply and critically about their own values and beliefs about social work with adults.

The first author in this second part of the book is Louise Watch, who herself requires support from services. In Chapter 6, her voice resonates with the determination and conviction of someone who has overcome many obstacles placed in her path as a person with disabilities. Her personal story is compelling particularly as it highlights the difference the views and values of professionals can make in enhancing (or limiting) opportunities, and the importance for her of interprofessional collaboration between health and social work/social care. However, the chapter offers more than an individual perspective, looking at the context of the development of social work with people with physical disabilities, starting with the exploration of different definitions and models of disability, and exploring the meaning and significance of relevant terms. The chapter highlights the importance of a rights-based approach to working with people with disabilities, alongside the challenges for promoting independence, choice and control in social work with adults.

Chapter 6 also looks at the development from a social model perspective with the ultimate goal of independent living to approaches which afford fresh ideas and solutions based on interdependency and mutual cooperation. Personalization will be explored in terms of wants, hopes, aspirations, solutions and fears, with examples and personal narrative. By examining these fundamental features of working with people with disabilities, the chapter aims to enable those who work within social work and social care to understand the complexity – and the possibilities and benefits – of working effectively alongside people with physical impairments.

Rights, choice, inclusion and control have been key words in the learning disability agenda from the days of Wolfensburger's Normalization theory and O'Brien's five accomplishments right through to current day with *Valuing People Now* (DH 2009). Often highlighting aspects of her work with individuals experiencing transitions and changes in their circumstances, in Chapter 7 Julie Potten, a practitioner in Adult Services with nursing qualifications and a very strong commitment to social work skills and values, examines how practitioners continue to face the ongoing challenge of how to ensure the recognition of rights, choice and control becomes a reality for the adults with whom they work. Practitioners are required and inspired to promote independence and opportunities for people with learning disabilities while also balancing issues of capacity, professional duties to safeguard along with public and organizational expectation of the management of risk and the pressure of finite resources and complex social situations.

Chapter 7 additionally explores some of the tensions in working with adults, looking at how the use of individual budgets, while providing genuine opportunities for many people with learning disabilities who use services, may also provide challenges in working with individuals with more complex needs due to severe and profound disabilities. The chapter considers the relevance of the Mental Capacity Act (2005) and analyses issues for those who lack capacity or where the practitioner has to negotiate with social and family situations to ensure service users have equality in their access to choice and control. This chapter offers further analysis of the use of the multidisciplinary approach as a way to provide a seamless, effective and accessible service for people with learning disabilities and their networks.

Chapter 8 looks at the situation of a group of people who are sometimes overlooked in terms of their relevance to the picture of social work with adults. Keith French, a social work practitioner who works with people with sensory disabilities, looks at the issues of those with sensory impairments from the point of view of a social worker who is himself deaf and who therefore has a dual perspective when working with people who experience difficulties with hearing or vision, or both. This chapter investigates some of the issues relating to specialist roles in adult social work within the current context of practice and raises awareness of the dilemmas and conflicts that inform the process of working with people with sensory disabilities, highlighting the notion that people with sensory impairments are more likely to receive paternalistic services. The chapter will explore the ways in which society views people with sensory disabilities and analyse the need for greater awareness and understanding of the role of the social worker in relation to working in a meaningful way with people with sensory disabilities to challenge the discrimination and marginalization that many people in this group experience. It also examines the impact of the changes brought about by the personalization agenda for specific service users within this group.

One of the key areas of work within Adult Services is that of working with older people. In Chapter 9, Mark Wiles looks at the emerging demographics and highlights the issues for society and for older people themselves of the 'ageing population' in the context of tighter budgets and the current 'rationalization' of services for older people. In doing so, he explores the challenges created by the personalization agenda, i.e. the restructuring of the relationships of state and individual to give more responsibility to individuals to meet their own welfare needs. He argues that there is increasing pressure on the time and resources available for work with older service users, but particularly those with dementia, who face the double discrimination brought about by ageism and the prevalence of the medical model in most dementia care. Ageism is a reality experienced by all people as they age and this is informed by the culture we live in, exemplified by the emphasis we place on youth and physical strength, autonomy and independence (Thompson 2005). Having highlighted how structural and organizational factors impinge on work with older people who use health and social care services, the chapter further considers how social work knowledge, skills and values can contribute to much-needed improvements in practice.

Chapter 10 focuses on the work that is carried out by social workers based in a multi-professional Mental Health Team. While one chapter cannot encompass all the complexity of working with adults who are experiencing mental health difficulties, Charley Melville-Wiseman, taking a feminist perspective, examines a number of key themes that are relevant to the role and responsibilities of the social work practitioner. These include the complex issues facing social workers based in integrated health and social care, multidisciplinary mental health services, including the importance of considering the complexity of relational needs, balancing the benefit of relationships to enhance mental well-being while identifying risks that may be present within some of those relationships. Mental ill health often results in the need for some or a significant amount of support from others. This chapter therefore identifies the issues inherently associated with a disparity of power, both perceived and actual, and considers the subsequent possibility of abuses of that power. The challenges of promoting social perspectives in mental health and recovery while working within the strongly endorsed medical model are explored. This is a complex task, and although social workers are trained and equipped to challenge discrimination and social inequality, resisting pressures to meet targets while addressing these issues is not easy when they are not prioritized in the service.

The last 'practice-led' chapter considers the role and remit of the social worker working with people with life-limiting conditions. While this is rightly regarded as a specialist area of social work, Marilyn Russell, who works in a multidisciplinary team based in a hospice setting, argues that many social workers who work with adults are likely to engage with service users and their families who have experienced losses and who may be going through the bereavement process. In many cases, the experience of loss or the way in which the terminal stage of someone's illness is handled, can significantly affect the way in which their family or network manage to cope with the ensuing bereavement. Chapter 11 looks at some of the key social work theories, skills and values that inform good practice with individuals and families facing terminal illness and life-limiting conditions.

Because of the emotional impact of the work, this aspect of social work requires good use of support from the rest of the multidisciplinary team as well as guidance and supervision for the practitioner. Although all social work carries emotional pressures and good supervision is essential to promote considered, quality practice and to maintain the well-being of practitioners, this chapter takes the opportunity to identify problematic areas within emotionally laden practice and to explore the value of reflection in managing the emotional impact on the worker.

In Chapter 12, the Conclusion, Georgina Koubel draws together some of the themes and threads that have emerged from the previous chapters. Not all adults will need to access social services and certainly not all adults who would like services would be eligible for such assistance. Social work with adults involves working with a wide range of adults who need support from services, some of whom may be extremely vulnerable. Some may need safeguarding and support, while many others may need assistance to gain or maintain independence or to promote dignity, choice and autonomy in the ways they choose to live their lives. Many are likely to have experienced marginalization, stigma, discrimination and social exclusion. While the principles, values and theories that underpin social work provide important parameters for work with adult service users, there are real challenges ahead for social work with adults in terms of partnership, power-sharing and person-centred practice. Balancing issues of resources, rights, risks and responsibilities will continue to frame the development of social work with adults in the future. In view of the need to continuously critique and question the role of social work with adult service users, a model to promote reflection is presented for consideration.

Although the future of social work in general, and in adult services in particular, is extremely difficult to predict, there is a risk that procedural and simplistic models will prevail. The development of Personalization and the increased implementation of Independent Budgets may provide opportunities and freedom for many but for others the challenges of taking on the level of risk and personal responsibility may prove too great. In such complex cases, there is still a need for social workers to be involved to work in partnership with people who experience discrimination and marginalization. In order to ensure that social work with adults holds on to its fundamental knowledge, skills and values base, practitioners in this area have to critically understand, apply and consciously reflect on the nature of their roles and tasks and their relationships with service users, colleagues and the wider community.

Because social work is a challenging and exciting area in which to work it requires motivation and commitment, which come from personal experience as well as professional education and development. Each contributor has therefore provided a paragraph outlining where his or her energy and interest comes from. These can be found at the beginning of each chapter.

References

Cree, V. E. (ed.) (2003) *Becoming a Social Worker.* Abingdon: Routledge.

DH (Department of Health) (1998) *Modernising Social Services.* London: Department of Health.

DH (2001) *Valuing People.* London: HMSO.

DH (2009) *Valuing People Now.* London: HMSO.

Gray, M. and Webb, S. A. (2009) *Social Work Theories and Methods.* London: Sage Publications.

Howe, D. (2009) *A Brief Introduction to Social Work Theory.* Basingstoke: Palgrave Macmillan.

Laird, S. E. (2008) *Anti Oppressive Social Work: A Guide for Developing Cultural Competence.* London: Sage Publications.

Shakespeare, T. (2000) *Help.* Birmingham: Venture Press.

Thompson, N. (2005) *Age Discrimination.* Lyme Regis: Russell House.

Thompson, N. (2012) *Anti Discriminatory Practice.* Basingstoke: Palgrave Macmillan.

Trevillion, P. (2005) *Social Work Skills: A Practice Handbook,* 2nd edn. Maidenhead: McGraw Hill.

Part 1

The context of social work with adults

1 The evolution of social work

Georgina Koubel

Those who do not learn from history are destined to repeat it.

(George Siddhartha)

Once upon a time, way back in the mists of the early 1970s, I was sitting on a train. Two women stood near me, talking quietly and earnestly to each other. Something in what they were saying caught my attention. They were discussing the situation of a family who were finding it very difficult to cope and the psychological implications for the children within that family of parents who found it both emotionally and materially difficult to meet their needs. I can't say I remember any of the details of what they said and I had never heard of social work but something within me resonated and I knew that this was an area I would have to explore further. I can't even remember how I found out what a social worker was, but I did, and within a few years I was on a social work course and for many years worked as a social worker, initially with the whole range of people using services and later specializing in working with adults. My interest and concern to understand the way people work, my fascination with the relationships between people and with the complex and sometimes contradictory interconnections between society's perspectives and its more disadvantaged members continues to intrigue and challenge me as an academic as much as it did when I was a practitioner.

Introduction

In order to understand what social work is actually about, and to develop the ability to stand back from the demands of practice and cultivate a more critical perspective on the issues that are covered in considering the process of social work with adults, it is important to understand where the concepts that inform social work have come from and how they have changed over the period in which social work has been part of society. Without this broader perspective, it becomes too easy for social workers and other practitioners to get caught up in the day-to-day pressures of applying *this particular policy* and meeting *those particular targets*. This can potentially lead to practice that runs the risk of becoming routine, reactive and unreflective, forgetting the knowledge, skills and values that make social work the unique and meaningful interaction with individuals, groups and communities that it should be. The aim of this chapter therefore is to enable practitioners within the profession to gain and retain the ability to think carefully about what they are doing and why they are doing it.

It is particularly important that those working in Adult Services should have a critical awareness of the changes and developments that have informed the evolution of social work. This will enable them to develop an objective understanding and a critical eye when considering the context and environment in which social work with adults operates. The first chapter will take a brief overview of the history and evolution of social work with adults from the Poor Law, paying particular attention to the transition from the political indifference of *laissez-faire* (let them be) through the collective principles of the welfare state to the beginnings of the 'modernization' agenda that led to the developments of care management and the changes that have emerged as a result. There will be analysis of the role of the social worker with adults, drawing on the underpinning and often contradictory concepts of charity and social justice that make social work so complex and interesting. Using reflective exercises and case examples, the chapter will start by considering:

- Where does the notion of social work with adults come from?
- Who are the kinds of adults who will need to engage with social services?
- What do you understand by the *laissez-faire* approach to welfare in the nineteenth century?
- What is the difference in considering the collective principles that underpin the Welfare State?
- What do you think are the principles that underpin current social welfare policy with adults?

Learning outcomes

By the end of the chapter, readers should have developed their understanding and awareness of:

- the social, political, legal and policy context of social work with adults, particularly the transition from a *laissez-faire* model of welfare to the collective principles of the welfare state model;
- how notions of stigma, the concept of the 'deserving' and 'undeserving' poor and issues relating to resources and dependency have affected the historical development of social work with adults;
- the need for understanding of different perspectives in social work and social care in order to maintain critical reflection and analysis of the context in which practitioners operate.

The intention is to ensure that practitioners in Adult Social Work develop the habits of reflection and critical analysis (Brown and Rutter 2008; Knott and Scragg 2010). Throughout the book we will look at ways in which practitioners can be helped to develop habits of critical thinking and reflection, which are no more than the ability to question where necessary practices that may be taken for granted, and to think consciously and conscientiously about their own practice. For practitioners, understanding how the tides of social work ebb and flow can help to avoid the sense of being flooded by the demands of the job or overwhelmed by the inevitable changes and challenges that will arise. Crucially, this level of awareness provides the opportunity for a better and more considered engagement with people who use services.

Clearly this is a lot to cover in a relatively brief account so I have separated the evolution of social work into two chapters. This, the first part, will look at how social work has evolved from the early days of the Poor Law to the comparative consensus around the roles and functions of social work that appeared to operate following the development of the welfare state up to the end of the 1970s. The development of social work will necessarily be considered initially within the wider context of the concepts, perspectives and ideologies that have contributed to the formation of an idea that could be called 'social work'.

The following chapter will look at the modernization of social work and will focus more specifically on issues relating to social work with adults. In some ways this division reflects the changes that have been taking place within social work in the move from generic, inclusive services to increasingly specialized and marginalized practice. We will consider these ideas in more detail as we go on.

The first question we ask of anyone who applies to become a social worker is what they think social work is. In fact we split it into three questions:

- What is social work?
- What do social workers do?
- Why are social workers necessary?

Over the next two chapters (and in fact throughout the book) we will try to address the issues that underpin these three deceptively simple questions.

Defining social work

In his helpful basic introduction to social work, Horner (2009) highlights two contrasting definitions that will help to explore the diverse elements that inform social work. The first is from the Association of Schools of Social Work and International Federation of Social Workers (2004 cited in Horner 2009: 3), which claims:

> The social work profession promotes social change, problem solving in human relationships and the empowerment and liberation of people to enhance well-being. Utilizing theories of human behaviour and social systems, social work intervenes at the points where people interact with their environments. Principles of human rights and social justice are fundamental to social work.

Another definition is provided by Jacqui Smith, a former Labour Home Secretary, who saw the role and function of social work somewhat differently. She says:

> Social work is a very practical job. It is about protecting people and changing their lives, not about being able to give a fluent and theoretical explanation about why they got into difficulties in the first place. (Social work training must equip) social workers to demonstrate the practical application of skills and knowledge and their ability to solve problems and provide hope for people relying on their support.
>
> (DH 2002b)

Reflective exercise

- What do you think are the key similarities and differences between the opinions expressed in these two statements?
- Which of these statements fits more closely and coherently with your own understanding of social work?
- Which statement do you prefer?
- Why do you prefer it?

Both statements highlight the importance of social work being knowledge-based and make it clear that the function of social work is to help and support those who need services. Jacqui Smith's view focuses on the importance of the practical application of this knowledge and uses some interesting language around the role of social work being to 'solve problems and provide hope' for people who use services. There are some differences in emphasis in relation to the importance of the practical application within the IFSW definition but they also talk about the importance of problem-solving and enhancing well-being.

There are, however, a number of crucial differences, and these are important because they lead us back to the sources of social work and reflect the diversity of the origins of social work. Both definitions emphasize change but in the IFSW version the key term is 'social change' while Jacqui Smith's summation talks about changing people's lives. In this latter definition it is the people (or their lives) that have to change while in the IFSW definition it is the role of the social work profession to promote social change. In other words, intervention depends on where the problem is located, whether social work operates to address the inequalities of society that need to be challenged on a political or structural level, or within the lives of people who need services, which can be improved by social work intervention at the level of the individual or family.

A further fundamental difference is that the IFSW places the principles of rights, empowerment and social justice at the forefront of their definition while the statement by Jacqui Smith, without any overt reference to social work values, makes social work practice all sound rather simple and straightforward. Of course it's not a matter of one or the other but the ethical challenges that practitioners are facing are often more complicated than outsiders appreciate.

> Most decisions in social work involve a complex interaction of ethical, politi-
> cal, technical and legal issues which are all interconnected. Our values will
> influence how we interpret the law.
>
> (Banks 2006: 12)

Within the media, the most common representation of social work is that of a
statutory social worker who has either misused her power to intervene inappropriately
or who has failed to intervene when she should have done. While it is easy enough to
look in hindsight at what should have happened and to find a scapegoat to blame for
the terrible things that can happen to children and vulnerable adults, these tragedies
do highlight the need for social workers to acknowledge the power they possess and
to acquire the skills and reflective capacity to sensitively balance the care and control
components of the job. This tension can lead to limited public understanding of the
social worker's remit and a lack of appreciation of the difficulty of the decisions that
sometimes have to be made in respect of children or adults who may be vulnerable.

> It is the fact of social work's potency – being replete with assumed and ascribed
> power – that, to a large degree, explains its contested and controversial identity.
>
> (Horner 2009: 5)

One way of trying to understand these issues is to look in a bit more detail at the
origins of social work and how it has developed into the collection of knowledge, skills
and values that inform social work as it is practised today.

Social work as an identifiable concept can arguably be traced back to the inception
of the Charity Organisation Society (COS) which as:

> ... the first organisation to which social work today can trace a direct lineage,
> was called into being and given the task of coordinating both voluntary asso-
> ciational charity and the state provision under the Poor Laws.
>
> (Pierson 2011: 17)

This assertion already contains the seeds of further questions, such as the issue
of the relationship between social work, charitable organizations and the state.
While this appears to be a modern conundrum in view of cuts to welfare services and
the promotion of the Big Society and the assumption of individual responsibility
(Koubel and Bungay 2012) rather than depending on the state to provide, the question
of who should receive services and who should provide them has been a contested area
for centuries.

A brief historical overview may help to clarify why and how social work came into
being. In order to make sense of what social work means, we have to draw some links
with the way in which society has developed and the beliefs and ideas that informed
people's attitudes and values in relation to work with vulnerable or disadvantaged
individuals.

The role of the Poor Laws is particularly interesting, as these provided the main
source of support for people beyond any provided by their own families or community.

This was the role of the parishes, which were charged under the Poor Law with the provision of 'material relief' in cash or kind to people who would otherwise be completely destitute. From early times there was a relationship between religion and assistance or alms, and in the normally settled and largely unchanging medieval society where everyone knew their place, there was an expectation that those with money and status owed some kind of obligation to those who for whatever reason were unable to support themselves. However, the reasons for the formation of the original Elizabethan Poor Law in 1601 (and perhaps even more so with the later amendment of the Poor Law in 1834) could be seen to have been the fear of challenge, if not revolt, by the poorest classes just as much as a commitment to the ideal of Christian charity and help for the needy (Pierson 2011).

With the advent of the Industrial Revolution, individuals and families flocked in great numbers from the countryside to the towns and cities. There, it was believed, there were opportunities to achieve through paid employment a standard of living that would have been impossible to aspire to in their small agriculturally based communities. The Industrial Revolution was undoubtedly a time of great development and change in the United Kingdom, and not a few individuals made great fortunes from the industry and ideas generated by these changes. However, for others this mass migration to urban centres had a number of unfortunate consequences.

The first of these was that individuals who had impairments or disadvantages could not compete in situations of fierce competition within the marketplace. As people flooded into the new conurbations such as Manchester, Liverpool and London, rural communities became fragmented and disconnected. The parishes that had supported the few older and disabled people in their midst were no longer able to do so. Additionally there was a strong belief among industrialists and politicians, who were the people who held the power in the towns, that the only way this revolution could work (to their advantage) would be to limit to the absolute minimum any intervention by the state. This was called *laissez-faire,* which basically means let it be, don't interfere.

> Thus the picture of the early nineteenth century is of a piece: rapid movement from country to city, poorly built urban housing, poor sanitation and the doctrine of laissez-faire all arrived, historically speaking, at the same time.
>
> (Pierson 2011: 7)

The concept of laissez-faire also led to a hardening of attitudes towards those who were for any reason unable to compete in this harsh new world. In 1834 the Poor Law Amendment Act was passed, limiting the provision of 'outdoor relief', i.e. the benefits that it had been possible for people to receive in order for them to remain living in the community. The notion of 'less eligibility' was introduced to ensure that no one could live better on 'relief' than they could even on the lowest of wages. In addition to the hardship this caused many people, there was a deliberate attempt to deter people from even applying for help by the use of the weapons of shame and stigma, so that in addition to their travails, people were made to feel guilty about even asking for help.

Reflective exercise

- Some of the concepts we have been talking about may have struck a chord with you. Think about the way society now regards people who require help or assistance and try to answer as honestly as you can the following questions:
    - Do you think as a society we still have the concept of the 'deserving' and the 'undeserving' claimant for benefits and services?
    - Do you think notions of shame and stigma still affect people who access services, perhaps particularly social services?
    - Going back to the earlier discussion about human rights and social work values, do you think everyone should be entitled to services if they need them?
    - Should people have to meet some kind of eligibility criteria and if so how do you think this should be decided?
    - Who, at the end of the day, should pay for these services?

These questions also challenged individuals in the nineteenth century who were thinking about those people who were unable to support themselves. Charitable societies were set up to address the problems of those who were seen to be indigent through no fault of their own; these often included an awareness of the plight particularly of orphaned children, and sometimes those who were severely and visibly disabled were cared for in hospitals. Others who could not provide for themselves or their family (through age or illness, for example) had to enter the work houses or the poor houses as they were known in Scotland. Conditions were extremely harsh, and in addition this inability to remain independent was seen as a source of stigma and shame.

However, the struggle to survive within the unmitigated market economy of the industrial revolution was so severe that it did lead to an increase in awareness among some elements of the emerging Victorian middle classes. Authors such as Charles Dickens and other philanthropists highlighted the plight of the 'poor and needy'. Although there was a general belief that those who fell into poverty were usually themselves to blame through their own weakness of character and intemperate habits, there was also a dawning recognition that for some the conditions of the industrial society contributed at least partly to their plight. Poor housing and sanitation, for example, led to many illnesses that made people unable to work, and within some quarters of society, there was a recognition that there were people who through no fault of their own might be in need of external assistance to acquire the Victorian virtues of thrift, individual responsibility and sober behaviour (Pierson 2011).

The Society for the Organisation of Charitable Relief and Repressing Mendacity [sic] was founded in 1869. It was soon to change its name to the Charity Organisation Society, the organization that could be said to have 'invented' the key philosophies and principles that underpin modern-day social work. Often it was remarkable individuals who led the reforms at this time, and the Head of this innovation, Octavia Hill, was no exception. She believed that people who required assistance should be valued and respected, and that a supportive and empathic relationship could aid them in changing their behaviour and improving their circumstances. She recognized the impact of poor housing and the damaging effects of poverty, although she did not necessarily see it as a relevant part of the help provided. She set up a system of regular lady visitors who went to see the families to help them with issues of budgeting, child care, and so on. They became a contact outside the family who would be there to help and support people – so long as they also made some effort to help themselves.

The role of the Charity Organisation Society (COS) visitors was to form an empathic, caring relationship with those they visited on a regular basis but also to carry out assessments as to whether, with their support, these families and individuals could be helped to acquire the important Christian values of honesty, sobriety, self-reliance and hard work. Some small amount of money or other material support might be made available if the people could demonstrate their commitment to these values but in general the COS did not see its remit as the provision of 'relief' or benefits. However, it was believed that these empathic and supportive relationships could help people change their ways and aspire to these qualities. This process was called 'casework', and the values underpinning it included ideas of active citizenship and the view that people should be seen as more than merely economic units of production.

Reflective exercise

- Does this sound to you like the kind of issues and values that social workers might be interested in today?
- Are the processes familiar from your understanding of social work?
- Are there aspects of the way this was set up that you would disagree with?
- What other ideals and values do you think social workers use today?

If we look back at the original definitions of social work, it is possible to see that another facet of social work is the recognition of the changes and developments that society needs to undergo. Although the COS could acknowledge the influence of poverty and the environment, they focused their interventions on the needs of individuals and families. However, among other people at the time, such as T. H. Green who lectured at Oxford University and influenced the emerging ideas of the Liberal Party (and later the Labour Party), the belief grew that the state had a responsibility towards its populace. He and other philanthropists highlighted the necessity not simply for people to change their ways but for the place of social reform in promoting the well-being, not just of those who needed assistance but of the whole population.

Other groups such as the workers' guilds, particularly in the North of England, located the community rather than the state or the individual as the target for intervention, and many provided assistance within their local communities. In other parts of the country the rise of the settlement societies, where individual workers would go to live among the poorest members of society to enable communities to support and enable each other through educational, social and cultural events, led to another way of looking at social work which later became known as community work (Healy 2012).

At this stage we can start to see a number of threads which are being braided together to form the different elements that make up social work today. The work of the COS with its casework and emphasis on the importance of the 'therapeutic' relationship, individual home visits, assessment of needs and the provision of help and support (not necessarily material) to facilitate personal change or growth reflects pretty closely the processes of social work today.

The idea of targeting neighbourhoods or communities as both a point of intervention and a potential source of support is one that has been adopted by social work, and in the early days of integrated social work community workers were very often qualified social workers who were employed by the local authority to carry out work with the community. While today this function has largely been ceded to the independent and voluntary sectors, it remains an important component of social work and we will look at it further when we look at the modernization of social work in Chapter 2.

Ideals of citizenship and social reform also fed in to the development of social work and this led to the recognition of social justice as a legitimate concern for social workers and a key principle which would inform social work activity. This was later taken up by the cause of 'radical social work' (Bailey and Brake 1975) and there are still campaigners who argue that the real purpose of social work should be to support the changes in society that are needed to promote equality and combat the disadvantage that many users of social work services experience rather than to engage in 'casework' with individuals and families. While these views have been instrumental in transforming the perception of receiving services for some people in society, for many the alleviation of pressing practical difficulties remains a more urgent focus (Coulshed and Orme 2012).

This variety of views around the role of social work led to the recognition in the early part of the twentieth century that social work was not a simple matter of 'helping out' by kindly but uninformed middle-class ladies, but could more accurately be seen as a skilled and complex activity which was based on a range of knowledge, skills and values that should and could be taught to potential members of this group of workers. The COS continued to develop their notion of social work through setting up the first social work training programme at the School of Sociology in London, soon to be renamed the London School of Economics.

Many aspects of this method of training would be familiar to social work students today. These included the construction of a 'scientific' knowledge base for social work which borrowed eclectically from other scientific disciplines, including the development of ideas from America about a psychological basis for casework, and an emphasis on practice placements to support the development of a distinct set of skills and values. Ultimately, though, social work, as today, was seen to be about people and their engagement with an individual social worker or practitioner at the point where a personal problem intersects with the concerns of society.

> Social work can be defined as an exercise in engaging with people to facilitate the telling of their story around a particular problem relating to their well-being, that is to articulate what has happened to them and why. Its interactive base makes social work *a relational profession*.
>
> (Dominelli 2004: 5, original italics)

The Charity Organisation Society (COS) believed strongly in the importance of the individual relationship between the practitioner and the service users, and this is still very much a keystone of social work today. Nevertheless, it is that pesky relationship between social work and society that keeps undermining the idea that it is simply a matter of a meeting of two minds with the aim of one helping the other. Those who supported the aims and objectives of COS realized that beyond the alleviation of individual problems social work could provide a moral impetus for the improvement of society. Influential socialists like Beatrice and Stanley Webb who supported the universal approach to reducing poverty also understood the importance of using social work as a stabilizing influence (Gray and Webb 2010).

These arguments, about the provision of welfare, about who should receive it and how it should be funded, continue today. In addition to the growing recognition of poverty and disadvantage that was becoming apparent as a result of the tumultuous changes wrought by the Industrial Revolution, concern about the poor physical state of volunteers involved in the Boer War (1899–1902) led to a number of significant pieces of legislation giving individuals rights in relation to school meals and medical inspection within the limited state education system (Powell and Hewitt 2002). In 1908, the Liberal Party introduced the Old Age Pensions Act, bringing in the first non-contributory benefit for older people who had no means of support. The early part of the twentieth century also saw the emergence of the Labour Party and thus an increase in the influence of those who believed that the state should actively intervene to alleviate poverty and disadvantage, potentially forming the basis for the development after the Second World War of the welfare state.

The welfare state

Some elements of the welfare state such as the universal provision of free health and education services are so inculcated into the way we live that it is hard to imagine a time when they weren't there. Now we may argue about the cost, quality and extent of such services but it is important to remember that these benefits 'available to all' are fairly recent phenomena. Looking back as far as medieval times there had been some acknowledgement through the Poor Laws that the state should assume some responsibility for the 'impotent poor' (people who were 'aged, blind, chronically sick and lunatics' as classified by the Poor Law of 1601) but charitable organizations like churches and hospitals supplemented this meagre provision around health, education and welfare, and as we have seen from the earlier discussion about the views and values of society there was no consensus that all people should have access to services.

Wars such as the Boer War and the Second World War seem to have exerted particular influence in terms of the development of welfare. After the grinding poverty and unemployment characterized by the Depression of the 1930s, the physical condition of recruits once again raised anxieties about their fitness to fight when the call came at the start of the Second World War in 1939. For a number of reasons, the end of the war in 1945 led to a radical departure in our understanding of the meaning of the role of welfare in society and the ways in which a range of services were provided, not least the role and remit of social work.

Reflective exercise
• Why do you think the experience of being at war led to the development of the welfare state?   • What do you know about the key ideas and principles of the welfare state?   • How do you think this changed our understanding of social work and particularly the role and remit of social work with adults?

There is an underlying perception that as a result of the Second World War the population felt that they had undergone a common experience. Men and women from different sectors within society had found themselves in close contact with one another and formed friendships within the army and through war work that would have been impossible in the class-bound structures that operated prior to 1939. Many people had been injured in the war, both men in the army and women at home, so that it was felt that these people, disabled through bombing, were owed something by the nation they had sacrificed themselves for. Children had been evacuated and homelessness was a common result of the aerial bombardment. There was a recognition that the war had been won through the collective efforts of people working together, and a feeling that collective effort could, as it had done in winning the war, have the potential to bring about the changes that could improve society and make it 'a land fit for heroes'. It also brought another dimension to the debate about whether and how much the state should be involved in the provision of welfare benefits, including health, social work and social care (Blakemore 2003).

The Labour Government elected in 1945 at the very end of the war heralded a period of rapid and intense change in British society. At any time (as we shall see later when we look at the modernization of social work) there is a close relationship between the political beliefs or *ideology* of the party in power and the social policies they choose to implement (Bochel *et al.* 2009). Building on some of the legislation introduced in the earlier part of the century by the Liberal Party but with a strong commitment to the ideals of equity and fairness for all its citizens, the views of the Labour Party formed an ideological basis for the implementation of the legislation and policies and practices that underpinned what came to be known as the welfare state.

Enduring notions of the 'deserving' and the 'undeserving' poor had not been completely eradicated by the war. Not everyone agreed that it should be the responsibility of the state to provide for all the welfare needs of its citizens, and even at the time there were those such as a number of Conservative politicians who expressed concerns that such a system could lead to an overarching level of control by the state and the potential for increased dependency on the state. Lord Beveridge himself, the author of the Beveridge Report which underpinned the changes that were to take place in Britain after the end of the war and who produced the Beveridge Report in 1942, actually preferred the term *welfare system* to *welfare state* as the former term suggested that although 'a structure of welfare services and social security exists, ... it is not provided or organised solely by government' (Blakemore 2003: 275).

Nevertheless there was an unprecedented level of consensus that what Beveridge called the 'five evil giants' that were held to be responsible for the ills of society could and should be tackled through a system of government intervention. He called these 'evil giants' disease, squalor, idleness, ignorance and want (Alcock *et al.* 2003). Even these terms now sound old-fashioned and even archaic. But if they are restated as chronic illness and disability, poor housing, unemployment, lack of education and poverty, we can see that they are still very much part of the picture of our present society, and they are issues that loom large in the perspective of social workers trying to engage with people who still experience many of these areas of disadvantage.

In the latter part of the 1940s legislation was introduced to deal with all of these elements as part of the wider vision of universal provision for everyone. The idea was that people paid in (through National Insurance) when they could afford it and then were entitled to payments through unemployment or sickness benefit if they needed it. This entitlement or right to benefit was the really radical idea, and removed from many the sense of shame or supplication that had been a key fixture of previous welfare programmes. The Beveridge Report effectively reversed the idea of 'less eligibility' so beloved of the Poor Laws by proclaiming that the payments, although never over-generous, should be sufficient to take account of food, clothing, fuel, light, rent and household sundries (Kennett 2001). Although the link to National Insurance contributions meant that not everyone was entitled to these benefits, with women and older people particularly unlikely to be in employment at the time, this was a genuine attempt to develop 'a new birthright, a part of citizenship not a deprivation of it, paid as of right' (Powell and Hewitt 2002: 38) for people anywhere in the country who needed to claim support from the state.

Legislation introduced the concept of free, accessible health and education for all. In relation to social work, the introduction of the National Assistance Act in 1948 brought together perhaps for the first time recognition of the state's responsibilities towards a group who could be loosely defined as 'vulnerable adults' (Wilson *et al.* 2008). Under section 47 of this Act, power was given to the local authority to provide services to promote the welfare of adults, i.e. in the words of the Act those individuals

> aged 18 or over who are blind, deaf, dumb or who suffer from mental disorder of any description and other persons who are substantially and permanently handicapped by illness, injury or congenital deformity or any such disabilities as may be prescribed.

Once again the language used may feel uncomfortable to modern ears but in many ways this Act paved the way for many of the changes that have informed the development of social work policy and practice in relation to older and disabled adults over the next 50 years. Services such as meals on wheels and residential care for older people, alongside day centres, home adaptations and hospitals for disabled people and access to psychiatrists and asylums for those with mental health problems, meant that people who needed assistance were not left to struggle alone. Help was available.

Despite the apparent consensus that social work was a 'good thing' for society, helping people and developing psychological and sociological perspectives towards meeting the needs of those who accessed services, the shame and stigma attached to applicants for services, established over so many years, were hard to remove despite the changes that had been introduced. While health and education, those universal services accessed by almost everyone, became fully embedded in British culture, social work struggled to develop its own sense of identity. One of the problems was that at this time social work was fragmented, with Children's Services, Mental Health Services and Welfare Services (which dealt mainly with the needs of disabled and older people) being administered from different government departments. Initially each of the separate elements of social work – the Charity Organisation Society with its emphasis on individual casework, the Settlement Movement and its commitment to community regeneration, the hospital almoners (who had in fact provided some of the earliest forms of social work for people in hospital) and the other established areas of practice within probation and aftercare and within psychiatric social work settings – had all seen themselves as specialists within their own fields. This question of the relative merits of general and specialist practice in social work informed the debate about the role of social work throughout the 1960s (Wilson *et al.* 2008).

The problems with social work at that time were held to be that as a result of these specialisms, practice was fragmented, with poor communication among practitioners. As many as three different practitioners might be visiting one family at any time (one in relation to the children, one looking at the needs of grandparents and another addressing mental health needs, for example) and this was seen as a duplication of resources as well as being confusing and uncoordinated for the family. Unification also, importantly, related to the belief that Social Services should be meeting the needs of the whole community and that a single, accessible point of contact would help to combat the stigma that stubbornly persisted about people seeking assistance.

In 1970, the recommendations of the Seebohm Report were accepted. From this point, social work was to be amalgamated into one unified Social Services Department which would be run by each local authority. Social workers at the time were termed 'generic' workers, which meant that they worked with groups across the spectrum of those who sought services. This had the advantage that one individual could be the contact person for all members of a family or group but it also placed a high expectation that the social worker would have knowledge of all specialist areas as well as general knowledge of social work policies, principles, theories and procedures across a range of service areas.

Another problem was that those who had developed their specialisms felt that these were being undermined by those new 'generic' social workers, and within the new departments there was felt to be a hierarchy of importance, with children and families practice being given priority over work with adults. Partly as a result of these tensions there was some disagreement or at least lack of clarity about what the role of social work should actually be. The apparent consensus about social work which had been anticipated through its role within the wider welfare state system was beginning to be seriously undermined by, among other things, the development of radical social work. This brings us back to the question we first started with: what is social work?

Among others who believed that social work should go back to its social justice mandate, Bailey and Brake (1975) argued cogently that social work should be working to transform the social conditions that placed people in a position where they needed help from social workers and vehemently countered the idea that social work was merely about the use of the psychological perspective of 'therapeutic casework' to meet individuals' immediate needs. The 1970s also saw the development of a more rights-based model of community work which reflected many of the ideals of the Settlement Movement of the 1880s, when Canon Barnett and his supporters set up the first settlement in Toynbee Hall in Whitechapel (Wilson *et al.* 2008). Community work drew on the strengths within the community to facilitate change and the promotion of social progress rather than expecting the change to come from the individual through the effects of the relationship with an individual social worker.

The discussion of what social work is cannot really be divorced from the notion of what social workers do. Throughout the chapters in this book, particularly in those which focus on the experiences of practitioners and service users, the connections between what social work is and what social workers do will become more explicit. To return to the question of why social work is necessary, it should be apparent by now that the reasons for the existence of social work cannot be explained without understanding the relationship between social work and society. And in order to understand this relationship we need to acknowledge the complexity of the relationship social work has with itself.

If we look at the two definitions highlighted at the start of this chapter, it is possible to discern the two tributaries that form the social work river. Clearly these two elements – whether social work is about the transformation of society or the changes required from the individual – continue to inform discussions and debates about the role and remit, indeed the very nature, of social work. Although it would be fair to say that in many ways the COS's relationship-based model of casework is more common within social work, there are also elements of the radical agenda – including areas such as the empowerment of service users, the model of social workers and service users working in partnership and a social construction of disability and vulnerability – that can be seen to inform the developments that took place in the latter part of the twentieth century and the first decade of the twenty-first century. This has raised huge challenges but has also opened up immense opportunities for the development of the role of social work with adults. These we will explore in more detail in Chapter 2 – the modernization of social work.

Looking back now, the changes that needed to be made in relation to the welfare and well-being of adult service users could not have taken place without these changes in laws and attitudes but at the inception of the welfare state there was still a very long way to go. Many people with physical and learning disabilities were still living mere 'half-lives' in hospitals and institutions, as you will see explored in other chapters in this book. There may have been a move to provide universal benefits for all but that did not mean that society had reached the stage where people with disabilities and mental health problems were not still considered at best objects of pity and at worst dangerous and 'a threat to established notions of discipline and normality' (Swain *et al.* 2005: 23).

References and further reading

Alcock, P., Erskine, A. and May, M. (eds) (2003) *The Student's Companion to Social Policy*, 2nd edn. Oxford: Blackwell.

Bailey, R. and Brake, M. (eds) (1975) *Radical Social Work and Practice*. London: Edward Arnold.

Banks, S. (2006) *Ethics and Values in Social Work*, 3rd edn. Basingstoke: Palgrave Macmillan.

Blakemore, K. (2003) *Social Policy: An Introduction*, 2nd edn. Buckingham: Open University Press.

Bochel, H., Bochel, C., Page, R. and Sykes, R. (2009) *Social Policy: Themes, Issues Debates*, 2nd edn. Harlow: Pearson Education.

Brown, K. and Rutter, L. (eds) (2008) *Critical Thinking for Social Work*, 2nd edn. Exeter: Learning Matters.

Coulshed, V. and Orme, J. (2012) *Social Work Practice*, 5th edn. Basingstoke: Palgrave Macmillan.

Cree, V. E. (ed.) (2011) *Social Work: A Reader*. Abingdon: Routledge.

Dominelli, L. (2004) *Social Work: Theory and Practice for a Changing Profession*. Cambridge: Polity Press.

Galpin, D. and Bates, N. (2009) *Social Work Practice with Adults*. Exeter: Learning Matters.

Gray, M. and Webb, S. (eds) (2010) *Ethics and Value Perspectives in Social Work*. Basingstoke: Palgrave Macmillan.

Healy, K. (2012) *Social Work Methods and Skills: The Essential Foundations of Practice*. Basingstoke: Palgrave Macmillan.

Horner, N. (2009) *What is Social Work? Context and Perspectives*, 3rd edn. Exeter: Learning Matters.

Kennett, P. (2001) *Comparative Social Policy*. Buckingham: Open University Press.

Knott, C. and Scragg, T. (eds) (2010) *Reflective Practice in Social Work*. Exeter: Learning Matters.

Koubel, G. and Bungay, H. (eds) (2009) *The Challenge of Person-Centred Care: An Interprofessional Perspective*. Basingstoke: Palgrave Macmillan.

Koubel, G. and Bungay, H. (eds) (2012) *Rights, Risks and Responsibilities*. Basingstoke: Palgrave Macmillan.

O'Sullivan, D. (1999) *Decision Making in Social Work*. Basingstoke: Macmillan.

Pierson, J. (2011) *Understanding Social Work: History and Context*. Maidenhead: McGraw Hill/ Open University Press.

Powell, M. and Hewitt, M. (2002) *Welfare State and Welfare Change*. Buckingham: Open University Press.

Swain, J., French, S. and Cameron, C. (2005) *Controversial Issues in a Disabling Society*. Maidenhead: Open University Press.

Wilson, K., Ruch, G., Lymbery, M. and Cooper, A. (2008) *Social Work: An Introduction to Contemporary Practice*. Harlow: Pearson Longman.

2 The modernization of social work

Georgina Koubel

After a short break from social work in the late 1980s/early 1990s, I returned to practice outside London to find that the world of social work had dramatically changed. The language, the processes and the priorities had been transformed. Social workers had become care managers and clients had morphed into service users. It was both disorienting and alarming – what would my role be? How would it be the same and how would it be different from before? But it was also exciting; the new world seemed to hold the promise that the pressing concerns of women, ethnic minorities and in particular the voices of people who used services could finally be heard. I chose to go deliberately into Adult Services despite the fear that the new jargon and the new systems would confuse and confound me. They did. For a few days after I started my new job I wondered if I had completely misjudged the situation and made a terrible mistake. But as soon as I started reading the files and going out on visits it became clear to me that the needs of the individuals accessing services were pretty much the same, and that social work knowledge, skills and values – and hopefully a few more for good measure – would form the backbone of high-quality care management practice.

Introduction

This chapter will critically examine the changes that have affected social work with adults within the modernization agenda, highlighting the key issues that have emerged within the move from universal to residual provision and from generic to specialist services. Looking at how and why social work has developed in the way it has will help us to trace the inception and implementation of the modernization agenda not just in social work but in health and social care and in society more generally. The form and function of social work has always been related to its role in relation to the society it serves. Kennett (2001: 6) emphasizes this relationship between social work and society, asserting 'the belief that assumptions and explanatory frameworks do not emerge in isolation'. For those who are familiar with social work as it is practised in Adult Services today, it may be hard to imagine how radical and far-reaching the change from social work to care management and community care appeared at the time.

This chapter will look at the modernization of social work and the particular challenges and opportunities that this has raised for service users and carers and for those carrying out social work with adults. The political ideologies underpinning changes within social work practice in the latter decades of the twentieth century will be explored, and their relationship with anti-discriminatory and anti-oppressive movements (Dominelli 2002) such as anti-racist, feminist and service user movements in disability and mental health will be analysed in terms of their significance for social work practice with adults. The chapter will integrate this critical understanding of the nature of health and welfare within the development of community care legislation and the notion of care management and the relationship between policy and practice. The chapter will further examine the significance of the care management model in terms of the move from collective to individual principles within the welfare system, leading to the 'marketization' or 'commodification' of care. This move towards the idea of care as a material thing which can be bought and sold within the context of free market policies is seen to take place within a reorientation of the relationship between the state and the individual in terms of rights and responsibilities (Koubel and Bungay 2012). The chapter will also trace the development of the Personalization agenda and the impact of this on social work with adults.

Using reflective exercises and case studies, the chapter will explore the changes brought about by the following:

- the move to care management;
- the valid contribution of social work skills (assessment, relational skills, active and sensitive communication skills, for example);
- the relevance of social work theories and approaches to developing critical reflective practice (Gaine 2010) in dealing with complexity and uncertainty; and, most importantly
- the primacy of social work values and their significance for understanding and interacting in partnership with service users and carers in ways that promote autonomy, choice, independence and empowerment (Adams *et al.* 2009).

Reflective exercise

Some of the ideas involved in community care may bear some closer inspection. Starting with a reflective exercise, think about how you understand the following terms:

- What do you understand by the term 'modernization' of social work?
- What is the relationship between modernization and care management?
- What is the impact of the commodification of care?
- What do you know about the Personalization agenda?

These are some of the key concepts that frame the current context of social work and social care that will be examined in this chapter. Having provided an overview of the political and legislative changes that have framed the modernization of social work and social care with adults, the chapter will go on to highlight the essential knowledge, skills and values required to undertake social work with adults and the opportunities and the challenges for those trying to carry out high-quality social work practice within the care management context.

Learning outcomes

By the end of the chapter, readers should have developed their understanding and awareness of:

- how the ideas of the modernization of social work has affected the models, approaches and principles that frame practice with adult service users;
- how the knowledge, skills and values of social work inform practice with adult service users;
- the ways in which these can at times challenge more procedural models of working within the adult services context such as care management;
- the importance of person-centred approaches, sensitive (anti-oppressive) practice and critical reflection in working with adults who use services.

There is evidence that social workers, particularly in social work with adults, are not always consciously employing social work knowledge, skills and values in their work (McDonald *et al.* 2007). Readers will be encouraged to reflect on the knowledge, skills and values that are most commonly used in social work with adults, in particular the importance of partnership and empowerment (Thompson 2007). The chapter will also explore the need for practitioners who work within adult social services to actively and consciously apply social work knowledge, skills and values in the current context in which services are provided for adults.

As we saw in the previous chapter, the 1970s had seen an unprecedented extension of professional social work and the expansion of statutory Social Services Departments. Despite the fact that many adults with disabilities were still incarcerated within institutions at this time (Parris 2012), the decades from 1970 saw the rise of increasingly challenging movements pressing for the needs of disabled people to be addressed in more radical ways so that they themselves could have greater say in the way services were provided. At the same time social work theories were being developed to address the interface between individuals and society. Both psychodynamic casework, which examined in depth the psychological and interpersonal elements of the difficulties people experienced, and radical social work (Bailey and Brake 1975), which emphasized the importance of systems and the structures within society, were part of the social worker's toolkit acquired through a greater emphasis on theory within social work education. Anti-racist and feminist perspectives, which were becoming part of mainstream thinking, also affected the development of social work.

Little was known of the lives of people within long-stay institutions but some researchers were beginning to take an interest. However, it was not a simple matter of exposing 'the tragedy' of disabled people's lives. Within the disability movement, a social model of disability (Oliver and Sapey 2006) was being developed to challenge accepted beliefs and attitudes towards people with disabilities. The acceptance of this model of disability, which moves the focus away from the impairment of the individual and relocates obstacles and discrimination within the structures and attitudes of society towards disabled people, has been a battle hard-fought, mainly by disabled people themselves. The social model of disability also highlighted the significance of language as a reflection of those attitudes. Before we go on to look further at the modernization of social work, stop and think about the following:

Reflective exercise

- When you think about people with disabilities, what words do you associate with them?
- Are there any of the words that you or friends use that you feel uncomfortable with?
- Why do you think it matters what words we use about people?
- Can you see it as part of a bigger pattern of prejudice and discrimination?
- What can you do about it?

We all use words every day without really thinking about them. When people do object to the use of certain words, it's easy to join in with the crowd who say, 'It must be political correctness gone mad!' or 'Can't these people take a joke?' So why does what we say matter?

Language is constantly changing. If you think back even to your own childhood there were certain words that were used at that time towards not only older or disabled people but in relation to black people, gay people, women and older people that we would be shocked to hear used today. You will notice that the people who have negative words used about them are the ones who are also discriminated against by society. Taking a leaf out of Goffman's (1963) analysis of the stigma that attached itself to people with disabilities and those connected with them, it seems as if even words can become 'tainted by association' to the point where there are some words we would never think of using today. It's odd to think that some of these terms which are now considered to be offensive were either purely medical terms that soon became insults, or that words which we would now consider unacceptable were in common parlance 20 or 30 years ago. If we accept that the words we use reflect the attitudes and values of the society we live in, then social workers who have a stated commitment towards social justice and against oppression and discrimination (BASW 2011) have a particular responsibility to be aware of the power of the words we use or condone. It is not unusual for students and practitioners to worry about whether they are using the 'right' words or if they could unintentionally offend service users. Thompson (2005) offers some very pragmatic advice:

> Be sensitive to the power of words to convey meaning. Don't get so hung up that you are afraid to speak, but work on heightening your awareness of the messages you are putting across in terms of the choice of terms you use. Discussing this in a group may be helpful in terms of finding alternative, and more neutral terms to replace ones which you highlight as discriminatory.
>
> (Thompson 2005: 48)

Community care

The relevance of these ideas about how we construct the world around us were of significance for social work at this time as it faced a range of challenges around the ability of social work to meet the expectations that had been set up for it through social policy and professionalization (Galpin and Bates 2009). 1982 saw the publication of the Barclay Report to review the roles and tasks of social workers. It noted that many social workers felt their work involved more than the individual casework, group work and community work that had traditionally been envisaged (Pierson 2011). The Barclay Report identified only two key roles for social work – social care planning and counselling. It also questioned whether the community should be involved in meeting the needs of those adults who used services rather than these services being provided by the state as had been envisaged in the raft of welfare legislation passed after the Second World War. Despite the impact of radical views and voices, at that time older and disabled people were still mostly cared for either by their families or placed by social workers within long-stay institutions (Priestley 1999). However, with the inception of modernization, social work with adults was about to undergo a major and irreversible transformation.

In 1988 the Griffiths Report (Griffiths 1988) presented a further challenge to traditional roles and tasks of social workers. Setting an agenda for change in social policy, the report proposed that the way services were provided could in itself be a barrier to change for people with disabilities and other service users. One of its conclusions was that community-based services would provide cheaper and better options for older and disabled people who had been living in long-stay hospitals. In those days there was perhaps a more collective sense of what was meant by the 'community' but there was also confusion about what was meant by the notion of 'community care': was this notion relating to ideas of care *by* the community, *for* the community or *within* the community? Many of these debates still continue today, many years later. The Griffiths Report was a central plank of the move towards Community Care, which was heralded by the National Health Service and Community Care Act in 1990 and which transformed the face of social work, particularly social work with adults. In order to understand the way in which social work and social care services are organized today, we need to stop and think about the meaning of Community Care.

Prior to 1990, the majority of welfare services were provided by the state. If you were an older person, for example, there would be a time when a social worker would come to see you, put in some home help to assist with some cleaning, shopping and personal care and arrange for you to go to the day centre if you were socially isolated. Later, when you found it more difficult to cope, they would arrange for you to go into Part III (of the National Assistance Act 1948) accommodation, or what we would now call residential care or a care home. All of these services were provided by the state via the local authority. It was unlikely that you would have to pay, at least until the final stage. It was familiar and pretty unvarying. There were very few options in terms of cultural choices or personal preferences. However, it was available to anyone who needed it and it was as a result very expensive.

There was always a voluntary sector from the days of the Poor Laws. These were often charitable and religious organizations that provided some care and services for older and disabled adults but their roles were seen as meeting preventative and support needs. The principle was that voluntary agencies should not offer the same services as statutory authorities. The NHS and Community Care Act 1990 turned this notion on its head. Whereas the welfare state had been based on ideals of collective and state responsibility for those who use services, the Conservative government in power argued for a version of welfare provision, where:

> ...the state's role should be restricted to funding and regulating the delivery of services, and not providing them. Large-scale state welfare agencies should be broken up and private and voluntary organisations should deliver services currently provided by government.
>
> (Cunningham and Cunningham 2012: 66)

The philosophy underpinning community care included the following elements:

* quality of life (including personal and physical well-being);
* individualization (but with the person being seen as part of their social networks);
* participation (user involvement; partnership and collaborative relationships);
* developing potential (building contacts and networks of support).

Care management

The NHS and Community Care Act 1990 stressed the need to separate the provision of services from those who purchased them: this came to be known as the purchaser/provider split. The role of social workers within the local authorities became one of assessment, care planning and monitoring and reviewing services which were provided by other private and voluntary organizations. Domiciliary care, which had been provided by home helps, now became the domain of a range of private agencies. This radically changed the role of social workers who had previously often been involved in long-term relationships with people who used services, and often with people who did not need tangible services but who gained support from their regular contact with a social worker. Even the name changed, and many social workers who had been employed in Social Services Departments were redesignated as care managers, and some social work departments decided that not all care managers had to be social workers (Payne 1995).

The passing of this far-reaching Act and the principles that underpinned it was viewed with some concern by many social workers. While they acknowledged and understood the perspectives of those who were arguing for a greater say for service users and a stronger voice for those who had been marginalized or oppressed by the kinds of services that had been made available to adult service users, there were also concerns that the particular skills and values that social workers brought to a situation could be lost. It was feared that in situations where the emphasis was on managerial rather than professional perspectives, there was a real risk of a decline in care standards as a result of cost-cutting measures (Hadley and Clough 1996).

The NHS and Community Care Act 1990 section 47 (1) stated that:

> where it appears to a local authority that any person for whom they may provide or arrange for the provision of community care services may be in need of any such services, the authority
>
> (a) shall carry out an assessment of his needs for those services; and
> (b) having regard to the results of that assessment, shall then decide whether his needs call for the provision by them of any such services.

The care manager, who may or may not be a social worker, would be the person who would carry out this 'assessment of needs' and decide on the basis of this how much assistance would be commissioned from an agency to meet these identified needs. At one time this determination was largely left to the professional discretion of the social worker. However, in further attempts to rationalize resources, those carrying out current assessments under the NHS and Community Care Act 1990 are required at the same time to undertake the role of gatekeeper of resources based on the local interpretation of a national framework of eligibility criteria (Fair Access to Care Services 2002). So although the individual applying for services may have the needs that are indicated in the NHS and Community Care Act, the person carrying out the assessment also has to make a decision as to whether the needs are of sufficient gravity to meet the eligibility criteria. Care managers should undertake the assessment, work on a care plan to meet the needs identified and, on the basis of this, commission services tailored to individual need from available providers rather than a 'one size fits all' provision (Thompson and Thompson 2005: 7). They also highlight an understanding of risk and how to address it as an essential part of the care manager's remit. A financial assessment would also be required, which was a role that social workers were often reluctant to take on.

Within the Care Management and Assessment Practitioners' Guide (DH/SSI 1991), the core functions of care management are set out as:

- publishing information;
- determining the level of assessment;
- the assessment of need;
- producing care plans;
- securing resources;
- monitoring the arrangements;
- reviewing the user's needs.

The ideology behind this move focused on the notion that 'care' could be 'commodified', i.e. that it could be bought and sold like any other 'commodity'. This, it was claimed, should promote the idea of the 'client' as 'consumer', based on the notion of empowerment which should give the service user increased choice and control over what services would be provided. We will return to the idea of empowerment later.

Community care, although it is now entering its third decade, remains a contested concept (Stepney and Popple 2008) within social work for a number of reasons. While social policy promoted the notions of self-determination and independence that would be supported by social work values, most practitioners are aware that many people who would previously have been supported by the 'welfare net' are no longer considered to be eligible for services. The argument that this would reduce the risk of dependency on the welfare state may have had some validity but it also meant there would be some people who would previously have been considered vulnerable who would be left without a level of support that they had previously become accustomed to.

> One of the many paradoxes of the care/case management role remains the highly inappropriate merger of opposing roles. For example, some care managers have highlighted the difficult task of spontaneously accommodating human need and risk while being embroiled in excessive office based rituals.
>
> (Carey 2008: 925)

There was a further argument that it was not possible to 'commodify' care: that care was a complex combination of relationships, duties, history and love that could not be reduced to a set of 'times and tasks', mere jobs that had to be completed within a specified timescale. Informal carers looking after their parents, spouses or adult children or even friends and neighbours provided far more than a mechanical and objective 'service' that could be measured in terms of the financial cost of the time involved (Twigg and Atkin 1993). Some carers, of course, are men but the fact that most carers, both formal (paid but often at a very basic rate of pay) and informal are likely to be women seems to say something about the value society places on the role of carer.

The question of the gender implications of community care provides another area of contention. Even in 1990 there was hardly an army of women living in the 'community' able and willing to give up their careers, their independence and often their roles as chief or sole breadwinner for their family in order to look after an individual who needed support (Orme 2001). There were also those who argued that it was not appropriate for adults to be 'cared for' by their families and that a system of payments to service users who could then determine and control their own services would be a better pathway to empowerment and autonomy (Morris 1993).

This perspective challenged the traditional views of some professionals who believed that service users could not be trusted to know what care would be best for them and who would not be able to understand the need for careful management of their finances to ensure they were able to get the care they needed. However, the tide was turning. By 1996 the Community Care (Direct Payments) Act was brought in to make this option available to service users. At the time it was only available to people with physical disabilities. Some professionals were very concerned about the risks involved (this was a time when adult protection was becoming an issue of concern for local authorities) but it also had the potential to make an immense difference to the lives of some people who used services.

Soon after it was introduced, a couple who we'll call Lynne and Vic approached social services to see if they could change from their present arrangement to the Direct

Payments scheme. They were a couple who had lived in hospital for many years but who had been rehoused in a specially adapted bungalow as part of the community care initiative. Both had complicated physical impairments and there were a number of carers going in and out over the course of the day. Lynne and Vic obviously appreciated that they were out of hospital in their own home where they could have a relationship (this had been forbidden in the hospital) and live with their own things around them. However, there were some things that they found hard to accept. Because of the number of calls every day, they were unable to build any kind of relationship with the carers. Often the carers, because they had to fit the calls in between other visits, came at 11 a.m. to get them up and returned around 6 or 7 p.m. to 'put them to bed'. Often they had to train the carers themselves in the specific needs and tasks required, as these were quite specialized, and sometimes one or the other of them was too unwell to even want to get up, or needed longer than had been allocated for the task to be completed. Sometimes they just didn't want to be bothered with people coming into the house at all but there was very little flexibility should they need to increase the hours on a particular day or wish to reduce or cancel the care on others. The amount and duration of the care had been determined by the local authority based on the assessment of their needs and had been designated as a set number of pre-specified 'times and tasks' which were commissioned from a local domiciliary care agency and which were, as care management demanded, SMART, i.e.

- specific;
- measurable;
- achievable;
- relevant; and
- time-limited.

With the advent of the Community Care (Direct Payments) Act in 1996, the social worker/care manager chose to argue on behalf of Lynne and Vic that they should be able to manage their own finances, employ who they wanted and organize the 'times and tasks' of the carers to suit themselves. What now may sound obvious was strongly resisted. The arguments focused around the potential risks to the couple if they employed unscrupulous carers and concerns about who would carry the responsibility if 'anything went wrong'. Underneath these reasonable objections there still appeared to be an assumption that it was impossible for service users to know what would be best for them – attitudes from the history of social work that it would appear some practitioners are still reluctant to acknowledge (Cunningham and Cunningham 2012).

There were concerns that service users might not use the money for 'care' but for other purposes, and questions raised about how the expenditure of money would be monitored. Certainly the move to greater choice and control for service users highlights issues of safeguarding and accountability but the care manager and the couple themselves together engaged in discussion with the Social Services managers who would make the final decision, and eventually it was agreed. For Lynne and Vic the experiment was a huge success and they both expressed their opinion that their lives had been immeasurably improved. They employed their own personal assistants who were able to be much more flexible, helping them to get up and go to bed when they wanted, providing personal care when the couple themselves found it helpful and leaving them alone when they did not want anyone else around. They were also able to save the money on days they felt either well enough to manage or not well enough to be bothered and did indeed sometimes spend the money on things other than 'care' to improve the quality of their lives. Importantly, they said, they could get to know the carers who would also know them but, most of all, they felt they had a sense of control over the way they chose to live their lives.

Although there were inevitable obstacles to overcome in terms of managing the finances and learning employment processes that Lynne and Vic had never been involved with before, for them the main obstacles in their way were the views of the social services staff who doubted their ability to manage the complexity of the tasks involved. Looking at some of the later chapters in this book, you can see how many of these issues and concerns remain in determining the process of Personalization which is now at least theoretically available to all eligible service users.

Policy and practice

While plans to limit the role of the state, reduce the cost of services and circumscribe the involvement of professionals like social workers sat comfortably with the familiar views of the Conservative Party to reduce public spending and limit the role and responsibilities of the state, the process was by no means overturned when the Labour Party were returned to power in 1997. The aims of the 'New Labour' party were explained in a Green Paper as a new contract for welfare which identified a 'third way' between the overarching provisions of the welfare state and the privatized, residual model of welfare promoted by the previous Conservative government. The rhetoric within the government's strategy made a commitment to universal and strengthened provision in health and education but with the avowed aim of promoting individual independence rather than encouraging reliance on the welfare state.

1998 saw the publication of the policy document *Modernising Social Services* (DH 1998) but by this time it would be fair to say that the modernization process, the move from traditional social work to care management and all that this entailed, was well on its way. The arrangements involved commissioning care services from a range of providers while social workers were mostly involved in devising and developing care plans to meet the needs they had pinpointed through the process of assessment.

Much of the demand for services came from older and disabled people who had a range and often a combination of health conditions and social disadvantages, and the value of closer collaborative working, particularly among practitioners from health and social care, became a significant aim for social policy drivers such as *Modernising Social Services* (DH 1998). While this had traditionally played a part in the development of good working relationships between individual professionals who found themselves engaged in negotiations to improve the chances of meeting the needs of their 'clients', the Health Act 1999 (for England and Wales) was intended to remove the systemic obstacles to interprofessional working with measures such as pooled budgets, lead commissioning and integrated providers in order to facilitate more effective integrated working, even partnership, among practitioners (Sharkey 2007).

Power, partnership and empowerment

However, partnership with other practitioners was not the only area that needed to change to complete the picture of modernized services for adults. Another highly salient element was that of partnership with service users. This goal informs many of the chapters that have been written in this book and is linked to concepts of power and empowerment. As empowerment is such an important feature of social work values, one of the main planks of the modernized agenda and person-centred approaches, a significant challenge to the marginalization of adults who use services and a source of considerable satisfaction for practitioners (Koubel and Bungay 2009), but also a concept which poses considerable contradictions for a number of service users, this is an area that will reward some reflection and examination.

Reflective exercise

Social workers, policy makers and service users all sign up to the importance of empowerment. Indeed, what could be more natural in terms of social workers' (and other helping professions') commitment to the rights, autonomy and self-determination of service users than wanting to 'empower' someone to have more control over their lives? But if this is so, why do service users keep telling us that the process of empowerment remains so challenging?

One way of trying to make sense of the contradictions inherent in the promotion of empowerment could be to look a little more critically at the concept of power. Power is often presented as inevitably a bad thing in social work, particularly with adults who are legally considered to be in a position to make their own decisions and take the consequences upon themselves. However, there are also times when people who use services appear to run risks that practitioners in the field of adult services, as those charged with a duty of care or with the challenge of professional accountability (Colyer, in Koubel and Bungay 2009), feel could put them in danger from themselves or others. Unless the person has committed a criminal offence or has a defined mental illness, or it can be proved that they do not have the capacity to understand the consequences of their actions, there is no legal remedy to permit intervention but many people feel that practitioners in health and social care are neglecting their duty of care when they 'allow' a service user to undertake what are perceived as risky activities. It appears that one of the most challenging areas for practitioners is the question of risk and the limits of their responsibilities, while one of the most challenging areas for service users is the risk of intervention by someone who feels they have your best interests at heart.

> With emotions of sympathy and generosity, and the urge to improve difficult situations on behalf of the other, comes a tendency towards control … Because a parent or carer or professional feels that they 'know what is best' for a person who needs help and is regarded as less competent to decide, they risk removing autonomy and control from that person.
>
> (Shakespeare 2000: 59)

The following model suggests different ways of thinking about power. What do these mean to you and how do you think they would affect your work with service users?

- Power to
- Power over
- Power with
- Power from within
- What other kinds of power can you think of?

Power *to* as a concept appears to be reasonably clear. It relates to the power any of us may have to do something. Just because we have the power to do it doesn't mean we have to do it, of course, but it gives an idea of the potential options and choices we might follow. A good example of 'power to' would be to go back to the earlier case example of the couple who wanted to use direct payments. However capable (or not) Lynne and Vic may have been to be able to manage their own care arrangements, it was not until the passing of the Direct Payments Act 1996 that local authorities could authorize the handing over of money directly to service users. This is an example of political power, i.e. that the policies and the legislation of the time allow certain policies (and not others) to be carried out. Even once they had that political or *structural* power *to* agree to the changes that the couple proposed, the local authority managers still had the power *over* the couple's future care. In other words, they could decide whether or not to carry out this policy; the legislation was enabling but it did not *require* the local authority to carry out this policy so the decision remained in their hands.

Rather than accept the stated concerns about the risks involved in giving per-mission for a couple with impairments and therefore historically viewed as unable to manage their own care via Direct Payments, the care manager and the couple worked together to develop a coherent argument for why Lynne and Vic should be able to manage their care package in the way that was envisaged by the Direct Payments Act. In a sense they harnessed the power they had as service users in a context where policy was driving a service user agenda with the *professional* power of the care manager, through the combined power of partnership or 'power *with*' to convince the local authority that this was a feasible prospect for them to agree to. Through this process, the partnership was able to challenge the local authority's unquestioning acceptance of the *cultural* ideas about the limited capacity and abilities of people with disabilities.

This model of power also informed the next step, that is to say the question of power *from within*. Both Lynne and Vic had spent the majority of their lives in hospital where they had had little opportunity to develop the skills and expertise needed to hire staff, manage their payments, train them in what they needed to do and make appropriate arrangements for when someone needed to be available. When they first started to manage their own care, there were many areas of the process that they felt unsure about or even convinced they would not be able to do. The care manager – and a finance officer – worked through the various elements required with Lynne and Vic and, importantly, remained with them until *they* felt confident to carry on alone, with the care manager just keeping a watching brief. Now Lynne and Vic offer support and advice to other individuals who are thinking of managing their own care arrangements through an Individual Budget. They have built up their knowledge and confidence about the advantages and pitfalls of managing your own budget to the extent that they have become the experts and their help is sought by others; this is the essence of *personal* power, or power *from within*.

As you can see, in addition to the model of power described within the reflective exercise, there are other ways of understanding power that can inform critical thinking and awareness. The references within the text (above) to structural, cultural and personal power are based on a model developed by Thompson (2007), which is applied within some of the other chapters of this book. The case studies and reflections in these chapters provide further opportunities to see how this model can be of assistance in trying to understand and promote empowerment in a way that is authentic and non-tokenistic, and which genuinely reflects and respects the choices and wishes of service users even when they do not accord with the latest government policy. Aspects of personal, professional and political power are further relevant concepts that social workers need to be aware of in working with adults around empowerment.

Empowerment is such an important concept but the question remains of whether practitioners working within the care management (sometimes now called case management) model can achieve the difficult balancing act required to maintain adherence to the social work values, skills and knowledge that are worthwhile and essential to forming good relationships in practice while also reaching out to absorb the changes and transformative opportunities for working alongside and in partnership with service users. Soon after the publication of *Modernising Social Services* (DH 1998), commentators from academia and the disability movements were already warning about the risk of routinized and unthinking approaches to developing services for people who used adult services (Priestley 1999; Drake 1999). The risks are there. Without striving to maintain the highest standards of ethical, person-centred and ethnically sensitive practice, the modernization of services could become a 'process' which could be as dehumanizing as the earlier processes of stigma and institutionalization that preceded the introduction of social work and community care.

Conclusion

Modernization places a responsibility on social workers to work within the legal framework, although the legislation surrounding Adult Services is somewhat complex and fragmented (Mandelstam 2008). The NHS and Community Care Act 1990 builds on but does not replace a range of previous legislation such as the National Assistance Act 1948 and the Chronically Sick and Disabled Persons Act 1970. You will see in future chapters that practitioners in Adult Services consider the array of legislation on offer and select those that are most helpful to them. Apart from the NHS and Community Care Act, the two most frequently applied pieces of legislation when working with adults are the Human Rights Act 1998 and the Mental Capacity Act 2005.

Following the Direct Payments Act, and the publication of documents such as *Independence, Choice and Wellbeing* (DH 2005) and *Our Health, Our Care, Our Say* (DH 2006), the rollout of the Personalization agenda has extended the opportunities to receive a direct payment and manage their own budget to a much wider range of people (Gardner 2011). Based very firmly on a social model of disability (Henwood and Hudson 2008), personalization further extends the very purpose of modernization, enhancing the process of transferring power and provision of services from the state to the individual. For many this has proved a transformational opportunity, although, as various authors in this book explore in forthcoming chapters, a model that has distinct advances for some does not necessarily mean that individual budgets are the answer for everyone using services (Carr 2010).

For practice to be truly person-centred and aligned with social work values, it is apparent that a solution needs to take account of the many uncertain and complex situations that social workers engage with, and of the wide range of challenges and opportunities that inform practice in Adult Services. Social workers and social care practitioners should welcome any system that combats the historical stigma and discrimination associated with disabled and older people, and which explores ways of genuine power-sharing and partnership with service users. Personalization heralds the promise of more control for service users and their networks but this inevitably raises issues of accountability, and the balance of rights, risk and responsibilities in working with adults. It is these conflicts and dilemmas from the perspectives of those who use services and from those who work in Adult Social Services that will inform the accounts of the various authors who have contributed to the forthcoming chapters in this book.

References and further reading

Adams, R., Dominelli, L. and Payne, M. (eds) (2009) *Critical Practice in Social Work*. Basingstoke: Palgrave Macmillan.

Bailey, R. and Brake, M. (eds) (1975) *Radical Social Work*. London: Edward Arnold.

Banks, N. (2006) *Ethics and Values in Social Work*. Basingstoke: Palgrave Macmillan.

Barclay, P. M. (1982) *Social Workers: Their Roles and Tasks*. London: Bedford Square Press.

BASW (British Association of Social Workers) (2011) *The Code of Ethics in Social Work*. Birmingham: BASW.

Carr, S. (2010) *Personalisation: A Rough Guide*. London: SCIE.

Carey, M. (2008) Everything must go? The privatisation of state social work, *British Journal of Social Work*, 38: 918–35.

Cunningham, J. and Cunningham, S. (2012) *Social Policy and Social Work*. London: Sage Publications.

DH (Department of Health) (1998) *Modernising Social Services*. London: DH.

DH/Social Services Inspectorate (1991) *Care Management and Assessment Practitioners' Guide*. London: HMSO Publications.

DH (2005) *Independence, Choice and Wellbeing*. London: DH.

DH (2006) *Our Health, Our Care, Our Say*. London: DH.

Dominelli, L. (2002) *Anti Oppressive Social Work Theory and Practice*. Basingstoke: Palgrave Macmillan.

Drake, R. F. (1999) *Understanding Disability Policies*. Basingstoke: Macmillan.

Gaine, C. (ed.) (2010) *Equality and Diversity in Social Work Practice*. Exeter: Learning Matters.

Galpin, D. and Bates, N. (2009) *Social Work Practice with Adults*. Exeter: Learning Matters.

Gardner, A. (2011) *Personalisation in Social Work*. Exeter: Learning Matters.

Goffman, E. (1963) *Stigma: Some Notes on the Management of Spoiled Identity*. Englewood Cliffs, NJ: Prentice-Hall.

Griffiths, Sir R. (1988) *Community Care: An Agenda for Action* (Griffiths Report). London: HMSO.

Hadley, R. and Clough, R. (1996) *Care in Chaos*. London: Cassell.

Henwood, M. and Hudson, B. (2008) Checking the facts, *Guardian*, 13 February.

Kennett, P. (2001) *Comparative Social Policy*. Buckingham: Open University Press.

Knott, C. and Scragg, T. (eds) (2010) *Reflective Practice in Social Work*. Exeter: Learning Matters.

Koubel, G. and Bungay, H. (eds) (2009) *The Challenge of Person-centred Care*. Basingstoke: Palgrave Macmillan.

Koubel, G. and Bungay, H. (eds) (2012) *Rights, Risks and Responsibilities*. Basingstoke: Palgrave Macmillan.

Leadbetter, C. (2004) *Personalisation Through Participation: A New Script for Public Services*. London: Demos.

Mandelstam, M. (2008) *Community Care Practice and the Law*, 4th edn. London: Jessica Kingsley.

McDonald, A., Pustle, K. and Dawson, C. (2007) Barriers to retaining and using professional knowledge in local authority social work practice with adults in the UK, *British Journal of Social Work*, Advance Access, 25 April.

Meagher, G. and Parton, N. (2004) Modernising social work and the ethics of care, *Social Work and Society* 2(1), available at http://www.socwork.de [Accessed 15 November 2012].

Means, R. and Smith, R. (1998) *Community Care: Policy and Practice*, 2nd edn. Basingstoke: Palgrave Macmillan.

Morris, J. (1993) *Independent Lives? Community Care and Disabled People*. Basingstoke: Macmillan.

Newman, J., Glendinning, C. and Hughes, M. (2008) Beyond modernisation? Social care and the transformation of welfare governance, *Journal of Social Policy*, 37 (4): 531–57.

Oliver, M. and Sapey, B. (2006) *Social Work with Disabled People*, 3rd edn. Basingstoke: Palgrave Macmillan.

Orme, J. (2001) *Gender and Community Care*. Basingstoke: Palgrave Macmillan.

Parris, M. (2012) *An Introduction to Social Work Practice*. Maidenhead: McGraw-Hill.

Payne, M. (1995) *Social Work Theory and Community Care*. Basingstoke: Palgrave Macmillan.

Pierson, J. (2011) *Understanding Social Work: History and Context*. Maidenhood: McGraw-Hill/Open University Press.

Priestley, M. (1999) *Disability Policies and Community Care*. London: Jessica Kingsley.

Shakespeare, T. (2000) *Help*. Birmingham: Venture Press.

Shakespeare, T. (2006) *Disability Rights and Wrongs*. London: Routledge.

Sharkey, P. (2007) *The Essentials of Community Care*. Basingstoke: Palgrave Macmillan.

Stepney, P. and Popple, K. (2008) *Social Work and the Community*. Basingstoke: Palgrave Macmillan.

Swain, J. and French, S. (2008) *Disability on Equal Terms*. London: Sage Publications.

Thompson, N. (2007) *Power and Empowerment*. Lyme Regis: Russell House.

Thompson, N. and Thompson, S. (2005) *Community Care*. Lyme Regis: Russell House.

Thompson, S. (2005) *Age Discrimination*. Lyme Regis: Russell House.

Twigg, J. and Atkin, K. (1993) *Carers Perceived: Policy and Practice in Informal Care*. Maidenhead: Open University Press.

3 Empowering and safeguarding vulnerable adults

Felicity Elvidge

My original aspirations to be a professional artist were revised while a student at art school and a number of twists and turns of fate led me to train as a registered general nurse. I worked in the acute sector for a number of years but creative painting was a constant saviour, enabling me to 'be myself'. One day I visited an old family friend who had been a prolific amateur painter, now resident in a care home. I asked her where, in her room, she kept her painting tools and her response was that 'they don't allow that in here, it's too messy'. The care home was driven by the medical model of well-being and had a very good reputation for physical care but complete disregard for the social element of residents' needs. I was left with a huge sense of injustice. How can you provide care for someone if you are ignoring their essence of self? Surely this is abuse? This fuelled my move into social care and informs my role as safeguarding coordinator with a particular interest in care quality and how, if quality is poor, this can descend into abuse.

Introduction

This chapter provides an introduction and overview of the challenges and complexities involved in safeguarding vulnerable adults. Using reflective exercises and case scenarios, this chapter will explore the history and development of adult protection and safeguarding. The chapter will consider the importance of person-centred safeguarding as a core value of good practice in the multi-agency context and not solely as a procedural response to abuse. This will be linked to relevant theoretical models of practice within social work and social care. Issues of risks, choice, capacity and vulnerability will inform the analysis and case scenarios will include consideration of the relationship between adult safeguarding and domestic violence. The chapter will start by exploring the following questions to identify a number of the key concepts in the context of safeguarding vulnerable adults.

- What is abuse? What are the main signs and symptoms of adult abuse?
- What do we mean by the term 'vulnerable adult' and where does it come from?

- What are the differences in the terms 'safeguarding' and 'protection'? What is the significance of these for work with vulnerable adults?
- What are the main policies, procedures and theoretical models which inform social work and care management practice with vulnerable adults?
- What are the main challenges and dilemmas in safeguarding vulnerable adults?
- What are the key strategies for applying policies and procedures in the process of safeguarding vulnerable adults?
- What is the relationship between safeguarding vulnerable adults and domestic violence?

Learning outcomes

By the end of the chapter, readers should have developed their understanding and awareness of:

- the history, development and social construction of concepts such as adult abuse, adult protection, risk, safeguarding and vulnerability;
- a range of theoretical frameworks which inform and underpin the role of the safeguarding coordinator and practitioners in adult social services;
- the challenges and dilemmas resulting from the modernization and personalization agendas for practitioners who work with vulnerable adults;
- the relationship between good interprofessional communication in adult safeguarding and ethical, person-centred practice with vulnerable people and their families, carers and networks.

The development of adult safeguarding policies and procedures and the roles and responsibilities of the various stakeholders will be discussed in the context of the social and moral implications of attitudes towards vulnerable people in society, including people who are subjected to domestic violence.

The chapter will include a number of case studies to enable readers to identify, explore and work on resolving some of the challenges, conflicts and potential contradictions for practitioners working in the field of adult safeguarding. This will be further analysed in terms of the benefits and tensions arising from the modernization of social care, the personalization agenda and the changing roles of service users and practitioners within social, health and 'commodified' (see Chapter 2) models of care.

History paints a disturbing picture of how society locates vulnerability within individuals, treating vulnerable adults as without value, burdensome and without personhood. Large families were the norm until the early twentieth century. Child mortality rates were high and medicine and social care had not yet developed to support sick or disabled children to thrive. Investing in a child who would be unable to contribute to the family income was generally counterintuitive; therefore they would generally not be encouraged to survive. Those who did survive, dependent on the nature and extent of their disability, would be excluded from mainstream community and forced into the 'sick role' (Parsons 1951). Thus disability became a medical, rather than social, construct, something which was deemed 'untreatable' or 'treatable', often by what we would perceive now as cruel, amoral and criminal interventions.

Mental illness, including learning disabilities, as recently as the sixteenth century, was universally thought to be caused by possession. 'Treatment' frequently meant being burned alive to drive out 'demons or devils'. In 1676 the new Bethlem Hospital (Bedlam) in London opened to treat psychiatric patients. Paying visitors were enticed in by a display of sculptures of people in tortuous suffering, giving a preview of the live entertainment available within. This was on offer for over 100 years and, along with the animals in the zoo, was rated as a top London attraction.

In the eighteenth century mental illness and learning disability were widely considered to be evidence of either a criminal mindset, brain damage or a moral failing on the part of the patient. Foucault (2006) describes the treatment of patients as brutal: forced purging, cold baths and starvation. Large institutions called 'asylums' were built when the Poor Laws of 1834 were introduced. These housed people then termed as 'feeble minded, imbeciles or idiots' for lifelong care (Wright and Digby 1996). It is significant to consider that Bethlem Hospital was co-governed with Bridewell Prison from the mid-1570s right up until 1948.

When the National Health Service (NHS) began in 1946 the asylums became hospitals although there was still no distinction between mental illness and learning disabilities until the 1959 Mental Health Act when the 'feeble-minded' became the 'mentally handicapped' as people with learning disabilities were then called. Even after this change in the label attached to them, people with learning disabilities were viewed as 'abnormal' and 'sick' rather than people to be encouraged, as others are, to reach their own potential. It was not until the 1980s that the idea of 'normalization' (Wolfensberger 1984) for people with learning disabilities was more widely introduced.

In a society where the popular media promote youth, beauty and celebrity as the primary states to which we should all aspire, it is plain to see how modern society feeds oppression. Bodies such as Action on Elder Abuse (www.elderabuse.org.uk) and the Partnership Boards (www.dh.gov.uk) are invaluable for those involved in safeguarding as victims, carers and practitioners to gather support and share experiences.

Vulnerability

Media coverage of Inquiries such as those into the deaths of Maria Colwell (Field-Fisher 1974), Victoria Climbié (Laming 2003) and Peter Connolly (Haringey Council 2009) highlighted the social vulnerability generated by the physical and emotional immaturity of childhood. This dominant construct of vulnerability implies that vulnerability arises from and is generated by individuals and their physical and mental characteristics and needs; inferring that victims have the cause of the abuse located within them rather than placing responsibility with the actions or omissions of others.

These ideas accord with the view that if all adults were able to effectively access support to enable them to live safer lives at the time they needed it, there would be no need for policies and procedures aimed at addressing the needs of specific groups of people (Association of Directors of Adult Social Services 2005).

This social model of vulnerability parallels the social model of disability, taking the stance that vulnerability, as with disability, is caused by the way society is organized, rather than solely because of a person's impairment or difference. Social, educational, environmental and fiscal designs commence with the blueprint of the physically and mentally able, with special measures and adaptations needing to be made for those who do not fit the blueprint. Societal support is the exception rather than the rule, placing people with a disability on the outside and excluded rather than inside and included, therefore potentially leaving them vulnerable (Martin 2007).

Guidance from the Department of Health in March (DH 2000: 8) on the protection of vulnerable adults from abuse tells us a vulnerable adult is defined as a person:

> who is or may be in need of community care services by reason of mental or other disability, age or illness; and who is or may be unable to take care of him- or herself, and or unable to protect him- or herself against significant harm or exploitation.

This definition was updated in the *Safeguarding Adults* guidance (ADASS 2005), saying that adults who 'may be eligible for community care services' are those whose independence and well-being would be at risk if they did not receive appropriate health and social care support. They include adults with physical, sensory and mental impairments and learning disabilities, however those impairments have arisen, e.g. whether present from birth or due to advancing age, chronic illness or injury. They also include carers: family and friends who provide personal assistance and care to adults on an 'unpaid basis', adding, 'They are not a self-defined community, but a group that has been created by social policy.'

Brown (2012: 41–53) suggests that 'the vulnerable' tend to be constructed in policy and social welfare practice as those who are less accountable for their circumstances or actions, and as those who have less 'agency' in the development of perceived difficulties in their lives. Brown expands on this, theorizing that the concept that the 'most vulnerable' must be 'protected' is rhetoric aimed at legitimizing reductions to state welfare provision. As spending cuts are made, creating and sustaining binary oppositions about the 'deserving' and 'undeserving' within society draws on notions of vulnerability and offers a rhetorical means of reassuring the public that those who need and 'deserve' services the most will not be affected, thereby bolstering the moral and economic credentials of the government of the time.

Clearly there are differing views on the meaning of 'vulnerable'. The report on the consultation on the review of *No Secrets* (DH 2009: 8) tells us that 90 per cent of respondents wanted the definition revised. What do you think?

- Would you rephrase or revise the term 'vulnerable adult'?
- If so, what term would you use?
- Is a 'special' term needed at all?

There was much support for the term 'adult at risk' to replace 'vulnerable adult'.

Reflective exercise

Before we go on to look at the process of social work with adults experiencing abuse, think for a while about the following questions:

- What is abuse?
- How do I know if it's adult abuse?
- What should I do if I suspect adult abuse has taken place?

What is abuse?

This question could inform a lengthy group discussion. However, *No Secrets* states: 'Abuse is a violation of an individual's human and civil rights by another person or persons', and continues:

> Abuse may consist of single or repeated acts. It may be physical, verbal or psychological, it may be an act of neglect or an omission to act, or it may occur when a vulnerable person is persuaded to enter into a financial or sexual transaction to which he or she has not consented, or cannot consent. Abuse can occur in any relationship and may result in significant harm to, or exploitation of, the person subjected to it.

> (DH 2000: 9)

Types of abuse

Again there might be different views on this question. *No Secrets* guidance (DH 2000) lists six main forms of abuse:

- *physical abuse*, including hitting, slapping, pushing, kicking, misuse of medication, restraint, or inappropriate sanctions;
- *sexual abuse*, including rape and sexual assault or sexual acts to which the vulnerable adult has not consented, could not consent or was pressured into consenting;
- *psychological abuse*, including emotional abuse, threats of harm or abandonment, deprivation of contact, humiliation, blaming, controlling, intimidation, coercion, harassment, verbal abuse, isolation or withdrawal from services or supportive networks;
- *financial or material abuse*, including theft, fraud, exploitation, pressure in connection with wills, property or inheritance or financial transactions, or the misuse or misappropriation of property, possessions or benefits;
- *neglect and acts of omission*, including ignoring medical or physical care needs, failure to provide access to appropriate health, social care or educational services, the withholding of the necessities of life, such as medication, adequate nutrition and heating; and

- *discriminatory abuse*, including racist, sexist, that based on a person's disability, and other forms of harassment, slurs or similar treatment.

The intent or motivation of the person carrying out abuse or neglect may determine the appropriate form of intervention but as the *No Secrets* guidance (DH 2000: 10) points out, '... any or all of these types of abuse may be perpetrated as the result of deliberate intent, negligence or ignorance'.

Many vulnerable adults may not even realize that they are being abused. For instance, an elderly person, accepting that they are dependent on their family, may feel that they must tolerate losing control of their finances or their physical environment. They may be reluctant to assert themselves for fear of upsetting their carers or making the situation worse.

How do I know if it is adult abuse?

Information that is initially received as an 'alert', a method of notification to the local authority that a vulnerable person has or is likely to have suffered harm, is very varied and will often contain broad information. To decide whether or not the information does constitute, or is likely to constitute, abuse the following must be determined:

The two key components are:

- a person who qualifies as a vulnerable adult in *No Secrets* (DH 2000) and *Safeguarding Adults* (ADASS 2005);
- actual or probable harm, most likely caused by action(s) and/or omission(s) by another person(s)

One common denominator among those who have less physical, mental or emotional strength by dint of age, chronic ill health or disability is that, compared with the majority of those around them, they have less power. It is all too easy to make misassumptions based on stereotypes of dependency. Simply equating old age with dependency, with all the disempowerment this entails, is clearly not acceptable (Thompson 2007).

An imbalance of power is always a factor in instances of abuse and we must be particularly aware of the dynamics of who holds the power when investigating cases of alleged abuse. So if, for example, there was a fracas between two learning disabled people of equal power and the fracas was not related to an omission on the part of any carer, then this would not be treated as adult abuse. If one learning disabled resident attacked another because of a lack of supervision, then this would be treated as adult protection. However, if the attack was carried out by anyone who had responsibility for the care of an individual deemed to be vulnerable, this would be a clear case of adult abuse.

Foucault (Gordon 1980: 116) tells us that power is something created by people to enable activity to take place. It is not something which descends from societal structures but operates from 'grass roots' level. Structural inequalities borne of, for example, economic systems and social class are best addressed at this base level. This theory is supported by the fact that inequality continues to exist between the roles of men and women within the family, and within the workplace, despite the Sex Discrimination Act becoming law in 1975.

Power is also about having the wherewithal to implement or disregard factors which affect the lives of others. This may be facilitated by social or financial status, higher physical or intellectual ability (in comparison to the vulnerable adult), by dishonesty, lack of acknowledgement of cultural difference, exclusion in decision-making and disregard for basic human rights.

Reflective exercise

- Think of times in your life when you were powerless. How did it make you feel?
- Think of times when you felt it necessary for someone else to have power over you, or when you have had power over another.
- Powerlessness: in a situation where a loved one has a terminal illness, for example, you may feel powerless; there is an absence of any vehicle whatsoever with which you are able to restore them to health. You may feel angry, frustrated and perhaps useless because the power needed does not exist. It is not there to be had.
- Power over: you may submit yourself to the power of the surgeon and anaesthetist when you have surgery. You may feel apprehensive even frightened, but you have been given a choice and trust them to act in your best interests. You give power over yourself only to those you trust. A carer may have power over the 'cared for' individual (who may also be a vulnerable adult). The cared-for individual may also have power over the carer in that the carer may feel duty bound to perform the caring role, in spite of his or her own frailties. As practitioners within health and social care, we have to be particularly aware of the power dynamic within relationships, including our own with colleagues, carers and particularly with service users.

Public authorities are, of course, made up of individuals from whom this culture of oppression and consequential abuse has arisen, therefore education, starting with our schools, underpinned by inclusivity, is a necessity. The application of this legislation must also be considered in other areas such as sexual orientation, disability, age and gender. Social workers particularly must have sound cultural knowledge of the communities with whom they practise, ensuring that all intervention and decision-making is based on cultural awareness. If people feel that their needs are poorly understood because of language and cultural differences, this creates barriers to accessing support, particularly in respect of abuse and safeguarding.

For many people who have just begun to understand the meaning of the term adult protection, the introduction of the concept of safeguarding may seem like just another complication. However, the difference is important because of the way it constructs the roles and responsibilities of society, professionals and service users.

Adult Protection refers to the multi-agency response to harm (or probable harm) to a vulnerable adult as a consequence of action(s) or omission(s) on the part of another person or persons.

Safeguarding relates to the umbrella of prevention of abuse and has a broad focus that extends to all aspects of a person's general welfare.

Responding to adult abuse

When responding to an allegation of adult abuse it is important to remember that the incident may be subject to a criminal investigation therefore searching questions must not be asked other than to establish whether emergency services, e.g. police and ambulance, are needed. Multi-agency policies (for example, Kent and Medway Social Services 2012) which govern adult protection require practitioners who become aware of adult abuse to:

- stay calm in your responses and listen carefully to what is being said;
- try to establish whether the information given is likely to have put other people at risk.

For example, if the person disclosing the abuse is describing a scenario in a care home where a vulnerable resident has been neglected by a member of staff, it is probable that other residents may be affected. Similarly, if a worker for a care agency is reported to you as having taken money from a vulnerable client, it is a possibility that he or she is financially abusing others.

In a case of domestic abuse, it is important to establish whether there are other vulnerable adults (e.g. an elderly relative) or children in the household. In all cases it is vital that the scenario is explored to identify whether there are any children at potential risk in relation to the disclosure. If so, then consultations must be made with the Children and Families' Safeguarding team. Practitioners are also required within the guidelines (Kent and Medway Social Services 2012) to:

- reassure the discloser that the information is being taken seriously, explain what will happen next and give them a contact number to raise further issues or ask any questions;
- make comprehensive and legible notes as soon as possible after the disclosure with a clear distinction between facts and conjecture – these could be used in future court proceedings so need to focus on clear times, dates, chronology, etc.

It is helpful where possible to use the person's own words, and to check whether there are any other witnesses who could verify their account.

Safeguarding principles and social work values

The safeguarding principles as described by the Department of Health (2011) are an essential tool to guide and audit best practice in safeguarding, being common denominators in all safeguarding activity, including responses to abuse. They are described as:

- *empowerment:* presumption of person-led decisions and informed consent;
- *protection:* support and representation for those in greatest need;
- *prevention:* it is better to take action before harm occurs;
- *proportionality:* proportionate and least intrusive response appropriate to the risk presented;
- *partnership:* local solutions through services working with their communities. Communities have a part to play in preventing, detecting and reporting neglect and abuse;
- *accountability:* accountability and transparency in delivering safeguarding.

The *Code of Practice for Social Care Workers* from the General Social Care Council (GSCC 2002) tells us that social work embodies a set of core values and principles. It is committed to the rights of the child; respects the equality, worth and human rights of all people, and their individuality, privacy and dignity; and challenges discrimination and prejudice. It provides a list of statements that describe the standards of professional conduct and practice required in social care to ensure that workers know what standards of conduct employers, colleagues, service users, carers and the public expect of them. Within the Code, social workers and all social care workers must:

- protect the rights and promote the interests of service users and carers;
- strive to establish and maintain the trust and confidence of service users and carers;
- promote the independence of service users while protecting them as far as possible from danger or harm;
- respect the rights of service users while seeking to ensure that their behaviour does not harm themselves or other people;
- uphold public trust and confidence in social care services; and
- be accountable for the quality of their work and take responsibility for maintaining and improving their knowledge and skills.

(GSCC 2002: 12)

It is clear to see the correlation between the safeguarding principles and the social work values and why safeguarding adults is best placed by *No Secrets* with Social Services as the lead agency, rather than, for example, with primary health who may have a range of other interests and drivers. However, this does not mean that other agencies can leave all the responsibility to social workers; indeed the main thrust of *No Secrets* and subsequent enquiries has stressed the vital importance of good interdisciplinary communication and clear lines of accountability.

Legal framework for intervention

Unlike *Safeguarding Children*, there is currently no one specific piece of legislation in England requiring National Health Service (NHS) or independent sector organizations to participate in a multi-agency service to safeguard vulnerable adults. However, Adult

Services are required, based on section 7 of the Local Authority Social Service Act 1970 to act on the guidance document *No Secrets* (DH 2000) to coordinate the development of policies, procedures and practices to safeguard vulnerable people. Local authorities must still find a basis in legislation for their safeguarding activities which the *No Secrets* guidance does not provide.

The person-centred approach which the safeguarding process supports empowers and enables adults to live as independently as possible. Placing the service user at the heart of the safeguarding process means that all those involved must explore and adapt the most appropriate civil, criminal and community care legislation and guidance as a way of promoting the most effective means of intervention with individuals and their support networks.

Local authorities are also subject to a duty to assess people's informal carers in their own right if:

- they are caring for a person who may be in need of community care services;
- they are providing substantial care on a regular basis; and
- they request an assessment.

Local authorities have the power to provide services to the carer. Clearly the current policy for more care to be provided in people's own homes, rather than institutions, places a greater burden on families and informal carers. The provision of support to the carer (though a power, not a duty) acts as a mode of prevention against the build-up of mental and physical stress which can potentially lead to the risk of abuse and neglect by informal carers.

Risk assessment

Determining the level of risk within situations where abuse may be suspected is one of the most challenging areas for social workers and other practitioners in this field of activity. Kemshall (2002: 18) tells us that 'Workers assess risk not only to determine eligibility for services, but also to prevent harm to users and avoid costly and damaging litigation.'

Risk assessment is clearly a core skill essential to the role of the social worker supporting vulnerable adults who may for various reasons refuse services or intervention, placing them at potential risk of harm either in care homes or in their own homes. Even where there is what appears to be supportive legislation, there can be contradictions between competing priorities that make intervention more difficult to determine (Koubel and Bungay 2012).

The National Assistance Act 1948 section 47, Compulsory Removal from Home, empowers a local authority (with approval from the community physician and a magistrate) to remove to hospital or residential care someone who is suffering grave chronic disease and living in insanitary conditions. As the person does not have to be mentally incapacitated or disordered, there is a view that s.47 of the 1948 Act is contrary in principle to Article 5 of the European Convention on Human Rights in that they would be deprived of their liberty (Mandelstam 2009: 173–4).

If such activity related to a person who lacked mental capacity, then the Mental Capacity Act 2005 would be an additional legal underpinning for the local authority's decisions and actions.

The term 'abuse' encompasses a continuum from minimal discomfort to extreme physical and/or psychological harm, prolonged pain and, in some cases, death. It is important to note that there is no direct correlation between the availability of criminal legislation and the degree of harm suffered. The following case studies help to explore some of the key issues and challenges that can arise within the sphere of adult safeguarding.

Case study

Mrs Patel lived in Home Lea residential care home. Her reviewing social worker found her in a poor state, unable to mobilize and in a low mood. Her teeth and glasses were missing and she appeared very underweight. The manager said Mrs Patel didn't need her glasses as she was asleep most of the time and didn't need her teeth because she only had soft food. Her care plan was incomplete and there was no record of the bruising and lesion presenting on her right elbow. Pressure sores were developing on her hips and heels, for which there was no care plan. There was no reference to her religious, ethnic and spiritual needs. Neither a drink nor call bell were in reach. The home was untidy and smelled of urine and there were very few staff on duty.

- What are the main priorities here?
- What are the key issues?
- What should happen next?
- Who should be held responsible for any abuse that has taken place?

The immediate safety of Mrs Patel was the priority and she was admitted to hospital. The next action was to look at scope and impact of the abuse, with regard to the question of whether any of the issues relating to the care of Mrs Patel suggest others could be at risk of harm.

Although Social Services is identified in *No Secrets* (DH 2000) as the agency with lead responsibility, it is imperative that this is understood within the context of the multi-agency collaboration. A common theme, particularly highlighted in Serious Case Review reports (e.g. Laming 2003), was that multiple agencies had contact and had concerns, but none had communicated with the other. In her final summary, Koubel (Koubel and Bungay 2009: 182–5) reminds us of the necessity for all professionals to work together to ensure that there is direct work with the individual concerned. In the case discussed above, a multi-agency strategy meeting agreed a plan for a joint investigation between the police, health representatives and Social Services. Other residents were deemed to be at potential high risk based on indications of neglect. Urgent health and social care reviews were ordered to take place for all residents.

Documents pertaining to the care of Mrs Patel were seized by the police. The Care Quality Commission inspected the home as a matter of priority (although not part of the investigatory process, it contributes to such investigations by sharing findings of regulatory activity). The CQC served several warning notices, communicating to the provider that these could escalate to closure and/or prosecution if the provider was not compliant with the Health and Social Care Act 2008 (Regulated Activities) Regulations 2010, and the Care Quality Commission (Registration) Regulations 2009 within a very short time frame. The owner said he could not understand the concern because these were all very old people.

Mrs Patel told investigators she felt very uncomfortable, intimidated and sometimes in pain. Her religion, Hinduism, encourages the acceptance of pain and suffering as part of the consequences of karma. It is not seen as a punishment, but as a natural consequence of past negative behaviour and is often seen as an opportunity to progress spiritually. While Mrs Patel's own beliefs around the significance of the abuse from her perspective would be acknowledged, this situation would still be treated as a case of abuse as she did suffer actual harm even though Mrs Patel may believe the harm had a spiritual purpose. Abuse by neglect was substantiated but it was determined that no crime had been committed.

The manager had only been in post three months and clearly lacked empathy and understanding as well as practical home management skills. Changes in need were not recognized, documentation was minimal and Mrs Patel's rights to basic dignity and respect were ignored. A culture had developed in the home where any deterioration was perceived as a normal consequence of old age, as discussed by Decalmer and Glendenning (1997). The political economy perspective illustrated by Phillipson (1997: 113) puts carers and the elderly person within a framework of social and political resources and ideologies that old age has a socially and biologically constructed status. This perspective, suggesting that people's contribution to society deteriorates with age, implies therefore that it becomes (theoretically) justifiable not to invest resources in the care and protection of elderly people as they have no value. This was the view of the acting manager who was named as a perpetrator of abuse by neglect as she dictated a culture of fear among the carers. Carers were also culpable as they followed her directive to neglect and did not 'whistle blow' to outside agencies, as was the owner who did not monitor the progress of the manager, despite her being new in post.

The manager and three carers were dismissed and referred to the Independent Safeguarding Authority (ISA), a British non-departmental public body set up following an inquiry headed by Sir Michael Bichard in the wake of the Soham Murders. The ISA was to oversee a new Vetting and Barring Scheme in England, Wales and Northern Ireland, which was to have required all those working with vulnerable groups to undergo an enhanced vetting procedure before being allowed to commence any relevant duties. In effect, if the evidence was accepted by ISA, this would mean that the individual concerned would not again be allowed to work with vulnerable adults or children.

In the case of Mrs Patel, she recovered quickly once she was rehydrated and well nourished. A new manager was appointed to the home and Mrs Patel eventually returned, with close monitoring in place for her and the service. Post-abuse care plans must be holistic and person-centred, not purely focused on physical care needs. Spiritual support for

Mrs Patel was sought from an appropriate community leader at her request. As a Hindu, Mrs Patel believed that all illnesses, whether physical or mental, have a biological, psychological and spiritual element. Treatments which do not address all three causes may not be considered effective – clearly an essential element to support her recovery and well-being.

The prevalence of institutional abuse clearly underlines the need to understand better how to intervene and manage institutional abuse from a proactive and preventative perspective, rather than a reactive, post-abuse and process-led perspective. Effective intervention at both service and case levels is necessary to prevent future abuse and to tackle poor quality care and low standards more widely. In order to identify where intervention is needed, robust, judicious systems must be in place. The main purposes of these systems are to:

- identify the provisions in need of support;
- identify the practices and processes within that provision likely to heighten risk to individuals of abuse by neglect;
- signpost care providers to appropriate sources of support.

Institutional abuse can be very challenging to unravel and, as the safeguarding investigations progress, multiple victims may be identified who have suffered harm as a consequence of neglect arising from holistic failings (Elvidge and MacPhail 2009). Balancing the economy of care as a commodity becomes increasingly problematic as the rising cost of living impacts upon business margins. The physical and mental demands of carers meeting needs in homes increases as local authority policy strives to keep people in their own homes for as long as possible, therefore agreeing to fund placements only for those with highly complex care needs.

Post-abuse support

Vulnerable adults may need particular support and enablement to identify and access housing and support groups, and to plan their future. The violence or threat of violence may continue after a victim has separated from the abuser therefore it is vital that vulnerable people in this situation are enabled to maintain their personal safety and this would constitute part of their 'post-abuse care plan'. It is critical that practitioners remember that the victim's perception and experience of the abuse is central, not how we or others might interpret it.

Case study

This situation provides a good example of the importance of the views and concerns of the service user. Mary Jane was 89 years old and suffered mild dementia. She had no family, few visitors, and employed private carers to help her wash and dress. Her daily routine varied little. The humanity perspective identifies the theoretical 'absence of meaning of lives for

elderly people and doubt and uncertainty which seems to infuse their daily routines and relationships' (Decalmer and Glendenning 1997: 113). Her most valued possession was a deco-
rated postcard which her husband sent her from overseas during the war; she had received
it on the same day as the telegram telling her he had been killed in action. She kissed it
goodnight every night and good morning every day. One evening she found it gone.

Mary Jane was inconsolably distressed and appeared to relive the bereavement and
loss of her husband. The police response was that there was no monetary value therefore
they would not be investigating it as a crime but acknowledged the theft. Despite the terrible psychological effect the theft had on Mary Jane, this case was impossible to progress
as the carers denied taking the card. The outcome of the investigation therefore was that
abuse was confirmed but with insufficient evidence to identify the perpetrator.

Cambridge *et al.* (2006) derived information in respect of elder abuse in both community and institutional settings from a large local authority in England. It was found
that although only 14 per cent of the population were aged over 65, around 60 per
cent of adult protection alerts related to older people or older people with mental
health problems. Almost half of alerts related to people in residential or supported living services. Older people were found to be more vulnerable to neglect and financial
abuse than younger people and a staggering 64 per cent of the 'alerts' relating to older
people were for those living in residential services (institutional abuse). Overall, the
data provided by the study suggest that the combined characteristics of gender, age
and placement in residential care place vulnerable adults at particular risk of abuse,
especially those made vulnerable by the frailties of old age.

Reflective exercise

Consider the following statements:

1   By its very nature, abuse – the misuse of power by one person over another – has
    a large impact on a person's independence. Neglect can prevent a person who is
    dependent on others for their basic needs exercising choice and control over the fun-
    damental aspects of their life and can cause humiliation and loss of dignity.

    (ADASS 2005)

2   In an effort to produce outcomes that reached prescribed targets within limited bud-
    gets, the nature of care planning and provision is increasingly under pressure to adopt
    an administrative or bureaucratic orientation, making it more and more difficult for
    professionals to honour their professional ethical code.

    (Elvidge 2008)

Reflecting on statements 1 and 2 above, how can we improve quality and safeguard adults
within current economic constraints?

Koubel and Bungay (2012) discuss this paradigm extensively, describing the tensions between the medical and social models of care and how these models are themselves divided between acute and community services supported by various professions, each confident in the dominancy of its own professional discourse. This has to be viewed in balance with the primary perspective of individuals and their rights, not made easy by the frequently abstract concept of 'rights' held by professionals purporting to 'uphold' them for the individual.

Pulling together the differing professions to pool expertise in order to achieve the best outcome for the individual is exactly the sort of multi-agency, holistic approach that is advocated by *No Secrets* (DH 2000) for the protection and safeguarding of vulnerable adults.

Brown (2011) stresses the importance of understanding the impact of emotion on decision-making, particularly in safeguarding. Decisions are not always made in a linear way and social workers will have to take into account the importance of history and memory, motivation and drive, mood and stability, and openness to influence when assessing the mental capacity of vulnerable people, especially in the context of self-neglect and domestic abuse. However, for the social worker, as highlighted in the following case study, a range of theoretical frameworks can help to analyse and plan within complex situations. Domestic violence also comes under the umbrella of safeguarding when a vulnerable adult is involved.

Case study

Brian Kettle moved in with his 64-year-old stepmother, Irene, after his father (her husband and carer) died. Irene suffered from bipolar disorder characterized by extreme mood swings with episodes of depression and mania. Brian, 53 and divorced, was very active in the local community organizing charity fundraising events and also on the board of governors for the local primary school. He told associates that Irene, having no other family, was his responsibility.

Approximately six months after Brian had moved in, a neighbour raised concerns to her general practitioner, describing Irene as having become very quiet and withdrawn to the point where she had not seen her for several weeks. This led to a hospital admission where Irene was found to have one arm broken in several places, weight loss and multiple bruising, particularly to her wrists, arms and shoulders. Irene described how Brian had taken over her life, cutting her off from the outside world and taking control of her finances. She was too afraid of repercussions to seek help. Police arrested Brian, who explained Irene would not 'do as she was told' and that his father had always had 'trouble' with her. He asserted he had not been physically aggressive towards her (despite forensic evidence to the contrary). He became very angry during the police interview, stating he had given up valuable time to look after her; that she was very 'difficult' and he had to restrain her to stop her from hitting him, adding, 'You know what it is like with these old people ... '

Thinking about the situation that has been described, consider the following questions
- Is this abuse? What kind of abuse is it?
- What theories could help us understand what is happening in this scenario?
- What legal and ethical frameworks can help to determine the best way to help Irene address and manage the situation?

Physical abuse is clearly evident in the broken bones, bruising and weight loss. Psychological abuse may be another key factor as Brian has kept Irene isolated from others, including care givers in relation to her mental health needs. Financial abuse looks like a probability though we are not told at this stage whether he is misusing her finances, only that he has taken control of them. Brian's dominance and control in the relationship may also indicate domestic violence.

Neutralization theory (Tomita 1990) holds that internalized social norms and moral standards are neutralized within the perpetrator of deviant acts through a process of rationalization or justification of the acts. Brian clearly puts the blame on Irene, ignoring her mental health needs, asserting that she had been 'trouble' to his father. Some techniques of neutralization are denial of responsibility, denial of injury to the victim, blame attributed to the victim, condemnation of those who disapprove of the abuse (he became angry with the police officers) and appeal to higher loyalties, the defence of necessity ('she wouldn't do as she was told') and the rationalization that the abuse is but a minor deviation from a life filled with good deeds (after all, he was a leading light in charity work and a school governor).

Irene was assisted to give evidence under the Achieving Best Evidence (ABE) guidance set out as a range of special measures to assist vulnerable or intimidated witnesses as prescribed by the Youth Justice and Criminal Evidence Act 1999 (Home Office 2002). She was supported by a social work practitioner trained to interview alongside the police, and the interview was pre-recorded to present as evidence. ABE is a joint police and local authority responsibility in respect of child witnesses, but not so for vulnerable adult witnesses. However, many authorities implement the principles of ABE in order to enable joint working in the best interests of the vulnerable adult. Brian was prosecuted for the infliction of grievous bodily harm under section 20 of the Offences against the Persons Act 1861. The Home Office-led Multi Agency Public Protection Arrangements (MAPPA) database showed that Brian had been a perpetrator of domestic abuse towards his ex-wife but she had chosen not to pursue a conviction. Had someone noted earlier that all was not well (perhaps by Irene not attending a GP or mental health outpatient appointment) it could have been possible to identify that he was known as a perpetrator via the MAPPA database and appropriate early interventions could have been discussed. However, Tomita (1990) also notes that the 'victim' may also neutralize or justify the abuse and it is possible that Irene may have totally refused intervention earlier. If she has mental capacity, Irene is within her rights to make 'an unwise decision'. In such cases the only recourse for the worker may be to record his or her concerns and alert the other agencies involved about the possibility of future harm.

Mirrlees-Black (1999) suggests that domestic violence occurs in all sections of society irrespective of race, culture, nationality, religion, sexuality, disability, age, class or educational level, clearly indicating the need for the application of social work knowledge, skills and values. Another aspect of abuse that is becoming more prominent within the work of safeguarding adults is the emergence of what has been termed disability (or older person) hate crime.

Hate crime

One of the areas of abuse that challenges the perspectives and values of social work and social care practitioners is a particularly unpleasant process which may be carried out against people just because they are considered by some members of society to be vulnerable. Hate crime is any offence against a person or property that is motivated by the offender's hatred of people who are seen as being different, by race, religion, disability, age, sexuality or gender. An example of disability hate crime is the case of a 49-year-old man who was sent by his mother, his main carer, to the hairdressers. After having his hair cut he went to church and was told that he had the word 'fool' shaved into his head. The hairdresser was prosecuted.

It is important not to be restricted by the above definitions, but to remember that multiple forms of abuse may occur in an ongoing relationship or an abusive service setting to one person, or to more than one person at a time, making it important to look beyond single incidents or breaches in standards, to underlying dynamics and patterns of harm. Phillipson (1997) describes the mistreatment of older people as an enduring feature of our social history often typified by intergenerational conflicts, e.g. an older person's financial dominance and control over property; single daughters 'obliged' to stay and care for older parents; intergenerational household conflicts between grandparents and grandchildren, both cultural and financial.

The interactionist theory of abuse (Blumer 1969) arises from interaction between family members, driven by conflicts of perception and beliefs which shift within the paradigm of social and biological ageing, changing role definitions within the social groups with which the older person was interacting. Thus, someone may find their previously dominant provider and protector spouse's personality radically change to one of vulnerable and challenging dependence as a consequence of dementia. The carer/spouse retains the memory blueprint of how their partner used to be, along with the complex emotional history of their relationship and may therefore become a perpetrator of abuse because of frustration provoked by their spouse's apparent refusal to embody their previous personality and all that entails.

Legal framework: another way of dealing with abuse?

In Scotland, the Adult Support and Protection Act 2007 gives local authorities new powers to enter settings where abuse of adults is suspected of taking place and remove and ban perpetrators from these places. Here, tensions are evident as contradictions are posed to the idea of the autonomy of the adult. The Act also creates the responsibility for local authorities to establish a statutory adult protection committee to develop strategic interagency working (Fennall 2008: 66). Unlike in Scotland there is no single statutory framework for adult protection in England and Wales. Instead practitioners engage with a range of legislation including the Mental Health Act 1983, the Mental Capacity Act 2005, the Safeguarding Vulnerable Groups Act 2006 and the inherent jurisdiction of the civil and criminal justice systems. In this context practitioners often have to rely on professional judgement, expertise and consultation to find suitable remedies.

Case study

Alan, who is 62, has been the main carer for his son Mark, 38, for a number of years, since his wife was killed in the car accident which caused brain damage to Mark. Alan, an ex-army officer, has always declined help, saying that he can manage, and anyway, he sees it as his duty as a father. In recent months, Mark has become more and more challenging to manage as his frustration manifests as trying to fight off his father, biting him at any opportunity and clenching his limbs tightly to his body, making care interventions almost impossible. He is admitted to hospital with severe constipation and has pronounced bruises on his forearms. Alan admits that Mark has been difficult recently but he wants to continue to care for him as that is what his wife, Mark's mother, would have wanted. The duty senior decides that there is no mal intent and tells the hospital team that Mark can return home once he is fit for discharge.

Three months later, Mark is admitted to hospital with bruising, dehydration and a fractured wrist. Alan admits he cannot cope and the injuries were sustained as a consequence of him attempting to deliver care he could not achieve.

Consider the following issues in relation to the above

- What are the main issues here?
- How can we understand the decisions that have taken place?
- What else do you think could be done to help Alan and Mark?

The weak point here was the sole decision made by the duty senior who may not have been experienced in safeguarding matters. Just because Alan was expressing a desire to care for his son, this did not mean that he was able to achieve this safely and neither should it have discounted the initial bruising as 'not abuse' because it was presumed no harm was intended. At the point the initial bruising was identified, a case conference should have taken place in order that a multi-agency informed decision could be made. Sharing the decision also shares the ultimate consequences of that decision.

Some instances of abuse will constitute a criminal offence which may lead to criminal proceedings. Vulnerable adults are entitled to the protection of the law in the same way as any other members of the public. However, sometimes it is deemed not in the public interest to prosecute, as was the case with Alan who completely acknowledged the abuse he had perpetrated because of his stubborn refusal to seek help. Mark wished to stay with his father who now accepts carer support.

Within any safeguarding investigation, the designated senior officer must focus on the needs and wishes of the vulnerable adult and conduct the orchestra of support, investigation and intervention from other agencies to assess the level and seriousness of the risks while at the same time ensuring the person's rights are respected. Social work values require that we try to see an incident of safeguarding as an opportunity, sometimes through advocacy or other support services, to enable and empower the victim towards his or her chosen outcomes. This may involve a complex network of practitioners from a variety of disciplines or it may be carried out by a single practitioner. The vulnerable adult, by whatever definition you prefer to give, must always be the centre of the safeguarding activity.

References and further reading

ADASS (Association of Directors of Adult Social Services) (2005) *Safeguarding Adults: A National Framework of Standards for Good Practice and Outcomes in Adult Protection Work.* London: ADASS.

Blumer, H. (1969) *Symbolic Interactionism.* Englewood Cliffs, NJ: Prentice Hall.

Brown, H. (2011) The role of emotion in decision-making, *The Journal of Adult Protection,* 13 (4): 194–202.

Brown, K. (2012) Re-moralising 'vulnerability', *People, Place & Policy Online,* 6 (1): 41–53, available at: http://www.extra.shu.ac.uk/ppp-online/issue-1-300312/doc [Accessed 5 July 2012].

Cambridge P., Beadle-Brown, J., Milne, A., Mousell, J. and Whelton, B. (2006) *Exploring the Incidence, Risk Factors, Nature and Monitoring of Adult Protection Alerts.* Canterbury: Tizard, University of Kent.

Decalmer, P. and Glendenning, F. (eds) (1997) *The Mistreatment of Elderly People,* 2nd edn. London: Sage Publications.

DH (Department of Health) (2000) *'No Secrets': Guidance on Developing and Implementing Multi-Agency Policies and Procedures to Protect Vulnerable Adults from Abuse.* London: Department of Health.

DH (2009) *Safeguarding Adults: Report on the Consultation on the Review of 'No Secrets': Guidance on Developing and Implementing Multi-agency Policies and Procedures to Protect Vulnerable Adults from Abuse.* London: DH.

DH (2011) *Statement of Government Policy on Adult Safeguarding.* London: HMSO.

Elvidge, F. (2008) The impact of law and ethics on evidence-based practice – a case study in social care, *The Kent Journal of Practice Research,* 2 (1): 49–54.

Elvidge, F. and MacPhail, G. (2009) The 'quality in care' model of quality assurance and safeguarding for older people in institutional care, *Journal of Adult Protection,* 11 (1): 28–37.

Fennall, F. (2008) Adult protection: the Scottish legislative framework, in A. Mantell and T. Scragg (eds) *Safeguarding Adults in Social Work.* Exeter: Learning Matters.

Field-Fisher, T. G. (1974) *Report of the Committee of Inquiry into the Care and Supervision Provided by Local Authorities and Other Agencies in Relation to Maria Colwell and the Co-ordination Between Them* (Chairman T. G. Field-Fisher). London: HMSO.

Foucault, M. (2006) *History of Madness.* London and New York: Routledge.

Gordon, C. (ed.) (1980) *Power/Knowledge: Selected Interviews and Other Writings, 1972–1977.* New York: Pantheon.

GSCC (General Social Care Council) (2002) *Codes of Practice for Social Care Workers* [Online]. General Social Care Council, Available at: http://www.gscc.org.uk/cmsFiles/Codesof-PracticeforSocialCareWorkers.pdf [Accessed 23 January 2012].

Haringey Local Safeguarding Children Board (2009), *Serious Case Review: Baby Peter* (online), available at: http://www.haringey/scb.org/executive_summary-peter-final.pdf [Accessed 5 July 2012].

Home Office (2002) *Achieving Best Evidence in Criminal Proceedings: Guidance for Vulnerable and Intimidated Witnesses, Including Children*. London: Home Office.

Kemshall, H. (2002) *Risk, Social Policy and Welfare*. Buckingham: Open University Press.

Kent and Medway Social Services (2012) *Revised Multi Agency Adult Protection Policy: Protocols and Guidance*. Maids-tone: Kent and Medway Social Services Departments.

Koubel, G. and Bungay, H. (eds) (2009) *The Challenge of Person-centred Care: An Interprofessional Perspective*. Basingstoke: Palgrave Macmillan.

Koubel, G. and Bungay, H. (eds) (2012) *Rights, Risks and Responsibilities: Interprofessional Working in Health and Social Care*. Hampshire: Palgrave Macmillan.

Laming, Lord (2003) *The Victoria Climbié Inquiry* (Chairman Lord Laming). London: The Stationery Office.

Mandelstam, M. (2009) *Safeguarding Vulnerable Adults and the Law*. London: Jessica Kingsley Publishers.

Martin, J. (2007) *Safeguarding Adults*. Dorset: Russell House.

Mirrlees-Black, C. (1999) *Domestic Violence: Findings from a New British Crime Survey Self-completion Questionnaire*. London: Home Office.

Parsons, T. (1951) *The Social System*. New York: Free Press.

Phillipson, C. (1997) Abuse of older people: sociological perspectives, in P. Decalmer and F. Glendenning (eds) *The Mistreatment of Elderly People*, 2nd edn. London: Sage Publications.

Thompson, N. (2007) *Power and Empowerment*. Lyme Regis: Russell House.

Tomita, S. (1990) Denial of elder mistreatment by victims and abusers: the application of neutralization theory, *Violence and Victims*, 5 (3): 171–84.

Wolfensberger, W. (1984) A reconceptualization of normalization as social role valorization, *Mental Retardation*, 34: 22–5.

Wright, D. and Digby, A. (eds) (1996) *From Idiocy to Mental Deficiency: Historical Perspectives on People with Learning Disabilities*. London and New York: Routledge.

4 Collaborative working with service users

Yolaine Jacquelin with Donna Francis and Ian Devereux

This chapter reflects the views of three people. The main author is Yolaine Jacquelin who works as a training manager in Adult Social Services. The additional voices are supplied by two people, Donna Francis and Ian Devereux, who use support services.

Yolaine says:

> Donna, Ian and I share a goal: to change professionals' perception of service users as 'other' through collaboratively working within the training of a social care workforce. Our reasons for this specific goal are very different. As for me, I worked in social care for over fifteen years before becoming involved in training and I am committed to empowerment principles and to tackling inequalities and upholding strong ethical values around fairness and justice as stated in the principles underpinning the *Code of Ethics for Social Work*.
>
> (BASW 2002)

Ian became severely disabled through illness and in the first year after the illness, he became conscious of 'the slow realization that whilst my life had changed irrevocably I was still the same person. My opinions did matter and being able to talk to people about my experiences might have some value.'

Donna says:

> I have a form of dwarfism called Spondyloepiphyseal Dysplasia Congenita (SEDc). This is a rare condition and is genetic and I was born with it. It causes painful joints and in my case none of my joints have formed properly. I am just under 3 feet 7 inches tall. I use an electric wheelchair for long distances and wear a hearing aid and glasses. Even though I have SEDc I am the same as anyone else and have the same aspirations and dreams as individuals without SEDc.

Introduction

Using an ongoing project of involving service users in the training of social care staff within a large local authority, known by the acronym TREND, this chapter will explore the principles, dynamics, approaches and drivers, as well as the joys and challenges of attempting to translate into practice the underpinning social work values inherent in the concept of collaborative working with service users.

Learning outcomes

By the end of the chapter, readers should have developed their understanding and awareness of:

- the application of social work values and commitment to the avoidance of a tokenistic approach to involving service users in the development of social work with adults and social care practice;
- the process of collaboration with service users and carers, analysing the drivers and approaches required to extend the role of service users in developing partnership and participation in practice;
- the role and contribution of service users to the training and development of practitioners in social work and social care, analysing the challenges and dilemmas that arise from actively embedding a partnership approach to involving service users within social work training and education;
- the emotional impact for users of moving from being recipients of services to learning facilitators with a real opportunity to influence current and future practice in social work with adults.

Practitioners in social work and social care choose to work in a profession committed to a set of fundamental principles they are required to adhere to and put into practice. The British Association of Social Workers (BASW) is the professional association for social workers in the United Kingdom. It has a duty to ensure as far as possible that its members discharge their ethical obligations and are afforded the professional rights which are necessary for the safeguarding and promotion of the rights of service users.

BASW issued a revised *Code of Ethics for Social Work* in April 2002. The primary objective of the Association's Code of Ethics is to express the values and principles which are integral to social work, and to give guidance on ethical practice. It is binding on all members. The code emphasizes that social work is committed to five basic values:

- **Human dignity and worth** (Every human being has intrinsic value. All persons have a right to well-being, to self-fulfilment and to as much control over their own lives as is consistent with the rights of others)
- **Social justice** (This includes: The fair and equitable distribution of resources to meet basic human needs; Equal treatment and protection under the law and identifying, seeking to alleviate and advocating strategies for overcoming structural disadvantage)
- **Service to humanity** (Service in the interests of human well-being and social justice is a primary objective of social work)

- **Integrity (**Integrity comprises honesty, reliability, openness and impartiality)
- **Competence** (Proficiency in social work practice is an essential value)

(BASW 2002: 2)

Reflective exercise

- What are your personal values? Where do they come from? How did you acquire them? How do people around you know you hold these values?
- What messages (positive, negative or silent) did you receive about people who are different from you as you were growing up? Which of these messages do you still hold as true? Which of these messages have you challenged and replaced? How and why did you decide to challenge this conditioning?
- How do you feel when you meet someone who does not share your values? How would you work with someone who challenged your values?

Parrott (2006) argues that our personal values form an intrinsic part of our identity, guide our behaviours and shape the person we are. He goes on to state that our values are developed within a specific cultural and societal context and they are constantly challenged by new ideologies and discoveries which present us with new ways of thinking and re-evaluating the values we hold. These personal values we hold and feel strongly about may not be shared by others, hence the need to have a set of professional values to guide us in our social work practice and the development of 'codes of practice' to protect all parties involved.

Working with someone who challenges your values can be difficult but also an opportunity to reflect and challenge yourself. Having open discussions with the intention of really understanding the other person's viewpoint is helpful for both parties. However, there are times when the other person might be at risk of being in breach of their professional code of conduct, or their employment contract or the law if their remarks are deemed offensive and it is perfectly acceptable to remind them of the framework they have agreed to work within. Exploring challenges to your values is a good use of supervision.

Labelling the people we serve

The concept of 'values' is complex and multi-layered and as a professional working within social care, I am interested in the translation of these sets of beliefs into behaviours which should have a positive impact on service users.

I have chosen to use the word 'service user' as a shorthand term to describe the people who currently use health and social care services. However, this term presents challenges as this could mean that people are thought of *primarily in terms of their use of services, which may not be how they would define themselves'*, as pointed out by Beresford (2000: 489).

Beresford (2005) goes on to highlight a number of reasons why the term is problematic:

- it presents people as if their main and perhaps sole identity is through their consumption of public services (services which they may dislike and reject);
- it ignores the fact that many service users have no say in whether or not they receive services. They are involuntary service users who are compelled to use services against their wishes;
- it reduces the complex identities which people have and suggests artificially that they all have something in common.

Service user organizations, such as Shaping Our Lives, A National Network of Service Users and Disabled People, give their own reasons, on their website, to question the term 'service user':

> The term 'service user' can be used to restrict your identity as if all you are is a passive recipient of health and welfare services. That is to say, a service user can be seen as someone who has things 'done to them' or who quietly accepts and receives a service. This makes it seem that the most important thing about you is that you use or have used services. It ignores all the other things you do and which make up who you are as a person.
>
> (www.shapingourlives.org.uk/definitions.html)

It could be argued that both Beresford and the organization mentioned above have a narrow understanding of the concept of 'services'. Until the advent of the personalization agenda, the term 'services' may have been used to mean the services provided solely by Health and Social Care organizations. However, the term now encompasses all generic services used not only by people with a physical disability or sensory impairment, people with a learning disability, people with mental health problems or people with a long-term condition but also by all members of the public (think universal services such as leisure and educational services). This, in turn, could imply that we are all 'service users' of public services. This might help Health and Social Care practitioners to appreciate that the term 'service user' refers to just one aspect of someone's identity and not the whole of it and that it should not imply a passive acceptance of services but rather an active engagement and level of choice and control with those services.

Within the TREND project (TREND is an acronym put forward by one of the members for Training Enables Never Disables and the project is a commitment to the proactive participation of users of services within a local authority in-house training delivery programme), we often had heated discussions about the particular use of the term 'service user' as it was written in all the policies we worked to. Some members strongly objected to the term on the grounds that it diminished their sense of self; others, like Ian, identified more with the label 'person with a disability'.

None of the group members identified with terms such as consumers, customers or clients as all these seemed to imply that, first, there was an element of choice as to where you could purchase your 'services', secondly, that you could purchase any service you wanted (as opposed to services that meet the user's eligible needs as assessed by a case manager following prescribed standards and procedures) and lastly, that you did the purchasing yourself where in most cases the purchasing was done on their behalf by a case manager. These statements mirror Sarah Bank's arguments against the use of the term 'consumer' or 'customer', as she argues that these terms 'serve to hide the fact of social worker as controller' (Banks 2006: 115).

However, she also notes that a consumerist approach to social work, with its implied notion of consumer rights, does challenge the power base of professionals. Banks also explores the label 'citizen' and warns of the dangers of the narrowness of some of the interpretations of the term which could imply citizens are equal members of a community enjoying equal rights. It is difficult to imagine that some members of our society, such as men and women with a learning disability still living in segregated settings such as long-stay hospitals, would feel they are citizens enjoying the same political, civil and social rights as other members of the community they belong to.

Whereas the word 'citizen' was never mentioned in our discussions, the term 'persons' or 'individuals' was often used by members as a preferred term with an emphasis on 'we are all people, I am just like you, I just need more support'. Banks (2006) reminds us that our understanding of the concept of 'personhood' needs to encompass the wider issues of the specific cultural and social context in which the individual is placed and acknowledge the power differentials between the person who needs the support and the person who has the authority and knowledge to make the support happen. For the people I work with, the most important factor for them is not to be perceived as 'other' by practitioners (which they feel is loaded with negative connotations and implies being a lesser being) but rather as 'same as', but with different support needs. What we learn from this is that whatever term we use to refer to the people we work with, it is important to explore the values and assumptions underpinning the terms we use and pause to reflect on the issues of power that the naming of others we perceive as different bring to both the practitioner and the users' perceptions of themselves.

Reflective exercise

- In what ways are the labels we use to define groups important to think about?
- In what ways are your rights and responsibilities different when you are a client, a consumer, a citizen or a service user?
- What and where is your community? What are your rights and responsibilities as a member of that community? Pause and think about who is excluded from your community. Do they, in turn, have a community of their own that they can actively choose to belong to?

The notion of community may be understood in terms of place, control, identity, inclusion and exclusion, freedom and restraint. Some people look back to an idealized dream of cohesive community (Means and Smith 1994). While communities can be inclusive, supportive and enabling there is also the problem that certain groups may be excluded from some communities, for example lesbians and gays, disabled people, deaf people, black and ethnic minority people, the travelling community, people who are homeless, people with enduring mental health problems, the working class (from gated communities in affluent parts of the UK).

Translating values into practice

As stated earlier, I am interested in the challenge of translating social work values into practice and exploring the ways in which the values and stated commitment of social work can actively engage with the risks, rewards and reality of incorporating the input of service users into social work practice with adults and social work education in a way that is meaningful and empowering for all involved. The concept of the service user as equal expert was the starting point for the TREND project I set up which sought to equip current users of services with the skills to make an impact on in-house training and practice. Following a successful project involving Mental Health service users, I became keen to extend the project to people who used adult services.

The decision to include a recruitment and selection process was based on the premise that being a service user does not automatically mean someone will be an effective trainer. The target group for recruitment and selection was current service users who were able to talk about their experience and present a balanced perspective. This meant there was a degree of self-selection and that some users were excluded because the very nature of their intellectual impairment meant they would not have been able to access some more abstract concepts. A person specification setting out the required experience, knowledge, skills and personal resources was circulated far and wide through case managers, local organizations, the private and voluntary sector, etc.

This is how Ian found out about it:

> It was towards the end of 2008. My care manager sent an email to my wife, which had been circulated throughout social services, asking for 'service users' who might be interested in joining the Social Services training team. After reading the material, one Friday afternoon, I immediately rang the organizer. I will always remember her saying, at the end of the 45-minute conversation, that she was going home with a smile on the face and looking forward to meeting me; well, I can honestly say that the feeling was mutual.

Donna found out about the project in a different way:

> One day I was reading one of the newsletters that we get emailed from a local charity and I saw an advertisement about service users being trained as co-trainers for Social Services. This looked amazing and something I could see myself doing. I had already been involved in teaching and training at the university and at the church I go to. I applied straight away.

There were two stages to the selection process. The first stage was an interview with an in-service trainer and an external trainer/facilitator to assess individuals' potential to deliver training and their ability to use and share their service user experience in a constructive way. The second part of the process involved an informal group discussion about the potential benefits of service user and carer involvement in training and development for both the practitioner learners and themselves, with the purpose of assessing individual motivation for involvement in training. Feedback was offered to all participants.

Here is Donna commenting on her experience of the course:

> I thought the TREND project was a great opportunity for service users to show professionals what it is really like to be at the receiving end of services. I sometimes found it hard to admit that I would need support for the rest of my life and not be able to do everything myself even though I am fiercely independent – sometimes I would rather struggle than ask for help. This was a great opportunity to show professionals that we are people first and foremost, people who have the same aspirations and dreams as them. People who are like them but just need extra support to do things that they may even take for granted. As the TREND training progressed I realized that this was the message I wanted to take to professionals – that we are the same as anyone else; we may just need extra support to do the things we want and need to do in our lives.

We receive ongoing feedback about the impact of service user involvement in training courses through evaluation and it is clear that practitioners value their input. Members of staff who had attended the courses cite working alongside service users as equal partners as the main impetus for wanting to change from a 'doing for' the user to 'working with and alongside' the user based on self-directed support and personalization principles. 'Working alongside' users does not underplay the real tensions and challenges that may be experienced when users and professionals work together. Ongoing issues of power, empowerment, and the extent to which users are equal partners will be further developed throughout this chapter.

We have already noted that one of the principles of social work is 'Respect for the dignity and worth of all human beings' (BASW 2002: 2). In the context of social work practice, this means that social workers 'have a duty to respect service users' rights to make informed decisions, and ensure that service users and carers participate in decision-making processes' (2002: 2). Within a social worker–service user relationship, this would mean doing as much as you can to build a rapport with service users, and supporting them to actively engage in the processes we use to enable them to live the lives they want.

At an organizational level, the principle of 'ensuring users participate in the decision-making process' (BASW 2002: 3) could encompass a range of activities currently used such as: involving users in staff interviews (with an equal vote to paid staff), speaking at conferences, training, working as 'mystery shoppers' to assess the quality of services, as assessors of care during major contract renewals, actually writing policies or mission statements and being active members of the most senior board with as powerful a voice as anybody else around the table (SCIE 2007; Warren 2007). The language used to describe how far the voices of users are embedded in the organizational principles reflects the different opportunities offered to service users in those very organizations: people can participate, be full partners, be involved, collaborate or co-produce (Beresford and Croft 1993; Braye 2000). It is not my intention to examine the meaning of these words as I agree with Braye (2000: 9) that 'the terminology is less important than the intention behind the actions it describes'.

Reflective exercise

Thinking of an organization you have worked for, either as a member of staff or a volunteer . . .

- At what level were service users involved in decision-making processes?
- What were the factors in place that made this possible?
- What were the barriers to participation?

Depending on the client group you worked with, the extent of their intellectual impairment, and the organization's commitment to user participation, your experience might range from people being supported to choose their own clothes, deciding the menus for the week, writing the person specifications for the recruitment of a new member of staff, to user-led organizations where members make all the decisions. It is important to note that, traditionally, 'participation hierarchy gives higher status to participation in policy making and resource allocation than participation in everyday activities' (Hernandez *et al.* 2010: 716). This does not just apply to service users, either, as the same disparity of status can be reflected in the contrast between the wages we pay policy makers and the wages we pay care staff. Warren (2007) reminds us to be mindful of thinking of a hierarchy of participation and advocates supporting people to engage in whatever way they can at whatever level is meaningful and accessible to them.

One model which challenges the traditional hierarchical perspective is the 'whole systems approach' (Wright *et al.* 2006). It is a model endorsed by the Social Care Institute for Excellence (SCIE 2007) and it sets out four elements which need to be there for an organization to support user participation effectively:

- a person-centred culture within the organization;
- a structure that has resources to make engagement happen;
- effective practice, and
- systems for review and evaluation.

You might like to look at your own list of factors that make participation possible in the organization you chose, check out which ingredients were in place and think about what more the organization could do.

Barriers to genuine participation can be grouped under two main headings: the individual level and the organizational level (Warren 2007). Within both levels it is important to explore professional attitudes and assumptions, poor communication with service users and carers, service user and carers' perceptions and experiences, institutional structures and practices and lack of practitioner time, as well as professional and organizational resistance.

Within the wider framework of the political and economic climate, one of the most vexing obstacles encountered in setting up the TREND project was the real difficulties of wanting to pay users the appropriate rate for their input and the challenges of a benefit system that is neither flexible nor entirely helpful.

The practice guide published by the Social Care Institute for Excellence (SCIE 2007) provides some useful examples of organizations working to embed the concepts of 'participation'. An underpinning quality these organizations have in common is their willingness to engage actively with the challenges and benefits that sharing power with users of their services will inevitably bring.

Power and empowerment

Social work practice has always concerned itself with the imbalance of power between the professional and the service user. Thompson (2007) warns us that the discourse around power is complex, multi-layered, and has a wide range of meanings depending on one's theoretical perspective. He offers a useful approach (known as the PCS model of power) for exploring issues of power whereby we can think of three interlinked models: the psychological or personal (that is an individual's ability to achieve his or her own ends); the cultural or discursive (the capacity of language to create structures of power) and the structural (where a person fits in the social hierarchy).

There were a number of reasons that I wanted to be involved in a collaborative project with service users, and one of those was my strong belief and commitment to empowerment. I had first encountered the term in the early 1990s when working with mental health clients who were being supported not only to voice their opinions of the services they were getting but also to shape the direction of new services. I then rejoined the client group I was familiar with (men and women with a learning disability) and, as part of the management team, was able to help turn around a team culture from a 'doing to' users to 'doing with and alongside'.

Empowerment does mean a lot of different things to different people but I like Thompson's definition of empowerment as one of 'helping people gain greater control over their lives and circumstances' (Thompson 2007: 21) as it seems to me to go to the crux of the matter. It needs to be said that this is not using the term 'helping' to refer to powerful professionals helping the helpless (Shakespeare 2000) but rather as all parties helping one another and bringing different skills, perspectives and ideas in an interdependent manner.

Current drivers

One of the basic reasons why we involve people who use services in decision-making processes in social care is quite simply because we have to by law and the impetus is also driven by central government policy and guidance. Some of the key pieces of legislation and guidance include:

- Health and Social Care Act 2001 (patients must be consulted in the planning and delivery of services);
- *National Service Framework for Mental Health* (DH 1999);
- *Valuing People* (DH 2001a) and *Valuing People Now* (DH 2009), specifically for the involvement of people with a learning disability;
- *National Service Framework for Older People* (DH 2001b).

Warren (2007) also reminds us that tackling inequalities and upholding strong ethical values around fairness and justice is one of the underpinning tenets of social work practice.

I do not believe that the current inclusive agenda would have made such effective progress if service users themselves had not been so vocal in demanding to be involved (see Chapter 6 for more details on this). Warren (2007) offers a comprehensive list of factors which might explain the development of user participation in social work practice. Among those listed are ideologies such as the social model of disability, the emergence of self-help groups and the influence of international user movements. Mention must also be made of the financial climate, as involving service users makes economic sense: if we listen to what people want, we are less likely to commission services they are not interested in.

Having looked at issues of power, empowerment, approaches and drivers required to push the concept of user participation I now turn my attention to the specific involvement of users within training, analysing challenges and dilemmas and exploring the benefits to all parties concerned.

The role and contribution of service users to the training and development of practitioners in social work and social care

I will be returning to the TREND project described earlier as a vehicle to explore the themes highlighted above and include within this analysis the emotional impact for users of moving from being recipients to learning facilitators in social work training. Prior to starting the project, a lot of discussion took place as to the extent of the role users could play within the training, how far we were able to commit, in terms of human and financial resources, to spending time beyond the training course to equip people with the knowledge needed to co-facilitate and how to measure the effectiveness of the users' contribution.

We were keen to avoid tokenism because we embraced the notion of meaningful participation and did not want to be seen as just ticking boxes. Thompson (2007) goes as far as stating that not carrying through one's principles of empowerment and commitment to purposive user involvement is tantamount to abusing one's professional power. The reality of putting those principles into practice, however, faced us with a number of challenges and dilemmas which I will consider now. When I reflect on those discussions, I am quite critical of them in the light of what I have learned from working with users:

- we were focusing on the intellectual part of the training where we probably felt, at the time, the power resided as opposed to thinking about the emotional impact of hearing someone's story and connecting with the person at a deeper level than the rational (Warren 20007);
- we were defining the role people should have as opposed to focusing on creating opportunities and ensuring the resources were in place for service users to decide for themselves the role they wanted to play (Carter and Beresford, cited in Warren 2007);
- we were in danger of going against our principle of inclusivity by defining the role as intellectually demanding and therefore not necessarily opening doors to users with intellectual impairments;
- we were focusing on service users being equal partners through having equal responsibilities, not as equal partners with unequal responsibilities but 'equally valued and respected for the work we do' (Jones and Hahn 2007).

The one thing we were clear about was that, to minimize the effects of tokenism and to equip users with a range of tools and techniques needed to be effective in presentation, we needed to design a course where, at the very least, people would build on their self-esteem and own skills so as to be able to confidently deliver their message to course participants.

Reflective exercise

Having just read about the value of simply hearing the service user's story and connecting with the person at an emotional level, take time to read part of Ian's story below and use the following questions to help you reflect:

- Are there aspects of Ian's story that resonate with your own understanding of disability?
- Are there any aspects that make you feel uncomfortable?
- What do you think this means in terms of social work values and issues of practice with disabled people?

Ian's story:

As a Director and Partner in two successful local businesses, I had given little thought to disability and the needs of the disabled. As a business we had ramps into our offices and a designated disabled toilet, all put in place by the landlord. We therefore thought we were 'doing our bit'. The fact that a wheelchair would have difficulty getting over the threshold and the toilet was completely inadequate had just never come up. Growing up I had a cousin with cerebral palsy, my new sister-in-law has Downs syndrome and I was learning how to help my wife with her daughter who is autistic. So I thought I knew all about disability.

I was completely absorbed by my impending second marriage to Denise and bringing our two families together and running our businesses. I had been feeling run down in the lead up to the wedding; but we just put it down to stress and my workload. I was therefore looking forward to a week off after the wedding. In the week after our marriage I started to feel progressively worse. Returning to work on the Monday I felt completely washed out, and suffering the usual jokes about man flu etc., came home and went straight to bed. I can honestly say that when I look back, from that Monday evening onwards I am in awe of what Denise has done and achieved ... if the roles had been reversed I could not possibly have done what she has. Were it not for her love, strength and determination, I would not have achieved or experienced many of the things I have over the last few years and will always love and owe her a huge debt for the way she has supported me and our family.

The following morning I could barely move, the doctor took one look at me and told Denise to drive me to A&E and not wait for an ambulance and she would ring ahead to warn them we were coming. I don't remember arriving but apparently two porters had to lift me from the car and wheel me into A&E. Twenty-four hours later I was in a coma with a virus attacking my spinal cord and brain stem and not expected to survive. The next thing I can remember is a string of cards over my bed, that was my birthday, May 6th, and I had effectively been in a coma since April 17th, and was now paralysed from the neck down. I was eventually stable enough to be transferred to Neuro-rehab and spent most of 2007 isolated from what was happening to my family, and basically being told what to do. This is the main reason I have always said that my illness happened to my wife and my family, not me; because I never lived through any of the consequences they had to deal with.

I was eventually discharged from rehab in late November 2007. This was an occasion of very mixed emotions as I was pleased to be leaving hospital but also had no idea what the future would hold. I was being discharged as a quadriplegic who had to be hoisted in and out of bed and needed 24-hour support, my wife already had an autistic daughter she was supporting and trying to run a brand new business from our bedroom just to keep a roof over our heads. Due to a mix-up with dates, my case manager never made the discharge meeting, and therefore we had no idea about any social services support, meaning that my wife spent the first couple of weeks trying to cope on her own.

It was at this time I also started to think about what the future would hold. It was apparent that I was completely unable to work or get around without a lot of help. I started to think that my future was daytime TV. It's difficult to describe the sense of loss and frustration you feel when you realize that you're incapable of doing the things you used to take for granted, but also had become a huge burden on those around you. To go from someone who felt in control of their life to someone who is dependent upon other people just to change the channel on the television is a very sobering and depressing memory. Coupled with this, the lack of ongoing physio input, and concern that if I didn't at least try I would never know what I could achieve. Life, such as it was, had the potential to become very depressing.

My case manager took one look at Denise and realized she was the person who needed help and support, not me. In essence, once I was up in the morning and sat in front of the TV there was little more I could do other than constantly ask Denise to do everything for me. It is difficult to overstate the impact that the care manager's support and guidance made in the early days after I was discharged from hospital. Upon seeing the situation he put in place a package of emergency support, which helped relieve the initial pressure on Denise, and allowed us time to take stock of the situation. My care manager spent a significant amount of time, meeting and getting to know all of us as a family and understanding us as people and finding out not only about the past, but also about any hopes we had for the future.

I think one of the hardest things for other people to understand is that while you might appear to the outside world to be confident, cheerful and getting on with your life, underneath it all in the quiet times when you're left with your own thoughts, usually in the early hours of the morning, you go through a huge range of emotions ranging from anger and 'why me?' to sadness at the problems and stresses you caused the family to fear and uncertainty for what the future holds. I also believe it's the uncertainty for the future which is the worst part of disability.

Obviously, a huge concern is financial, but just going down to the shop can become a major expedition. Just trying to find ramps on and off the footpath for an electric wheelchair to get up and down or wondering if there will be a properly accessible toilet at your destination becomes a major concern. You also feel incredibly vulnerable, especially if you're on your own: what would happen if I couldn't get up the kerb, or the wheelchair stopped for some reason. We hear all sorts of stories about disabled people being attacked or threatened in the street. And what would I do, if it happened to me?

While I wholeheartedly believe in the principles of self-directed support and allowing people to live their own lives – I for one could not possibly have achieved the recovery I have, without the support of people around me – there are negatives. By far the biggest frustration for me has been telling my story repeatedly to different professionals who all come with their own preconceived ideas. I've lost count of the OTs who try to get me to use modified cutlery, which I personally hate, and that hatred forced me to learn to hold a fork; although I still can't hold a knife, I keep trying. If professionals spent time to listen to and understand my personal goals, which have never really changed, they would understand far more about me. There is always a huge concern and fear around constantly changing professionals and their interpretation of 'the system'.

Becoming disabled has given me an insight into the NHS, social services and people as a whole. What's important to me is exactly the same as every other person – my wife, my family, security and the future, so why ask? The more sensible questions are: what makes me me, what do I want to do, what do I want to achieve, what are the problems and what is happening with the people around me? By all means offer me possibilities, but don't expect me to necessarily have or want the same needs or desires as other individuals like me may have chosen. What I want is the opportunity to live my life my way, and not be shoved into some box that says: because I'm disabled I should just accept I am no longer a full member of society.

Ian's personal story highlights the complexity of the individual's response to disability and the need for practitioners in health and social care to remember the essential *person* inside the disabled external presentation. It provides a good reminder of what people with physical or sensory disabilities experience every day and of the minimum provision needed (for example as we saw within the TREND programme) to ensure users' participation. These experiences included:

- venue accessibility: insufficient disabled parking bays, parking space too far away from the front door for someone with restricted mobility to walk to, heavy doors not opening automatically, accessible toilet with broken door lock, accessible toilet too small for a wheelchair user, having to ask for a key every time you need access to the accessible toilet;
- sensory impairment: loop system in place but not working, being assured there is a loop system in place and finding none;
- room too small to accommodate two wheelchair users even though you have specifically requested a large room to accommodate wheelchair users;
- accessibility of information: policies about service users not written in a user-friendly format or in font and colour accessible to someone with a visual impairment.

Aside from practical challenges, there are a number of personal challenges for service users that co-trainers and practitioners need to take into account:

- the debilitating and exhausting effects of living with a painful long-term condition which affects you physically, emotionally and intellectually and this meant I could not always rely on the presence of a co-trainer and had to ensure I had contingency plans ready;
- the emotional impact of sharing your story, your experiences, difficulties and joys with groups of strangers who may or may not value that experience (hence the importance of offering debriefing time after each session);
- as a trainer, I would sometimes find it difficult to listen to a service user's powerful experience when I had never heard it before and yet had known the person for over a year (we did not ask people to share their life stories as part of the training courses; we focused on presentation skills and how to engage people).

Despite all of the challenges above, and maybe because we recognized them and tried to meet them, the biggest challenge reported by the service users was organizational, within the widest sense of the word, as service users struggled to work within a complicated benefits system which disempowered and stressed them. Some users managed to get paid through an advocacy organization which took on the system or their behalf while some others continue to have to jump through hoops to get benefits. We need to continue to challenge systems so as to increase flexibility for users of services who may not be able to work full-time but should still be able to be paid for the work they do. If you want to find out more about user involvement and payments, I would recommend you read SCIE Guide 4, *Involving Users and Carers in Social Work Education* (SCIE 2009).

Aside from challenges, there were a number of dilemmas faced by both service users, trainers and the organization when trying to embed the principles of purposive collaboration. Dilemmas can be defined as 'a choice between two equally unwelcome alternatives' (Banks 2006: 13) and I propose to explore two key issues that have challenged and continue to challenge me as a co-trainer:

- the dilemmas faced in training by some professionals who regard the users involved as 'quasi-professionals' and deny the reality of their story;
- when a service user's concrete experience of current processes and procedures does not match the positive organizational messages to be given.

Some professionals dismiss the experience related to them on a training course either because they believe the user is almost a professional therefore the participant thinks the user's story loses validity or they dismiss the user as not being representative because he or she is seen as too eloquent (a remark that was said to one of the TREND members on a course I co-facilitated). These ways of challenging someone's narrative say more about the participants than they would care to admit if challenged. I think it highlights some of the concerns people have when they feel that their power base and their sense of professional identity are threatened and they resort to being patronizing, paternalistic and dismissive of attempts to learn from users as experts on their own lives.

For me to deliver training effectively and meaningfully implies that I believe in the messages that I am trying to convey, be it in presenting new policies, processes or ideologies. I would struggle to deliver messages that went against my own beliefs and values; however, this is a dilemma that has happened for some TREND members who struggled to be enthusiastic about new ways of working when these new processes were impeding their own lives or did not match the ways the ideas were represented in practice. In some instances, the users' experiences were harnessed to come up with better ways of matching processes to realities and feeding the ideas back up to policy makers. In others, some service users declined the offer of co-training as they felt they would not be talking with an authentic voice and therefore would compromise themselves.

Despite these challenges and dilemmas, I am convinced that there are huge benefits for service users, participants and the organizations in working collaboratively with users and this forms the final part of this chapter.

Reflective exercise
What do you think are the benefits of involving service users in social work training:
1   for the service user?
2   for you as a participant (you meaning student or practitioner)?

The benefits for service users of being involved in education and training have been well documented (Warren 2007), so I will just present the benefits that TREND members have highlighted:

- enhanced self-esteem and higher levels of confidence;
- a first step towards further studies or employment prospects;
- learning and practising new skills, networking, gaining a lot of knowledge about policies, legislation and how personalization principles translate into practice;
- making new friends, feeling good about discovering we have similar problems and can share ideas for sorting them out;
- a realization that organizational changes start with a change in hearts and minds and that service users have a crucial part to play in bringing about that change.

Donna sums up the group's common understanding that:

(Care management) ... is not just about filling in forms and getting a care package in place; it is about seeing the person behind the forms and getting to know them and what they want to do and achieve in their lives. This was a common theme that came out of our training together; we wanted professionals to see the people behind the forms and not worry about the paper work all the time but take the time to get to know us as people, fellow human beings.

Donna shares the following:

Through the TREND training I have met ten other people who want to change the way social care see disabled people and service users. I have met people who are passionate about being seen as an individual and not just a service user who needs help. It has made me more passionate to see disabled people get what they need. That is the thing to keep in mind: lots of the support we need is for aspects of our lives that we need, not necessarily want. For example, we would rather be able to cook for ourselves or get ourselves out of bed but instead some service users need help with this day in and day out for ever.

From the evaluation forms we asked social care staff to complete, I have gathered the following comments from participants about the benefits of attending a course involving co-training with service users:

- a better understanding of the exchange model of assessment;
- the service user's experience made me realize that I need to talk less and listen more as I am often in danger of offering solutions without even checking that the person opposite wants me to offer solutions;
- meeting someone with severe physical disabilities who sees him- or herself as in control of his or her life has made me reflect on my understanding of independence;
- I am going to refocus my energies on building a relationship with the people I meet, not on the paperwork I need to fill in although I understand the importance of getting that right too to effect changes in someone's life.

Donna tells us that:

> I like to think that what I have brought to the professional's training is the fact that service users are the same as anybody else and we want to be treated like that. I hope that the professionals I have come in contact with have seen me as someone filled with potential and someone who can live an independent life with the support that I need from social services. Without the support I get I cannot live an independent life. I hope that TREND has enabled professionals to see life from the other side – the service user's side.

Conclusion

The key issues in this chapter have involved the application of social work values and a commitment to the avoidance of a tokenistic approach to involving service users in the development of social work with adults and social care practice. Despite considerable advances in consultation and collaboration, there are still problems of labelling the people we work with based on traditional and taken-for-granted assumptions about 'service users'.

Collaborative working with service users implies a willingness to explore notions of power and empowerment. Within adult social work and social care, this involves thinking about approaches to empowerment and the current drivers for the involvement of users such as legislation, government policies, codes of practice and ethics, all underpinned over the years by user-led organizations demanding that their voices should be heard.

The previous part of the chapter focused on the role and contribution of service users to the training and development of practitioners in social work and social care and the importance of service users being equal partners through having different responsibilities within the training role, and ensuring users are supported to have the input they choose to have.

Looking at the TREND project as an example, it was possible to explore some of the practical challenges to user involvement such as accessibility, encompassing both access to venues and materials, highlighting the fact that the biggest challenge remains that of balancing the right to be paid for work done with the inflexibility of current benefit systems. Two examples of dilemmas were given: when a service user's narrative challenges the very processes he or she is expected to present positively and where participants dismiss the narrative either because the trainer status removes the label of service user or invalidates the user's story or where the user is dismissed as unrepresentative of a group. This latter dilemma is embedded within the professional power discourse (Thompson 2007).

It is too easy for practitioners to pay lip service to social work values or even to really believe in the principles and ethical frameworks that inform social work and social care with adults without fully appreciating the perspective of the people they work with who use services, or fully understanding the complexities and ethical dilemmas that can arise in trying to work effectively in genuine partnership with service users.

For Donna, the message is quite simple:

> As a reader of this chapter, I hope you have seen that, just because service users need to be assessed and need support, this does not mean that we cannot succeed in life and live independent lives. Disabled people are the same as anyone else in society and with the right support we can achieve and fulfil our dreams and aspirations. As professionals: see everyone as equals, listen to us and see how you can support us to live the lives we want to.

References and further reading

Banks, S. (2006) *Ethics and Values in Social Work*. Basingstoke: Palgrave Macmillan.

BASW (British Association of Social Work) (2002) *Code of Ethics for Social Work,* available at: http://cdn.basw.co.uk/upload/basw_112315-7.pdf [Accessed 21 November 2012].

Beresford, P. (2000) Service users' knowledges and social work theory: conflict or collaboration, *British Journal of Social Work*, 30 (4): 489–503.

Beresford, P. (2005) Theory and practice of user involvement in research, in L. Lowes and I. Hulatt (eds) *Involving Service Users in Health and Social Care Research*. Abingdon: Routledge.

Beresford, P. and Croft, S. (1993) *Citizen Involvement: A Practical Guide for Change*. London: Macmillan.

Braye, S. (2000) Participation and involvement in social care: an overview, in H. Kemshall and R. Littlechild (eds) *User Involvement and Participation in Social Care. Research Informing Practice*. London: Jessica Kingsley Publishers.

DH (Department of Health) (1999) *National Service Framework for Mental Health: Modern Standards and Service Models*. London: Department of Health.

DH (2001a) *Valuing People: A New Strategy for Learning Disability for the Twenty-first Century*. London: The Stationery Office.

DH (2001b) *National Service Framework for Older People.* London: Department of Health.

DH (2001c) Health and Social Care Act, available at: http://www.legislation.gov.uk/ukpga/2001/15/contents [Accessed 21 November 2012].

DH (2009) *Valuing People Now: A New Three-year Strategy for People with Learning Disabilities.* London: Department of Health.

Hernandez, L., Robson, P. and Sampson, A. (2010) Towards integrated participation: involving seldom heard users of social care services, *British Journal of Social Work,* 40: 714–36.

Jones, E. and Hahn, S. (2007) Working in partnership to deliver training, *A Life in the Day,* 11(4): 9.

Means, R. and Smith, R. (1994) *Community Care: Policy and Practice.* London: Macmillan.

Parrott, L. (2006) *Values and Ethics in Social Work Practice.* London: Sage Publications.

Shakespeare, T. (2000) *Help,* available at: http://www.leeds.ac.uk/disability-studies/archiveuk/Shakespeare/help1.pdf [Accessed 3 December 2012].

SCIE (Social Care Institute for Excellence) (2007) Stakeholder Participation Guide 17. *Practice Guide: The Participation of Adult Service Users, Including Older People, in Developing Social Care,* available at: http://www.scie.org.uk/publications/guides/guide17/ [Accessed 21 November 2012].

SCIE (2009) Guide 4: *Involving Service Users and Carers in Social Work Education,* available at: http://www.scie.org.uk/publications/guides/guide04/files/guide04.pdf [Accessed 3 December 2012].

Shaping Our Lives (SOL) (2003) *What Do We Mean by 'Service User' and 'User Controlled' Organisation?* available at: http://www.shapingourlives.org.uk/definitions.html [Accessed 21 November 2012].

Thompson, N. (2007*) Power and Empowerment.* Lyme Regis: Russell House Publishing.

Warren, J. (2007) *Service User and Carer Participation in Social Work.* Exeter: Learning Matters.

Wright, P., Turner, C., Clay, D. and Mills, H. (2006) *The Participation of Children and Young People in Developing Social Care.* London: Social Care Institute for Excellence.

5 Responding to difference, identity and globalization

Edith Lewis

This chapter was inspired by my own experiences of migrating from a country where I was considered as a member of the majority. Being a black person and in the majority in my own country of Zimbabwe I had never thought much about my identity as a social category but more as a matter of personal characteristics. Suddenly I was in a country where I was no longer part of the majority and where my identity was assigned based on my racial identity, gender and country of origin. I soon found out there was a tendency to make assumptions and generalizations about those who were considered to be different, such as immigrants or ethnic minorities, and this was perpetuated by the media. Coming from a former British colony, I was reminded of Foucault who argues that the way in which people think about, classify and categorize experience is influenced by wider social discourses and these reflect power within society (Foucault 1967). This chapter is informed by a number of case studies and my own experience not only as an immigrant in Britain but also as a practitioner in health and social care.

Introduction

Social workers work with some of the most vulnerable people and groups in society. It is therefore important to recognize the power relationships within British society and the impact this can have on those considered different. As an immigrant I soon found out how individual differences and similarities across groups of people can be lost when people are put into categories or boxes. There is a danger that when people are defined by their racial identity it can reduce them to one single defining aspect of their identity while overlooking other aspects of who they are, or being so aware of the requirement to consider someone's differences that we may be unaware of the similarities they may share with others in mainstream society. The risk for practitioners is that this may result in assuming that all people of similar groups have similar needs.

There is some interesting research evidence to show how children are inclined to see the things they have in common with each other rather than differences, especially when playing. However, as they grow into young people and adults, differences become more visible. In adulthood there may a tendency to emphasize differences rather than commonalities (Bhatti-Sinclair 2011).

This chapter will explore how social work practitioners can respond effectively to the impact of globalization by developing greater awareness of how they themselves perceive difference and identity, and the ways in which the people they work with from diverse backgrounds may perceive their own identities.

According to Bhatti-Sinclair (2011), the words black and minority ethnic are used to define people on the basis of colour, culture, religion, tradition, custom and country of origin or birth. However, ethnicity can be seen as having limited relevance to white Britain as the word is usually used interchangeably with race and almost always associated with colour and difference (2011: 170). What constitutes ethnicity, on the other hand, is subject to ongoing debates. When one looks at the racialized British society, ethnicity could be seen as 'a multifaceted phenomenon based on physical appearance, subjective identifications, cultural and religious affiliation, stereotyping, and social exclusion' (Berthoud *et al.* 1997, cited in Afkhami 2012: 6). It's important as a practitioner to recognize that classifying people into groups in a society is never easy. On the other hand, Britishness itself is a debated concept as people can have multiple identities. In order to examine the issues for social workers, consider the following questions as you read this chapter.

- How do we understand the terms difference, identity and globalization?
- What changes and developments in the world do social workers need to take into account?
- What are the key principles that underpin anti-discriminatory and anti-oppressive practice?
- How do these ideas inform culturally aware, ethnically sensitive practice in social work with adults?

Learning outcomes

By the end of the chapter readers should have increased their understanding and awareness of:

- globalization and what it means to social work practice and social work education in the context of adult social care. Examples will be given from both personal and professional experiences;
- issues of difference and identity, what forms these take and what this means to adults accessing social work, health and welfare services;
- recognizing and challenging practitioners' own cultural patterns; developing awareness of what forms these expectations and perceptions;
- an appreciation of how different people might respond to social work intervention, and the interpersonal skills, abilities and competencies required for culturally aware social work practitioners to respond ethically and sensitively to issues caused by globalization.

What is globalization and what is its significance for social work?

It is not particularly easy to define globalization and its consequences both for society and for social work. Globalization is one of those tricky concepts that can mean different things to different people. However, it is an area that social workers need to be able to understand; Lyons (2006) argues that it is a reality affecting all societies and sections within them differently and that welfare systems and social work practice are bound to be affected.

The International Federation of Social Work (IFSW) recognizes that:

> Globalisation is a continuing process which, while advancing global technological development and communications, also has a negative impact on the balance of economic, political and cultural power between individuals and communities. Social workers see and work with the causes and consequences of these processes.
>
> (IFSW)

The recent professional capabilities framework introduced by the British Social Work Reform Board advocates the need for social workers to understand differences in self and others, respect differences, challenge discrimination and oppression and challenge cultural assumptions (Social Work Reform Board 2011). In order to understand the implications of these requirements for social workers, it may be helpful to think about two particular elements of globalization that have had a significant impact on systems and ideologies in welfare in the UK.

1   Globalization can be seen as primarily a question of trade and finances, which means that commercial transactions are carried out across the world. On a positive note, this can break down protectionist national barriers and encourage cross-national communication and interaction, which may lead to innovations and developments that might not otherwise be possible. The focus within this context is the importance of material or commercial success rather than the well-being of the individual or the relevance of communities. This leads in social work, particularly in the arena of practice with adults, to prioritizing transactional rather than relational processes within social care. The care management model discussed earlier in Chapter 2 stresses the importance of the management of limited resources, with the emphasis on the 'efficient' allocation of goods and services, whereby the social worker is often carrying out the assessment and gatekeeping functions in relation to services. It reconfigures the 'client' as a 'consumer' or 'customer', which ideally provides additional choice for that individual and their family but also requires the social worker to apply financial rather than professional criteria in determining the availability of services. Those who have money can buy what they want; those who don't are subject to stringent eligibility criteria.

2   The other element that is particularly relevant to social work with adults is the recognition of the impact of globalized movements of people. As globalization continues to rise in Britain and other western societies, it has had and continues to have an impact socially, economically and culturally. When one explores the history of British immigration over the centuries there is evidence that migration has promoted significant social and political debates and policy changes. It is no longer the case that people will live in one place for their entire lives and live according to one set of national and cultural norms (Levitt 2004). It is important for social workers to realize that historically people have continued to experience forced migration due to slavery and continue to migrate out of choice or for either economic or political reasons. The movement of people worldwide has been recognized by the United Nations in 1948 as a fundamental human right.

(Law 2010)

Burns (2008), on the other hand, acknowledges that the changes brought by migration are often linked to ambiguity about identity and sense of place in the world for those who are migrating or have migrated. This means for first-generation immigrants that their identity might be directly linked to their country of origin while second-generation immigrants might see themselves as more British and with other multiple identities e.g. Black British, British Muslim, British Asian or British Indian. Hall (2000) asserts that identity is a process and is not fixed and is constantly changing. For practitioners it is important to recognize that defining people using one aspect of their identity, e.g. ethnicity, disability or sexuality *reduces* them to one aspect of their identity. There is a danger of overlooking those needs arising from other aspects of people's identity and there is a risk that this process will simplify the complexities of individual and social identities which are constantly changing and socially constructed. Although relating to disability, the following definition helps to clarify our understanding of what is meant by the notion of identity.

Identity is the way people view themselves, how they view themselves in relation to others, and how they are viewed by others.

(Swain and French 2008: 67)

Everyone who interacts with social workers will come with their own cultural, personal history, and their own expectations and values (Thornton 2008). It is therefore crucial for social workers to understand where their clients place themselves and how they perceive their problems rather than interpreting the problem solely from the social worker's perspective and understanding of identity, culture and difference. As social workers working with diversity, it becomes a prerequisite to understand different experiences and understand how people shape their sense of identity over time, especially for those who have migrated and those from black and ethnic minorities who have been born in what they might consider a foreign multicultural society (Seidler 2010) such as the UK. As social workers consider these factors it is also important to 'appreciate that identities are complex and that people often carry diverse identities, histories and traditions as a result of mass migration and a globalized economy' (Seidler 2010: 18).

Social workers by the nature of their work with vulnerable adults will tend to meet those suffering the negative impact of globalization. Social work values such as anti-discriminatory and human rights perspectives become a priority in social work practice in order to understand the impact of discrimination and poverty on migrant communities. The work of Bannerji (2000) and Williams (2001), cited in Sakamoto and Pitner (2005) acknowledges that issues of multiculturalism in the UK may be perceived as an approach whereby the dominant group tend to acknowledge only superficial cultural differences without addressing power differentials.

Most communities and workplaces in Britain are now multi-ethnic and multicultural and this requires practitioners to be sensitive and knowledgeable about how other people may identify themselves. Over the years migration has taken a significant role in constructing situations and the patterns of ethnic relations and how attitudes to those considered different are formed (Law 2010). Debates and arguments on the impact of immigration within Britain's communities continue in most political circles and at times there may be a tendency to stigmatize and view immigration negatively rather than looking at the positive attributes. It therefore becomes a prerequisite in social work practice to respond appropriately and challenge our own perceptions to meet the needs of those accessing social services regardless of their background.

Dominelli (2010a) notes that although there has been considerable research and literature on anti-discriminatory and anti-oppressive practice, social workers in practice and social work educators have tended to respond to local issues and have not necessarily engaged with the implications of globalization. As social workers struggling to make sense of different perspectives, ideologies and theories on the complexities of globalization, it is important to understand service users' narratives, the probability of complex identities and the way they may experience discrimination.

The impact of globalization on social work practice in adult social work

Globalization and the movement of immigrants is not a new phenomenon in British history. British history is characterized by movements of people from other nations who have settled for centuries and continue to settle for various reasons. There is evidence of migration of different nationalities into Britain from the Industrial Revolution, from Jewish families escaping persecution in their own countries, through the colonial era, the impact of the First and Second World Wars, and the 1950s, when many members of former colonies entered Britain as migrant workers at the request of the British government. Although the nature of migration and the number of people coming has changed over time, the impact of different waves of immigration at different times for specific purposes has made the British population more ethnically diverse than ever before. One of the legacies of the British imperial past has been the large inflow of migrants from former colonies, some of whom might be in need or in receipt of social care as adults (Gaine 2010).

A challenge for social workers is to appreciate how immigration laws and wider social policy reforms have continued to exclude those without British nationality and other categories of British citizens from accessing welfare benefits (Law 2010). There is evidence that immigration laws and post-war welfare reforms have continued to institutionalize racially exclusionary rules determining eligibility to welfare benefits including residence tests (Law 2008, cited in Law 2010). As eligibility criteria to accessing social care services continue to tighten it becomes even more important for social workers to understand how this can have adverse effects on those accessing, or seeking to access adult social work and social care services. While recognizing the impact of globalization on social work education and practice, social workers working with adults need to understand the impact of immigration policies on those individuals and families who have migrated to the UK and who may be in a position of accessing adult social care.

Globalization has also affected those social work practitioners who previously saw their work as serving the needs of local white communities and who placed the responsibility of responding to ethnically sensitive practice with those working mostly in inner cities where historically people who migrated have settled. In order to assess and meet the needs of all service users, social work practitioners will need to understand and be aware of different pathways into migration and the overall impact of globalization. This can also be addressed by practitioners recognizing the need to reflect on, and if necessary challenge their own assumptions, stereotypes and prejudices (Knott and Scragg 2010).

Exploring difference and identity

As globalization continues to have an impact in Britain today, the changes are often linked to the ambiguity or uncertainty about identity and a sense of place in the world for those who have left their home countries. There have been ongoing debates about identity in response to political devolution, with an increase in economic migration and global terrorism leading to politicians promoting the need for major debates on Britishness, a concept which is now linked for those applying for British citizenship. The original expectation by policy-makers, especially in the 1960s, 1970s and 1980s, was that those migrating to Britain should assimilate into the local host culture, and an ethnocentric approach was the norm. In sociological terms the word ethnocentric is seen as a belief in the inherent superiority of one's own culture or race. Some commentators have advocated the idea of assimilation but this remains a debatable concept. It can be difficult for people coming to a new country to be suddenly expected to leave their beliefs, culture and languages behind and become 'British'.

Law (2010) considers the history of race relations as not just the development of a set of ideas but as characterized by the operation of systems of dominance and governance. The starting point for most migrant workers has always been that of economic disadvantage. Globalization and the changes in demographics will continue to impact on how practitioners in social care will need to adjust and develop their skills and challenge their own assumptions, and at times those of others, in order to meet the needs of diverse communities. Increasingly those who migrated after the Second World War will be reaching retiring age and will be forming part of the older generation. The following case study provides a good example of how assumptions can affect the service people receive. It is also useful to think about how the issues of power can affect decision-making.

Case study

Mr Vishnamurthi is an Indian man in his seventies who has been admitted to hospital following a stroke. His speech has been affected, as has the movement in all his limbs. He can do very little for himself and needs help with feeding, dressing and all aspects of his personal care. During his stay in hospital his wife has visited every day bringing in the food he likes and helping to feed him. Although no one understands the language they use, she is observed sitting by his bedside for hours talking to him. It is clear they are very close, and a number of other people, thought to be family, have been seen to visit as well. It has been decided that nothing more can be done medically and Mr Vishnamurthi can go home. At the ward meeting, the consultant decides there is no point referring him to social services as 'these people, they look after their own'. This is agreed by the nurses and the social worker present at the meeting. Two days after discharge, Mr Vishnamurthi is readmitted following a very distressed phone call from his wife saying that she cannot cope with him and demanding that he be taken back into hospital.

As is apparent, the assumptions that were made about this family were not accurate and were based on a number of erroneous preconceptions. In fact, Mrs Vishnamurthi was alone with her husband and the expectations by the staff that there would be a wide extended family to support her proved to be unsubstantiated. Staff also acknowledged they did not like to ask about the cultural and other differences that might have been acceptable to the family as they were not sure how to approach this. There was also the question of getting an interpreter, which could have proved expensive and potentially have extended Mr Vishnamurthi's stay in hospital if no one was immediately available. This would have been inconvenient as there was pressure for the bed. Most worryingly, because of the ethnicity involved, the social worker seemed to forget all the things she knew about the needs of people with severe sudden illness and disability such as the sense of dislocation and depression, loss and helplessness that individuals and their families are likely to experience and which can lead to crisis (Payne 2005). Instead of offering more opportunities for support, recognizing the additional problems the family could be undergoing because of isolation and marginalization, she acceded to assumptions that were based on a broad and rather unconsidered view of what the needs of anyone from that ethnic background might be. The basic principles of respect for individuals and person-centred care that underpin all social work interventions were overwhelmed by an adherence to a model of 'difference' or 'otherness' rather than appreciating that many of the aspects of the situation would very likely be the same for the Vishnamurthis as they might be for anyone else in such a situation.

The fact that everyone agreed with the consultant's assessment may reflect on the power dynamics within the hospital team, and as a result this family experienced an extremely distressing situation that could have been avoided. It is therefore important for practitioners to challenge their own and others' perceptions and the language they might use when working with migrant populations in adult social care. It is particularly important also to be aware of whether the individuals with whom they are working are first- or second-generation immigrants who might have different perceptions of their identities. According to Lawler (2008), to be seen as a refugee or an economic migrant, for example, is to be positioned as without a meaningful identity. This provides a useful insight for practitioners who work with adults, as she goes on to say: 'Those denied any chance to name and define themselves tend to be defined in terms of a mass or a mob in contrast to the "white" who are defined as individuals' (2008: 146).

Sameness and difference

Within the UK the notion of difference has frequently been ascribed to people from black and ethnic minorities while making an assumption that the white majority share the same identity by the nature of their colour. Understanding and developing anti-racist practice has not looked at white identity and has tended to focus on issues of race, class and gender, for example (Bhatti-Sinclair 2011). There is a danger that the majority 'whites' continue to be the non-defined and then continue to label or categorize others. Frankenberg (1993: 197), quoted in Bhatti-Sinclair (2011: 76), was concerned that identity is generally defined relative to white cultural norms:

> Whites are the non-defined definers of other people ... whiteness comes to be unmarked or neutral category whereas other cultures are specifically marked 'cultural'. Similarly discussions of race difference and cultural diversity at times revealed a view in which people of colour actually embodied difference and whites stood for sameness.

As practitioners it is important to question how we perceive those that might be different to us. A starting point may be to look at the similarities and then work on meeting what might be different. For example, meeting the cultural needs or dietary needs of service users which may highlight difference does not necessarily mean that there are no similarities in other aspects of their life and how they might relate to you as a practitioner or to mainstream white society.

Reflective exercise

This is taken from a real scenario (details anonymized) based on a classroom discussion with student practitioners. A question was raised on elements of anti-discriminatory practice to consider when supporting social work students in practice. A student practitioner gave an example from practice and said she was currently working with an African–Caribbean family and according to the father the adults left a child of 13 or 14 years old looking after two other younger siblings who were respectively 5 and 7 years old. According to the father or the social worker's interpretation, could this have been seen as a question of 'black culture'? Before considering further the dilemmas in this situation, think about your own attitudes within this scenario.

- At what age do you think it would be acceptable to leave children on their own?
- Where did you learn how to make this estimation?
- Is this an area where you and your friends all agree?

The facilitator raised a question: what should be considered when faced with such a situation, i.e. is it culture, a black issue or is it that anybody can leave young children without adult supervision? The class gave different suggestions on what issues they would consider and what questions they would need to explore. These would include:

- How often does this happen and how long is the older child being left looking after the two younger siblings?
- How responsible was the older child and were there any aspects of potential risks to consider?

Further analysis of the situation revealed a number of different approaches to the subject. Some students asked whether this was legal or not and although it was established that it was not deemed illegal, there were some concerns raised. Good practice indicates that it would be important to treat each situation independently while exploring individual circumstances. A question was asked of the class (majority white students) whether any of the students would leave a child of that age looking after younger siblings. Their response was based on the issues above with some students indicating they would and some saying they would not; some responded that they would also consider the safety of the neighbourhood and the closeness of community support from neighbours. This led to the question of whether it was a cultural issue and at that point all students realized that this was an issue pertinent to any family regardless of their culture or background. What was significant was the need to consider the matter carefully without making assumptions about a particular ethnic or cultural group's attitudes and values.

The conclusion of the discussion was interesting as the student who had raised this as a 'cultural' issue suddenly realized this was not simply a black or cultural issue but what was needed was to explore the reality of the issues and then respond accordingly as a practitioner. It was established that it was important as a practitioner not to make quick conclusions based on race, culture or difference without exploring different explanations as potential interventions can be biased. If any potential risks were identified the safeguarding procedures would be followed. This raised a final but essential question for social work practitioners: does an issue requiring social work intervention become a cultural issue because it involves a black family but is not labelled as such when it happens to a white family?

Reflective exercise: Identity
<ul><li>Think of the years you were growing up to become who you are now.</li><li>What factors do you think have formed your identity or the person you are today?</li><li>How do you identify yourself? Consider gender, culture, race/ethnicity, etc.</li><li>Is your identity important to you or do you find yourself adopting different identities, or is it other people's problem?</li><li>At what stage in your life was identity more important?</li></ul>

The term identity can be difficult to define. Lawler sees the notion of identity as hinging on a paradoxical combination of 'sameness and difference' (2008: 2). While it can be easy to find differences based on race and ethnicity, it is important for professionals to see how we can share common identities as human beings, as men, women, white, black or British. It is also important to consider how people are unique and different from each other. Hence one cannot see an older person simply as European, Caribbean, Asian or African, as by so doing it can be easy for a social worker to make an assumption that every old person originating from these continents is the same and they have no identity of their own. Different generations, for example, can carry their own anxieties about identity and belonging and this can be different within a group of people originating from the same country. Equally there can be conflicts between different ethnic groups who might for a period seek alliances with each due to similar experiences of racism. This was the case for most African, Caribbean and Asian migrants in the 1970s and 1980s although later they sought their own distinct identities (Seidler 2010). This demonstrates the need for practitioners to avoid putting those accessing services into boxes as people tend to determine their own individual identities through separating from collective identities.

Cultural competence and critical consciousness

As social workers it is essential to develop critical consciousness. This requires us not only to examine our own various identities but to do the same for the clients who receive adult social work and social care services. People have many social identities which might include race, social class, gender, disability or sexuality and these tend to be influenced by the society one is living in, taking into account a range of historical, socio-cultural and political factors (Reed *et al.* 1997, cited in Sakamoto and Pitner 2005).

How professionals or practitioners position themselves within these various identity groups affects the way they perceive themselves and others. These identities can lead to privileges in some cases, disadvantage in others. A Black client, for example, may be from a middle-class background and enjoy a comfortable lifestyle but they may still be oppressed if they face racism because of their skin colour, disability or sexuality. Listening to clients' narratives is paramount in social work practice as different groups are usually knowledgeable and understand their narratives better than the non-oppressed groups (Butler *et al.* 2007).

Ethnicity and nationality are important aspects of identity for individuals who use adult social care services. A Black African, Caribbean or Asian person may be British by birth and nationality but may attach different importance and meaning to their ethnicity and nationality and consider their religion as their identity; in other words an individual may view being British Muslim as more important than British Asian or just being Asian.

The need to understand how identities are socially constructed rather than 'given' is important as a foundation to promote anti-discriminatory practice. For social workers this involves treating clients or service users as individuals rather than a homogeneous group, or seeing them all as being the same with undifferentiated 'cultural' needs and attitudes. It is no longer valid or possible to classify Blacks or Asians simply as having a structural or disadvantaged position in society, as people have different socio-economic experiences. It is not enough for practitioners to perceive everybody coming from a particular community as having the same needs or similar culture and language. Within any community there are likely to be some very different variations of language, culture, religion, norms and practices, etc., and the role for the practitioner may be to engage with the conflicts and dilemmas that these differences of perception may entail.

Reflective exercise

- Can you think of different ways in which these kinds of assumptions of treating people as a homogeneous group could affect social workers/practitioners?
- How can this understanding help us to think more sensitively about the individual needs and perspectives of people from diverse ethnic communities?

A personal example

I am originally from Zimbabwe but undertook my social work training placement in a predominantly white British county. I was taken aback to see that my supervisor assumed I had an understanding or would be able to provide answers on anything affecting black clients, especially those who considered themselves to be African. I was soon considered as a representative of all Africans and expected to address or respond to any issues the team was presented with. There were a significant number of black children who were privately fostered in the county and I remember a colleague questioning why African parents were using private fostering arrangements for their children.

The expectation was that I should understand this but it was a practice which shocked me and I could not understand why someone would give their child to be looked after by a stranger and not their immediate family members or grandparents. It was as much of a mystery to me as it was to some of the white practitioners, yet it was labelled an African problem. Later, after doing some research and watching some documentaries on TV on the issues of private fostering by some West Africans, I began to understand the problems of private fostering, especially in some West African countries, in particular Nigeria. In response I began to tell my colleagues how it can be misleading for practitioners to assume that a particular practice by a few African people can be seen as the prevailing norm without understanding the circumstances of each individual case.

Social work professionals will need to respond to some of the complexities and challenges of meeting the needs and understanding the perspectives of diverse communities. Cultural competence is therefore not only required by those professionals working in inner cities where there is a diverse ethnic mix, but is an essential component for all social workers. Ouseley (2007, cited in Bhatti-Sinclair 2011: 22) suggests that 'the answer to complex questions often lies in better listening and decision-making, which is based on human justice, equality and diversity'. This makes anti-discriminatory practice crucial to professional practice.

There is evidence that adult social care practitioners receive very little support or training to work with migrants, asylum seekers and refugees and often lack knowledge of the issues and problems (Dominelli 2004a, cited in Dominelli 2008: 188). Dominelli also recognizes that legislation employed in adult social care can restrict practitioners' capacity to work within social work values and ethics promoting social justice. Training becomes paramount in meeting the needs of an older person who, for example, may have migrated in the 1950s or 1960s in making sure the transition to old age is managed in a sensitive way. Understanding aspects of transition in old age and the impact of culture and migration is therefore important for an effective practitioner.

Case study

Shirley is an 83-year-old woman who migrated from Barbados with her parents when she was in her early thirties. For many years she lived with her husband until he decided to go back to his country of origin, Jamaica, where he died two years ago. Unfortunately, due to late contributions to her pension fund, Shirley relies on welfare benefits and sometimes struggles paying her bills and in buying food. She was recently diagnosed with arthritis and is considering relocating to Barbados where one of her sons is currently living with his family and Shirley's other grandchildren, who are all happy to accommodate her. She has also suggested the weather in Barbados might help with her arthritis. However, her daughter, who lives a few miles away from Shirley in the UK, is adamant that Shirley should stay in the UK where she can look after her.

- What issues would you consider when working with Shirley to support her with this decision?
- How might you deal with any aspects of transition?

With this case the social worker needs to start the analysis by thinking about whether and in what way issues of migration and identity are significant for Shirley and her family and to address these issues in a manner that does not make assumptions about what their views might be. As Shirley is an adult who has the right and capacity to make her own decisions, the social worker would need to take on the role of exploring her wishes and perspectives and working through the pros and cons of different options that may be available to her. This work with Shirley therefore should be informed with a commitment to the essential social work values of respect, autonomy and self-determination that underpin all good social work practice with adults (Banks 2006).

Personal values, attitudes, prejudices and beliefs can all affect how practitioners respond to people using social services. These values can be demonstrated both directly and indirectly in the professional relationship (Heydt and Sherman 2005). Challenging our own stereotypes and attitudes towards people who have been affected by globalization and immigration is crucial to ensure that we practise in an anti-discriminatory and anti-racist way. Some practitioners may be reluctant to raise issues of ethnicity and racial differences but culturally competent practice means being able to have honest and open discussions on issues of difference and identity, while not presuming that they are the only factors that may be of importance in any specific situation.

Developing self-awareness, according to Heydt and Sherman (2005), is important as a part of working towards the development of cultural competence, and at the same time helps develop appreciation of multicultural identities and the complexities brought about by migration. Cultural competence is more than just using the correct language or providing the right dietary needs. In some cases this might mean specific training to respond to particular needs of the communities and groups one is working in.

For white practitioners there is a need to recognize how, for those who come from the majority group, issues of difference are usually taken for granted and rarely questioned or are associated with culture. While this chapter has concentrated on black and ethnic minorities, practitioners will need to be aware of some cultural and language differences often ignored for others such as Irish, Welsh, Scottish and English users accessing adult social care. For example, the relevance and importance of religion in some Irish or Jewish communities and families may be overlooked. Those that are seen to be different have always been seen as having a culture. So if someone comes from an African country or a South Asian country the first visible aspect of the person's identity is not only their skin colour but their culture or religion. As practitioners it is important to explore evidence from literature on whiteness which demonstrates how white people's experiences are seen as human or universal experiences and how this allows white people to be seen simply as individuals while others are seen as minorities and members of a racial group (Dyer 1997 and Chambers 1997, cited in Jeyasingham 2012).

The chapter has tried to contextualize issues of globalization, difference and identity and how this can enable a better understanding of the importance of anti-racist and anti-discriminatory practice in adult social care (Thompson 2006). Many people accessing adult social work services may have already experienced disadvantage and/ or discrimination as a result of their age or disability as well as their ethnic origin and this makes approaching social services difficult enough. Migration is likely to bring a significant number of additional problems to the person or families. Immigration status also matters as it may determine who gets into the country, what they can or cannot do and their entitlements to welfare benefits (Dominelli 2010b). Practitioners need to be aware that accessing social care for most migrants can be an even more difficult process due to either language barriers or unfamiliarity with the welfare systems; such problems can also be coupled with restrictions imposed by eligibility criteria and immigration status.

To enable practitioners to practise in an anti-discriminatory or anti-racist manner there is a need to understand that cultural diversity and ethnicity issues are not just for non-whites. Everyone has their own unique identity and we all need to develop our skills and knowledge base to deal with a changing world. Social workers' commitment to social justice, social work values and anti-racist and anti-discriminatory practice is part of the process of challenging any residual negative stereotypes and unconsidered assumptions that may underpin engagement with adults who access services (Graham 2007).

Key principles underpinning anti-discriminatory and anti-oppressive practice

Social work values require that those taking on the role of the social worker must demonstrate a commitment to anti-discriminatory and anti-oppressive practice. Listed below are some key lessons from understanding issues of globalization, culture and identity that can be translated into awareness of how practitioners can promote working in an ethnically sensitive way. The process starts by each of us looking at the personal and individual responsibility we carry for the way we work, and the need within training, practice and supervision to:

- challenge our own beliefs, perceptions, attitudes, prejudices and assumptions;
- understand the impact of oppression and discrimination on adults, families or communities;
- be prepared for ethnically sensitive practice including disability or mental health awareness;
- understand the issues of difference, identity, culture, discrimination and prejudice;
- understand the role and the influence of the media in constructing our perceptions on difference, especially those who have migrated;
- understand as a practitioner that discrimination and disadvantage exist in society;
- appreciate that some groups suffer multiple and simultaneous discrimination;
- be aware of language and how it can label people in a negative way, e.g. the use of immigrant, refugee and asylum seeker;
- check own language and that of others around you and challenge other people and professionals around you as appropriate;
- challenge institutional and other forms of discrimination or oppression;
- establish any changes that are required in public and professional behaviour.

Conclusion

As practitioners there is a need for us to understand issues of diversity, culture, race and ethnicity in the context of British immigration and the British colonial past and its legacy in relation to power relations. Understanding some of the terminology used in defining difference, we need to be aware of the risk of using words such as 'race', culture and identity too loosely. It is important to recognize that culture is not a static concept but a fluid entity; varied ideas, customs and social behaviour within a society can be shared by people of different races, backgrounds and ethnicity.

In addition to being aware of our practice on a personal level, we also need to think how we can influence practice at the institutional level. This includes developing a greater awareness of organizational response and the law. It is therefore important for practitioners to be familiar with the changes brought by the Equalities Act 2011 and the challenges of using legislation. Diversity should not be just understood in the context of negative perceptions and assumptions or stereotypes of immigrants, which perpetuates racism and indifference. As practitioners it is important to recognize the debates on what constitutes Britishness for people of any origin. While Britishness might mean different things to different people, the starting point for practitioners will be to see people as individuals with different needs and give them an opportunity to categorize themselves while recognizing the impact of discrimination and oppression on their lives. This context will provide a better opportunity for social workers to examine how their own assumptions, biases and cultural worldviews affect the ways they might perceive difference and power dynamics (Sakamoto and Pitner 2005) and the implications for developing ethnically sensitive non-discriminatory practice.

References and further reading

Afkhami, R. (2012) *Ethnicity: Introductory User Guide*. London: Economic Social Data Service.

Banks, S. (2006) *Ethics and Values in Social Work,* 3rd edn. Basingstoke: Palgrave Macmillan.

Best, S. (2005) *Understanding Social Divisions*. London: Sage Publications.

Bhatti-Sinclair, K. (2011) *Anti-Racist Practice in Social Work*. Basingstoke: Palgrave Macmillan.

Bollard, R. (ed.) (1994) *Desh Pardesh: The South Asian Presence in Britain*. London: Hurst and Co.

Butler, A., Ford, D. and Tregaskis, C. (2007) Who do we think we are? Self and reflexivity in social work practice, *Qualitative Social Work: Research and Practice,* 6 (3): 281–99.

Chambers, R. (1997) The unexamined, in M. Hill (ed.) *Whiteness: A Critical Reader*. London: New York University Press.

Dominelli, L. (2008) *Anti-Racist Social Work,* 3rd edn. Basingstoke: Palgrave Macmillan.

Dominelli, L. (2010a) *Social Work in a Globalising World*. Cambridge: Polity Press.

Dominelli, L. (2010b) Globalization, contemporary challenges and social work practice, *International Social Work,* 53 (5): 599–612.

Dyer, R. (1997) *White*. London: Routledge.

Foucault, M. (1967) *Madness and Civilization: A History of Insanity in the Age of Reason*. London: Tavistock.

Gaine, C. (ed.) (2010) *Equality and Diversity in Social Work Practice.* Exeter: Learning Matters.

Graham, M. (2007) *Black Issues in Social Work and Social Care.* Bristol: The Policy Press.

Hall, S. (2000) Who needs 'identity'?, in P. du Gay, J. Evans and P. Redman (eds) *Identity: A Reader.* London: Sage Publications.

Heydt, M. J. and Sherman, N. E. (2005) Conscious use of self: turning the instrument of social work practice with cultural competence, *Journal of Baccalaureate Social Work,* 10 (2): 25–40.

International Federation of Social Work (IFSW) cited at http://ifsw.org, accessed 11 March 2013.

Jeyasingham, D. (2012) White noise: a critical evaluation of social work education's engagement with whiteness studies, *British Journal of Social Work,* 42 (4): 669–86.

Knott, C. and Scragg, T. (eds) (2010) *Reflective Practice in Social Work,* 2nd edn. Exeter: Learning Matters.

Laird, S. (2005) *Cultural Competence in Social Work.* London: Sage Publications.

Law, I. (2010) *Racism and Ethnicity: Global Debates, Dilemmas, Directions.* Harlow: Pearson Longman.

Lawler, S. (2008) *Identity: Sociological Perspectives.* Cambridge: Polity Press.

Levitt, P. (2004) *Transnational Migrants: When 'Home' Means More than One Country.* Washington: Migration Policy Institute.

Lyons, K. (2006) Globalisation and social work: international and local implications, *British Journal of Social Work,* 36 (3): 365–80.

Payne, M. (2005) *Modern Social Work Theory,* 3rd edn. Basingstoke: Palgrave Macmillan.

Powell, J. and Robison, J. (2007) The 'international dimension' in social work education: current developments in England, *European Journal of Social Work,* 10 (3): 383–99.

Sakamoto, I. and Pitner, R. (2005) Use of critical consciousness in anti-oppressive social work practice: disentangling power dynamics at personal and structural levels, *British Journal of Social Work,* 35 (4): 435–52.

Seidler, V. J. (2010) *Embodying Identities: Culture, Differences and Social Theory.* Bristol: The Policy Press.

Social Work Reform Board (College of Social Work) (2011) *Reforming Social Work Qualifying Education: The Social Work Degree,* available at: http://www.collegeofsocialwork.org/uploadedFiles/TheCollege/_CollegeLibrary/Reform-resources/ReformingSWQualifying Education(edref1)(1).pdf [Accessed 1 January 2013].

Swain, J. and French, S. (eds) (2008) *Disability on Equal Terms.* London: Sage Publications.

Thompson, N. (2006) *Anti Discriminatory Practice,* 4th edn. Basingstoke: Palgrave Macmillan.

Thornton, S. (2008) *Understanding Human Development.* Basingstoke: Palgrave Macmillan.

Williams, C. and Johnson, M. R. D. (2010) *Race and Ethnicity in a Welfare Society.* Maidenhead: McGraw Hill/Open University Press.

PART II

Working with different service user groups in adult services

6 Working with people with physical impairments

Louise Watch

As a young adult, I began writing for our *Five Villages Chronicle* in North Wales. I felt an innate desire to show that not all disabled people felt the need to chain themselves to the gates of parliament to tackle inequality. Instead, I simply shared life experiences from the ever-changing perspective of someone with muscular dystrophy. Without realizing it, I had started down an effective path that became my key passion – exploring how personal experience can be used to educate and challenge perceptions around disability and impairment. Importantly, how individual narratives can stir a passion and motivation in those who listen, to make equality, rights and interdependent living a reality for disabled people and their families.

Learning outcomes

By the end of this chapter readers should have developed their understanding and awareness of:

- the historical development of social work with disabled adults from a period when service users had little choice or control through personalization from the 1980s to the present day;
- the need to reflect on how and why social care has moved to a rights-based, citizenship approach and the implications of this on practice;
- how changes in social care have altered theories and approaches to disability – moving away from the social model and independent living to interdependent living;
- how each of the above affects the adoption of self-directed support by people with physical impairments;
- the impact of personalization on individuals and the wider community through user experiences and narratives;
- the importance of critical reflection on personalized outcomes and the concept of creativity.

Talking about disability

When we start to develop a wider and more in-depth understanding of the lives of disabled people, the varying use of language becomes apparent. It's something that constantly evolves as we find more meaningful ways to describe aspects of disability and new ways of thinking about what it means to be disabled. We also begin to see variations in definitions from a legal and political perspective, within the UK and globally.

First, let us reflect on who the term 'disabled person' applies to. Are all people with health conditions disabled? What about a person with HIV who feels physically and mentally healthy – are they disabled? What about Betty who is 89, has practical assistance for most daily activities yet doesn't identify with being a disabled person, stating 'it's just old age'. It is a very powerful thing for professionals to assign someone a label (or place on someone an identity) that is not one the individual would choose for themselves. If a person doesn't see themselves as a disabled person, then any support, information, services, benefits, etc. branded as such may be ignored. Equally, I have worked with families from a variety of ethnic communities where they actively avoided seeking support because of the stigma of being labelled disabled or 'needy'. Understanding the nature of 'help' and how disability is perceived among different cultures is essential in enabling people to access the support and services that is their entitlement.

There is also another way at looking at disability. As a wheelchair user, in some situations there is nothing that makes my experience any different to someone without an impairment. I don't always experience restrictions or disadvantage. If, on the other hand, steps bar me from a local pub then is my impairment to blame? If the steps are seen as the problem, rather than me, then solutions exist. This suggests a perspective where disability is not so much about having a medical condition; rather it is more to do with whether or not the person with the impairment experiences disadvantage or inequality. This approach (where society determines the extent to which inequality or barriers are experienced) is central to the social model of disability. Created by disabled people in the mid-1970s (Barnes and Mercer 2004), this model offered an alternative social interpretation of disability. It is one of many influential perspectives around the nature of disability and disabled people (Shakespeare 2006).

New perspectives/models or interpretations emerge all the time such as the Disability Diamond Theory (Sibley 2011). Within this perspective, the driving force is life itself. The focus is on setting goals and aspirations, understanding and having the means to remove barriers and develop self-confidence. It is a model based on real world application, to know one's limitations and to 'never discount anything'. Interestingly, it's a model that both disabled and non-disabled people can reflect on – asking us to consider how much we disable ourselves, limiting our own lives and degree of happiness in various ways. Debate continues as to whether models are progressive or regressive in relation to furthering the rights and inclusion of disabled people (Finkelstein 2001). However, we must understand that the approach taken will impact the way we work, affect the policies and laws we create, influence our attitudes and behaviours and ultimately affect the inclusion, rights, independence and participation of disabled citizens within our society.

Disability and impairment

The social model, albeit in an evolved form, remains the approach advocated by organizations of disabled people and the Office for Disability Issues (ODI), the government office leading on equality for disabled people in the UK. Conflict arises when social care organizations adopt a working ethos based around this emancipatory model (i.e. political and social liberation), while using a working lexicon that opposes its very backbone. We will now explore this in relation to looking at the differences between disability and impairment.

One of the most common expressions used in social care is the term 'physical disabilities', i.e. where disability is used to mean the person's bodily limitations or impairment/medical condition. Individuals may describe themselves in the same context, e.g. 'my disability is cerebral palsy'. However, at the heart of the social model lies the clear separation of 'disability' from 'impairment'. These terms mean two very different things within this approach. The person's medical condition became known as their impairment and a person with an impairment such as multiple sclerosis was not automatically disabled. This distinction was the most profound revelation in disability history, signalling a new era of inclusion and disability rights. Why was this distinction important? For the first time, the cause of disability (the disabling factor) was not the person's medical condition. Disability was externalized and was no longer a fixed or unchangeable part of the person's identity. Within this approach, society created the conditions which determined whether or not people experienced disability and therefore became disabled. Disability came to represent the experience of disadvantage, inequality, exclusion, oppression, etc. by people with impairments (and by association, friends, family, etc.). Someone who identifies with the experience of disability on a regular basis may define themselves as a disabled person and adopt this as part of their identity and culture.

Reflective exercise

- How has this interpretation of 'disability' benefited disabled people and communities?
- What sorts of things might disable people, from a social model perspective?

Like others, I understood the social model concept from lived experience rather than by name. I never felt inadequate or that I was the problem. The failure was in others not considering people who experienced the world differently and basing their approach on a medical model. The medicalization of disabled people attributes the limiting factor to the individual's medical condition. The emphasis, therefore, was on that person to accept treatment or equipment responsibly in order to restore normal functioning (Wolfensberger 1980), comply with rehabilitation or otherwise accept institutionalization if this was never attainable (Oliver 1998; NHS 1999). Attitudes like these were leading 'professionals to set limited objectives for their patients and clients' (Finkelstein 1981: 1). The goal was ultimately normalization – the state of being able to perform the role society expected of you and to shrug off the shame and stigma of being needy (Goffman 1963; Gill 1966; Shakespeare and Watson 2002). For amputees, in a world that had not considered adapting the environment, walking at 'normal height' with prosthesis was preferable to using a wheelchair. In reality, the person may have been able to mobilize in other quicker, easier or less painful ways but 'difference' was not an attractive option practically, socially or mentally. Critically, this option benefited the needs of the individual as opposed to a single solution addressing the barriers faced by many. This mindset also affects the development of mobility equipment. Little effort went into the practical or aesthetic aspects of wheelchair or prosthesis design, for example, when the emphasis was on cure or passive living/care. Taking on a more social/independence model is changing the way products are developed for disabled people in terms of function, style and being fit for an equal range of social experiences.

Institutionalization

It's a small step to move from seeing a person as defective or subnormal to being less human, less value to society or dehumanized (Armer 2000). It then becomes easier to exploit, segregate, isolate, abuse or even eliminate 'lives devoid of value' (Kendrick 2010). If normalization could not be achieved, people were encouraged to adjust to a passive life of being cared for, controlled by health and welfare professionals or well-meaning family/communities. Society comfortably allowed the 'sick' to live a life devoid of their responsibilities as citizens. The development of day centres in the 1960s fostered 'significant living without work' (Warnock 1978) and a long-standing culture of created physical and psychological dependence (Carter 1981). Working in centres that were being closed in 2010, I met many people finding it impossible to see a life outside these familiar institutional surroundings. A physics graduate was one of many people whose talents and visions were left to die as they developed the aptly named cabbage syndrome (Barnes 1990). One man admitted he could work having previously run an accountancy firm. However, he accepted the offer of daytime activities in the absence of any other support such as getting back to work. Neither the individual nor staff reviewed or questioned this over the years. Gaining independent living skills can be complex and a slow process – yet many people have made successful plans to live, work and experience leisure opportunities alongside non-disabled people.

The assumption that disabled people need or desire to go to specialized places or should be exempt from work-related responsibilities is still abundant. Public perception of disability in relation to work is very much politicized – particularly in light of recent benefit changes and difficulties ascertaining fitness to work. Arguably this has contributed to the rise of harassment and abuse of so-called 'benefit scroungers' (Walker 2012). Staff at the day centres were often institutionalized themselves with little to challenge their assumptions. Thinking I was a client, attempts were made to herd me into a hall with the general flow of people. Similarly, during recruitment of Direct Payment support staff, a social worker asked who her line manager would be. When I informed her that would be me she let out an audible gasp and in a shocked voice said, 'what, you ... but you're ... ' She wasn't the first person to find it incomprehensible that they would be managed by someone they could only see as a dependent client and not a person of authority. Power is a complex issue that can lead to abusive practice (Braye and Preston-Shoot 1995). Relinquishing this power to clients remains challenging for many social care staff in delivering personalization and has caused many to reconsider their career.

Reflective exercise

How might a person view themselves and social care services today if they experienced living at a time where society was predominantly influenced by:

- a medicalized approach towards disabled people;
- the social model approach to disability?

In summary, we have looked at a few of the different approaches to disability and reflected on how people with impairments have been viewed by society over time. An older person with a physical impairment (or multiple impairments) will find themselves much less disabled today compared to 30 years ago. People will therefore have varying experiences of life as a disabled person. We have also started to reflect on the consequences of adopting these different approaches. Not only are we more able to identify and change environmental barriers, but we can recognize other disabling factors such as policies which take little or no consideration of how they will affect people with impairments (either directly or indirectly). Financial/poverty-related barriers, attitudes, behaviours, and general lack of awareness or consideration can all affect people's wider independence. A person who has been influenced by a medicalized or stigmatized view of disability might find accepting social care support or adapting to life as a disabled person more difficult. They may be less aware of their rights or the services and support available to them, which we can now look at from a legal perspective.

Legal definitions of disability

If we understand that society disables people, then anyone who experiences difficulties (in relation to impairment) in their day-to-day life could consider themselves to be a disabled person. In 1995, the Disability Discrimination Act (DDA) made it unlawful, for the first time in the UK, to discriminate against people within employment and in provision of goods/services. Education and elements of transport were included over the next decade.

It is the Equality Act (Home Office 2010) which now provides us with a definition of disability when seeking legal protection against discrimination or harassment, arising from disability. It replaced six separate equality Acts, including the DDA (1995 and 2005), and includes the public sector duty which requires authorities to tackle discrimination and promote equal opportunities. A person has a disability 'if they have a physical or mental impairment which has a long term and substantial adverse effect on their ability to carry out normal day-to-day activities' (Home Office 2010: pt 2(1): 6). This definition is further clarified noting the inclusion of those with physical, sensory and mental impairments or severe disfigurement. Controversially, those with cancer, multiple sclerosis and HIV infection are singled out as being automatically considered disabled. Non-disabled people who are perceived to have a disability or who are associated with a disabled person are also protected.

Understanding the legal protection people have can assist social care staff in not only ensuring non-discriminatory practice, but importantly ensuring those whom they support are aware of their rights within the Act. When ensuring a person's human rights, there is a further definition that is applicable – that contained in the UN Convention on the Rights of Persons with Disabilities, ratified by the UK in 2009.

Specifically the Office for Disability Issues (ODI) 'supports the use of the social model' and recognizes that 'the International Committee drafted the Convention using a "differing approach to disability" particularly in the area of language' (ODI 2012a). As such in the UK it is referred to by the UN Convention on the Rights of Disabled People. All public bodies are bound to consider the Convention which explicitly states what these rights are for disabled people (although the rights themselves are covered in the various human rights treaties). The Health and Social Care Act 2012 confirmed that 'all publicly funded health and care providers should also consider themselves bound by the [Human Rights] Act' (BIHR 2012).

The varying views around disability, globally, incorporating wide-ranging experiences, attitudes, language, etc. are relevant to understanding the relationship between disability, identity and receiving help among different community groups where cultural and economic differences may impact on how social support is perceived or utilized. Moving to a rights-based approach has been a big shift in social care, set out in the 2007 *Putting People First* ministerial concordat that started the transformation of adult social care (DH 2007). Understanding how to use and apply human and civil rights can be an immensely powerful tool for practitioners, disabled people and their families.

Prevalence of disability

The estimated prevalence of disability in Great Britain is over 10 million adults (more than half over state pension age) who have a 'longstanding illness, disability or infirmity, and who have a significant difficulty with day-to-day activities' (ODI 2012b). An attempt has been made to determine, more accurately, the number of people who might meet the legal definition of disability by the inclusion of Question 23 in the National 2011 Census (ONS 2011).

Within social care, local authorities provide data on the number of people who receive services and their primary client group. In accordance with predicated trends, out of those aged over 65, over 80 per cent of male and female clients had a 'physical disability'. While there is much debate on the nature of disability and who might be

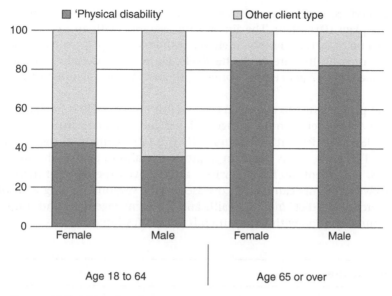

Figure 6.1 Percentage distribution of service users receiving services by client type, gender and age, England 2009–10

disabled, what is important is that our definitions (and how this materializes through our thoughts and actions) do not discriminate or limit the vision, goals and aspirations of disabled people. We must ensure our approach does not diminish our moral responsibility and obligation to 'promote, protect and ensure the full and equal enjoyment of all human rights and fundamental freedoms by all persons with disabilities' (UN 2008). This means having respect for the inherent dignity and worth of each person including the freedom to make one's own choices and have full and effective participation in society on an equal basis.

Health and social care personalization

One of the key criticisms of the social model of disability has been from disabled people with long-term health conditions. Someone with chronic pain or fatigue may argue that even the most inclusive society cannot remove disabling health factors. How a person manages their long-term condition (LTC) will impact on the level and type of social care support that may be needed. Equally, a person will only be able to optimize the management of their health care if they can engage with health and social care professionals in equal partnership.

The 2009 *Health Survey for England* found that nearly a quarter of men and women reported an illness that limited their activities in some way (NHS 2009). One way of improving services, treatment and management options was to introduce personal (health) care plans (DH 2006). The aim was for everyone with an LTC to have such a plan by the end of 2010. This would enable people to accept personal responsibility and manage their health care more effectively. However, nationally, only around 15 per cent of men and 17 per cent of women with an LTC had such plans by June 2009 (NHS 2009).

Is it that people refuse to engage in their health care or could it be that health care professionals are still reluctant to engage with patients in equal partnership? Evidence from the NHS Expert Patient's Programme (EPP 2002) highlighted significant power imbalances. This approach is based on improving health outcomes through training programmes, for patients and carers, where tutors have experience of living with an LTC themselves. Training can include disease-specific sessions, dealing with tiredness or pain, exercise and diet, mental health and stress management and, importantly, effective communication with family, friends and professionals.

Reflective exercise

If social or health care is done in partnership with service users and their families, recognizing each other's expertise, how might this relationship benefit:

* each partner;
* their organization/family or support networks; and
* the community as a whole?

The characteristics of an expert patient (Patterson 2002, cited in Fox 2005: 26) could arguably be adjusted in a social context to refer to characteristics seen in 'experts in independent living'. People who were confident, knowledgeable and expert gained the ability to work more effectively with their health care providers around decision making (Griffiths *et al.* 2007; Phillips and Cummings 2008). They were also better prepared and equipped to collaborate and work towards shared, mutually agreed goals and for mutual benefits. The same is true when working alongside people to explore social support. Partnerships are about doing things together, sharing risks and concerns, strategies, benefits, etc. A true partnership is one where things happen through mutual cooperation, consent and respect for each other's expertise.

What about the expert who encounters health or social care professionals who are unable to work in partnership or accept this fundamental power shift? Undervaluing the person's expertise can result in insensitive attitudes and overpowering, intimidating or controlling behaviours (French and Swain 2001). When a person's confidence is irreparably shaken, partnership working becomes impossible and the benefits of it are lost. I have had numerous experiences of negative attitudes around my health such as a physiotherapist who told me I would die if I didn't walk up three flights of stairs. This abuse of power served only to damage my mental health and ensure a future of non-compliance and distrust. People who are reluctant to access or be involved in their health care because of such attitudes (perceived or real) could also reduce compliance with health care advice or treatments. One older person with chronic impairments lost confidence in her GP, recalling, 'I remember the doctor saying to me "You keep quiet! I'm telling you what you must do!" He made me feel stupid' (Bentley 2003: 184). Accounts of providers that did not listen or include them in treatment decisions are also expressed by disabled people (Begum 1996), particularly those with multiple impairments (Barrett 2000). Overwhelming inequality in health care is also widely evidenced (Wilson and Haire 1990; Welsh Office 1996; Whitefield *et al.* 1996; DRC 2006).

Reflective exercise
• How will a person's experience of health care and interactions with health care professionals impact on their day-to-day lives and their social care support or assistance?

I recently returned to a local consultant for a respiratory review following treatment at another hospital. I started using a ventilator and medically the therapy was working. The consultant announced 'wonderful', informed me the quality of my life had improved and requested I write a note to the hospital thanking him for this outcome. I hadn't said anything. Where was the planning, management discussion and partnership working? He might have discovered that the therapy was impacting negatively on both my life and my husband's. I had no opportunity to discuss how it had changed my health and social care needs and returned home feeling let down and frustrated. Over the year, the consequence was that I had to close my business, return to benefits and rearrange my social care support. This in turn will affect my employees and so the ripple will continue, leading to major life changes that could have been avoided. I am not alone in experiencing attitudinal/power-based imbalances that break up planning around health and social care needs.

Social benefits of health planning

Health support plans can act as a useful mini 'health CV' that can be of great value when shared with family, carers, personal assistants, social workers, advocates, etc. An improvement in health management for patients may also lessen the level or duration of social care needed for some people. On the other hand, health support plans may also be a 'voice' for people, to enable them to access a higher level of social care by informing the assessment process and shaping their support plan so that the right level of social care support can be gauged.

My strategy for managing my health has a huge effect on how I live my life and the support I need to do that from day to day. I cannot separate my life into either health or social care. They are fused together to make one life and to break them apart within a personalization and rights-based approach is damaging. I have used information

successfully from specialists and charities to evidence the long-term costly consequences and social impact of not receiving a particular level of social care support or
equipment. Equally, those involved in the medical or therapeutic aspects of my life
need to understand my social care support plan. Charities and social enterprises often
provide vital community workers and advocates who can bridge the chasm between
social and health care. However, the funding of these is variable, often insufficient and
at risk where the numbers of people in the population who will benefit (i.e. people
with rare impairments) are comparatively low. These individuals can be overlooked,
going unsupported and experiencing the most inequality in health and social care.

Combining health and social care support

Early indications around the benefits of enabling people to take control over their health
needs are varied. For those who had personal health plans 67 per cent of men and 70
per cent of women said it had also improved their social care services (NHS 2009), but
when it came to people purchasing their own health services using an NHS Personal
Health Budget or PHB (DWP 2011a, 2011b; DH 2012), professionals still indicated concerns over letting patients take control. However, the pilot sites unanimously agreed with
health and social care integration, albeit not in the form of a joint budget. The person's
planned purchase may necessitate combined funding. For example, a lady I worked with
purchased a weekend break at a spa for relaxation. This helped reduce her chronic pain
and anxiety, and overall to manage her mental health better. At the same time she met
her social need for a break. Solutions need to be found that do not result in people having to divide elements of their lives into either purely health or social-related support.

Interestingly, personalization has seen many 'health and therapeutic' activities
becoming normalized from a social perspective. As a young adult I enjoyed horse riding as a fun social activity but for others it was deemed 'therapy' (Peacock 1994; Riding
for the Disabled 2003). Once given this label it attracts questions of 'appropriateness'
for social care funding that would not otherwise be asked. Simply by dropping the
label and seeing it as recreation with health benefits we begin to accept it as the person's preferred way of achieving social interaction and leisure opportunities. Similarly,
people now enjoy swimming, previously excluded under the label of hydrotherapy.

Those approving plans must retain the focus on the outcome and not the client's
chosen method of achieving it. In the mid-1990s, social workers found it difficult to
accept uses of Direct Payments. Today, NHS staff are experiencing the same anxieties
such as questioning the use of health funds to purchase a Wii Fit as opposed to funding
conventional health therapies.

The move from carers to personal assistants

During the emergence of the social model, disabled people began to recruit and employ
people to assist them, defining personal assistance as very different from 'care' (Jolly
2009: 3). Key elements were being able to have full control over who was employed,
what they did, how they were to assist and when. The number of people employed as

personal assistants (PAs) increased when Direct Payments were introduced and the professionalization and acceptance of personal assistance has since changed considerably. PA users often feel they have a better quality of support (and value for money) compared to using a care provider. They are free from policies such as that which caused a colleague to experience great humiliation at work when a care worker 'gloved up' at her desk to hold a sandwich to her mouth.

PAs now account for one-fifth of jobs in adult social care (Fenton 2011). The definition and role of a PA retains a level of consistency throughout the PA user community and across Europe. However, personalization in the UK has significantly diluted this with a variety of care and support roles wrongly being labelled as personal assistance. These roles often do not allow the person being supported to retain the level of choice and control over their assistance that would be paramount in a PA relationship. In response to these issues, the government launched their PA Framework in 2011 (DH 2011) to support the evolving PA workforce and their employees.

In their infancy, we now find those piloting personal health budgets having the same concerns that social care overcame some ten years earlier. A good example is a comment such as:

> [those] joint funded already have Direct Payments through social services and they either have a PA or agency staff ... That is fine when it comes to social care but if it comes to actual healthcare and it requires someone who is qualified ... they do not feel the risks involved are that important ... It's scary isn't it.
>
> (Jones *et al*. 2010: 2)

The individual went on to give the example of suctioning for someone with a tracheostomy tube yet families and personal assistants have been doing these aspects of care for many years. They are risk-aware and due to providing 1:1 support are often more 'expert' in meeting that individual's needs than nursing agencies can offer. In Europe support organizations controlled and run by disabled people offer training for PAs around a range of complex medical tasks and social care needs. Health care professionals work with assistants in enabling them to learn tasks once reserved for medically qualified staff. Some assistants are qualified in nursing, physiotherapy, etc. and, as a profession, being a PA should not be viewed as an unskilled job. The skills and abilities that people are looking for in a PA are as varied as the individuals they work with. However, financially, the amount of money available in a budget may not be enough to pay PAs in line with these and this remains a huge area of conflict. This may impact on the quality of the skills of the person that can be employed and in turn the disabled individual's quality of life. A low personalized budget for health or social care may mean people have to take risks and employ people with lower skills and abilities than are actually required.

Independent living

Life as a disabled person is oxymoronic. I'm an able dis-abled person, an independent dependent individual. Amidst a plethora of unhelpful definitions of independence, the most meaningful is that generated and agreed globally by disabled people and supported by organizations controlled by them. One such UK organization promoting Independent Living is Disability Rights UK, a merger of the National Centre for Independent Living, Disability Alliance and RADAR (http://disabilityrightsuk.org/). As a concept, independent living has lived alongside the social model approach for many years and is at the heart of rights-based social care. It was born out of the lived experience, desires and aspirations of people with a range of impairments and occurs when disabled people secure the same rights and freedoms as non-disabled citizens.

When providing training for social care staff over the past few years 90 per cent of participants, across five local authorities, described independent living, wrongly, as one of the following:

- government scheme;
- housing scheme to enable disabled people to live in their own home or supported housing;
- the ability to do things without relying on other people or 'being a burden';
- employing a PA;
- accessing support for the basic essentials of life;
- referring to equipment or adaptations.

What matters to people is that they can carry out their daily lives, according to their own preferences and without restrictions from a lack of assistance/support. People with impairments had a desire to be free from the rigid, prescribed menu of services and regain control over their lives. Life was about spontaneity rather than getting help only when it was convenient for others to provide it. Living was not simply about getting to and from bed, getting washed and dressed or eating and accessing the toilet. Neither was it about low-paid or tokenistic 'work' opportunities or perfecting basket weaving (which I still observed in 2011). This realization mobilized a desire for full inclusion and participation in every aspect of life.

Coalitions and Centres for Independent Living (CILs), under the management of disabled people, base their work around core areas including housing, employment, education, leisure, transport, etc. Services typically include peer support, advocacy, training, information provision and a local and national campaigning role around rights and equality issues. Many also include core services around employing and recruiting personal assistants, enabling people to access and use Direct Payments/Personal Budgets and facilitating the creation of support plans. A detailed history of the independent living movement in the UK and globally can be found on www.independentliving.org.

To facilitate the development of user-led organizations (ULOs), in 2011 the government announced £3 million funding to 'help organisations play an even greater role in shaping the decisions that will affect their lives', leaning on the 'experts' and 'ambassadors' approach (DPULO 2011). Disability Wales is working with the Welsh government in forming a valuable and detailed vision for independent living and 'citizen-directed support'. This includes a strong emphasis on working towards political change to enable 'access, involvement and social, economic and cultural inclusion' (Disability Wales 2011). Importantly, Article 19 of the UN Convention on the Rights of Persons with Disabilities emphasizes the right to personal assistance in achieving equality and independence.

How social workers can make a difference

In the 1990s I was one of a small number of people with complex physical impairments who negotiated with their local authorities to obtain cash payments in lieu of care services. As a socially isolated young adult my main glimpse of life was through the TV. Finishing my final year of A levels my career adviser spelled out a gloomy life of low-paid employment supplemented by benefits. I aspired to a career in medicine. Only one person outside my family believed in my potential – my social worker, Anne. Together we made a seven-month plan so I could go to university. Without her patience and support I would probably have moved into residential care and have potentially experienced long-term mental health problems.

We focused on my wants and needs, understanding that the social aspect of university life was just as critical to support as the academic side. Disability Living Allowance, Independent Living Fund, Disabled Student Allowance ... we had lists of things to apply for to bring together my budget. I would need a wheelchair-accessible Motability car (www.motability.co.uk), 24-hour care from volunteers and the skills to manage my three assistants. In terms of life skills, I had never shopped for food or clothes, had any social experiences or handled money. Often social work is about building up to the bigger picture, trying things out in small steps to achieve bigger goals. A person is more likely to manage and achieve success with this approach. In my case, we had limited time and resources so funding was found to have an assistant for four days so I could get used to directing them as to how and when I wanted to do things.

There were other barriers to overcome, with only three universities in the UK accepting someone with my level of impairment to undertake a biology degree. Campuses or accommodation were often inaccessible and the absence of disability equality legislation meant it was not unlawful to refuse to make any adjustments as it is today. I struggled getting funding for a laptop as I couldn't write by hand. Local villagers sent donations, shaming the education authority into funding one. Each of these issues impacted on the level and type of support I needed. Social worker visits became a weekly occurrence and we jointly visited two universities to see which was the best, first practically and secondly from an academic point of view. Once the results came through we ran the gauntlet of putting the plan into action. Then I began my new life – I was in control and experiencing life like any other student away from home for the first time. Those three years were the best and yet most difficult time of my life, taking huge risks and making many mistakes along the way. From this came opportunities to gain further degrees, full-time employment and to establish a business. I came off benefits, rented a house and got married.

People didn't make me independent – it happened through my own efforts, making choices, asserting my rights and having practical, personalized support. Independent living is not the goal of personalization, it is about removing the 'multiple social disadvantages that exist which prevent us from living with the full choices, self-determination, rights and control that non-disabled citizens [enjoy]' (Jolly 2009: 3). Human beings grow and develop from true immersion and the richness of their experiences. The micro details are important. I cannot describe the amazing experience of my first supermarket trip. I could have sent my assistants but I would never have discovered how much I hated the smell of fish, how cold the dairy aisle was or the pleasure of trying out new foods. When we interact with others in different environments, it shapes who we are, what we like, what we know of the world and how we choose to respond to other situations.

To deny disabled people the range of full human experiences and expression of themselves, through lack of social support, risks damaging both individuals and society. We must stop to think what are the characteristics of quality of life? However complex a person's impairment, there remains a moral and human duty to enable a rich life experience.

Today we acknowledge that we do nothing totally in isolation or independently from one another. Interdependence, as noted earlier, is a more meaningful way to describe our interactions with, and responsibilities for, each other. We can all be givers and receivers, helper and helped, each contributing different things into the social mix. It could be described as social mutualism – we are all interdependent, benefiting from the relationships we have with each other. The key mantra for social care is no longer simply control, choice, freedom and flexibility. Rather the progression to interdependent living has emphasized four more progressive fundamentals upon which to base social care/social work: human rights (fairness, equality, dignity and respect); personal responsibility; active citizenship and full community (public and political) involvement.

Moving to direct payment and personal budgets within social care

One of the ways social work and social care moved to enable disabled people to enjoy an enriched life began with the controversial notion that someone other than a trained professional could organize and purchase care/services – namely the 'service user'. Following nearly a decade of campaigns headed by the British Council for Organisations of Disabled People (BCODP) the Community Care (Direct Payments) Act 1996 allowed disabled adults to take up the offer of receiving 'cash in lieu of directly provided (social) services' (DH 2009). In 2003 the power to offer Direct Payments (DPs) changed to a duty to offer and make them available to everyone, regardless of age or impairment who:

- was eligible to receive support within the local eligibility criteria;
- met the DP eligibility criteria;
- was not specifically excluded within the Act; and
- had a need(s) that the local authority agreed to meet.

Direct Payments are now legalized under the Health and Social Care Act (2008) and its amendments. Specifically, the latter enabled adults who lacked capacity to benefit from payments alongside others formerly excluded under mental health and criminal justice legislation. Therefore, very few people fail to meet the criteria around eligibility.

Today over 154,000 children, adults and carers utilize Direct Payments (NHS 2010). The money can be used creatively and flexibly as long as purchases are legal and enable people to meet the goals agreed in their support plan. This plan typically contains details around accountability, e.g. what records to keep for financial monitoring, and any support that is needed to put the plan into action (including who will receive the funds or make the arrangements on behalf of the assessed person where appropriate). A young man with a learning difficulty very neatly explained the value of accessing payments by saying he would rename them rainbow payments. I asked him why and he replied, 'because they fill my life with colour'.

Relative and useful social care

When you are offered support, the assumption is that it will be useful and relevant. However, social care can also be restrictive if not carefully considered.

Case study

Jenny is 64 and the main carer for her daughter Katy whom she lives with. Katy has recently come out of hospital following a period of illness due to her long-term heart condition. Jenny is unable to leave Katy on her own for much longer than an hour and is finding it increasingly difficult to do food shopping and have time to herself. Social services have assessed their needs and arranged for home care for one hour a week. Jenny finds this restricts when she can go out, limiting her to the local shops on her bus route. These don't have the foods they prefer and are more expensive, adding to their home budget problem. Jenny feels the support is not working for her.

- What would be the benefits for the family and wider community of retaining the focus on effective and useful social care?
- What solutions might exist if Jenny and/or Katy had a personal budget in the form of Direct Payments?

It is helpful to think about what person-centred practice actually means to people who use social work and social care support. Social care hasn't always been about seeing people as individuals with unique qualities and multifaceted lives and relationships. While it may take some effort on the recipients' part, Direct Payments makes it possible to 'shop around' to see what type of support might be a best fit. Discussions with agencies might uncover some that are able to offer more flexibility around the time they can support, or require less notice to arrange a care worker. Sometimes it enables a person to think of a very different solution for more holistic support. Jenny prioritized the things that were most important to her at the time – to go into town, do the shopping and meet people she knew. On analysis, the bus route was taking up 40 minutes of her time away from the house. She used her Direct Payment to pay for a mobile phone to provide the reassurance of being in easy contact with Katy. The money was also used for taxi fares to reduce her travel time by half, enabling her to stay out longer and get home more quickly should she need to. These were things she could otherwise not afford and offered the ideal solution without the need to purchase expensive, restrictive home care on a regular basis. Jenny was able to find a cost-effective solution that was personal, relevant and useful.

The importance of keeping user-defined goals in sight cannot be overstated. When I left university, I had an agency carer. However, taming that 'just got out of bed' hair style was not one of their skills. How could I think about work (my goal) if I didn't feel good about the way I looked? Not only this, but I didn't have the fine control over when they arrived, meaning punctuality would be problematic. I was automatically excluded from seeking employment, ensuring that society was losing a tax payer and my skills contribution, etc. Support and assistance will only limit or remove disabling factors and ensure true opportunities for full and responsible citizenship if appropriate, user-defined goals are identified and the focus is retained on achieving them. My solution, a Direct Payment, did not cost the council any more than they were currently spending on my support. Only through taking control of who supported me, under my terms (tasks, skills needed, times of assistance, etc.) was I able to work. Equally, by working and having support late into the night I could do volunteering, socializing, and wield part of the huge spending power disabled people hold – estimated at £80 billion annually (DWP 2004). Solutions, with far-reaching benefits for everyone, don't have to be complex. However, they do require acceptance that there are many routes a journey can take – and like all good trips, planning, budgeting and knowing where you're aiming for is essential. With ever depleting budgets, enabling a person to optimize the use of their allocated funds, in a useful way, can be a challenge. It is easy to revert to merely keeping people alive and making sure they can eat, sleep and maintain some basic degree of hygiene. It is easy to brush aside dignity, civil and human rights. Social isolation can kill people (James 2001) and studies such as Holt-Lunstad *et al.* (2010) demonstrated that loneliness has an effect on mortality similar in size to cigarette smoking. With over 8 million people in England living alone it has led to campaigns, supported by the Department of Health, to tackle loneliness in old age (Campaign to End Loneliness 2012). However, local authority support services are being reduced to the extent that the human need for companionship and social interaction goes unmet.

Thorough assessment is critical in identifying not only the varied risks to a person's independence and well-being but also the long-term consequences to society of unmet social need. Understanding and articulating these will strengthen any support plan undergoing approval – a core skill of most independent living advocates/personalization workers.

Personalization brings opportunities for people to meet a range of needs simultaneously. An example might be a person who has funding for one hour of personal care and one hour of leisure time. If a person decided to get up in half an hour and spend 90 minutes chatting to people while having their hair done at the hairdressers then not only does that meet their needs but there are additional benefits for everyone. Personalization motivates people when there is freedom to choose based on personal interests. Plans can help people examine their lives and think about what is important to them, and prioritize their support. Through good planning, people are encouraged to do things they otherwise would not have had the opportunity to do and this enables integration of other, often suppressed aspects of their lives. Recent examples are the numerous Direct Payment recipients who have accessed a sex worker or prostitute by using funds towards travel and accommodation, personal care, etc.

Reflective exercise

- Is there a difference between one person's goal of travelling to experience sexual intimacy and another doing so to see the tulip fields to meet their leisure needs?
- How would you feel, as a social worker, if you were asked to arrange (or to agree a support plan) where the service user wanted to access a sex worker?

In 2010, media reports suggested personalization funds were being used to pay for prostitutes and exotic holidays, causing many local authorities to reconsider approving support plans (Pitt 2010). Indeed, many of the difficulties with personalization and the funding of social care lie with public misconceptions. It has also been challenging for some social care staff with regard to professional conduct and judging to what extent support can or should be provided. For others, sexuality issues impact on their personal or religious beliefs more within the context of personalization. When care was prescribed, staff didn't have to talk through or approve personal plans enabling gay people to socialize, form relationships or have a family, for example. Disabled people are pushing the boundaries of exclusion, informed of their rights and daring to mention those aspects of their lives that were previously ignored. Good social work allows people to feel confident in doing this and allows for discussion, debate and supportive risk taking across all areas of life.

What is a personal budget?

At one point my assistance funds were made up of five different sources and this pooling of funds is an example of what was briefly termed an individual budget. The social care element is called a personal budget. Upon assessment, every person whom the local authority has agreed to support is allocated a personal budget from which their social care/services/equipment will be purchased. Each individual (with support as may be required) is invited to make a support plan that is personal and relevant/ useful to them. This alone can be an empowering process if done effectively and there are a large number of resources to aid their creation for both staff and services users. One of the first decisions is whether or not to take it as a Direct Payment and make your own arrangements. Other options include the local authority using your budget to arrange support or requesting it goes to a broker or directly to a care provider. Systemic changes were introduced across adult services to implement this level of personalization.

What do these changes mean for social workers and their role in working with disabled people?

Staff across a range of social care agencies were required to use their skills and experience in different ways, adopting an adaptable work ethic. Changes in roles and responsibilities for social workers have been challenging yet promise many benefits. New partnerships have been forged within the community, for example working with a gym to encourage the purchasing of accessible equipment. This enables disabled people (regardless of whether they receive social support) to access that facility and have a presence in society. It is no longer acceptable for normal community activities to be routinely repeated exclusively for disabled people, hidden away in day centres or similar. Isolation and exclusion only serves to embed discrimination and provide grounds to nurture harassment, abuse and fear of difference. We have seen increased commitments from local authorities to work through co-production, i.e. working with disabled people as partners at strategic level such as in the delivery of personalization (ODI 2012c). We must not forget that independent living can occur, through personalization, regardless of place of residence, nature of impairment, level of capacity or age. Part of the vision of *Putting People First* (DH 2007) has been to ensure that people exercise maximum control over their own lives and and can participate as active and equal citizens, retaining dignity and respect. Ultimately people are experiencing social care that is radically different from its infancy. Disabled people are no longer passive recipients of prescribed services. The important element of interdependency and personal responsibility (of all citizens) has brought us back to what was first realized in the 1968 report by Frederick Seebohm, stating that social care should enable 'the greatest possible number of individuals to act reciprocally, giving and receiving service for the well-being of the whole community' (Seebohm 1968).

References and further reading

Armer, B. (2000) Selected issues surrounding the identity and social valuation of disabled people in contemporary industrial society. Unpublished MA, University of Leeds, available at: http://www.leeds.ac.uk/disability-studies/archiveuk/armer/MA%20dissertation.pdf [Accessed 23 November 2012].

Barnes, C. (1990) *Cabbage Syndrome: The Social Construction of Dependence*. Basingstoke: Falmer Press, available at: http://www.leeds.ac.uk/disability-studies/archiveuk/Barnes/cabbage%20contents.pdf [Accessed 8 January 2013].

Barnes, C. and Mercer, G. (2004) *Implementing the Social Model of Disability: Theory and Research*. Leeds: The Disability Press.

Barrett, J. (2000) *The Information Needs of Elderly, Disabled Elderly People, and their Carers*. Oxford: Disability Information Trust, available at: http://freespace.virgin.net/julie.barrett/Webpart1/Webpart1.htm [Accessed 23 November 2012].

Begum, N. (1996) Doctor, doctor: disabled women's experience of general practitioners, in J. Morris (ed.) *Encounters with Strangers: Feminism and Disability*. London: The Women's Press.

Bentley, J. (2003) Older people as health service consumers: disempowered or disinterested?, *British Journal of Community Nursing*, 8 (4): 181–7.

BIHR (British Institute of Human Rights) (2012) *Health and Social Care Act 2012: Briefing*. London: BIHR.

Braye, S. and Preston-Shoot, M. (1995) *Empowering Practice in Social Care*. Buckingham: Open University Press.

Campaign to End Loneliness (2012) Summit on tackling loneliness in older age, 15 March, available at: http://www.campaigntoendloneliness.org.uk [Accessed 3 April 2012].

Carter, J. (1981) *Day Centres for Adults: Somewhere To Go*. London: George Allen and Unwin.

DH (Department of Health) (2006) *Our Health, Our Care, Our Say: A New Direction for Community Services*. London: Department of Health, available at: http://www. official-documents.gov.uk/document/cm67/6737/6737.pdf [Accessed 25 November 2012].

DH (2007) *Putting People First: A Shared Vision and Commitment to the Transformation of Adult Social Care*. London: Department of Health, available at: http://www.dh.gov.uk/prod_consum_dh/groups/dh_digitalassets/@dh/@en/documents/digitalasset/dh_081119.pdf [Accessed 25 November 2012].

DH (2009) *Guidance on Direct Payments for Community Care, Services for Carers and Children's Services*. London: Department of Health.

DH (2011) *Working for Personalised Care: A Framework for Supporting Personal Assistants Working in Adult Social Care*. London: Department of Health, available at: http://www. dh.gov.uk/en/Publicationsandstatistics/Publications/PublicationsPolicyAndGuidance/DH_128733 [Accessed 25 November 2012].

DH (2012) *Personal Health Budgets*, available at: http://www.dh.gov.uk/health/category/policy-areas/nhs/personal-budgets/ [Accessed 8 January 2013].

Disability Wales (2011) *Manifesto for Independent Living*, available at: http://www.disability-wales.org/independent-living [Accessed 25 November 2012].

DPULO (2011) *Disabled People's User-Led Organisations Programme*, available at: http://odi.dwp.gov.uk/odi-projects/user-led-organisations.php [Accessed 8 January 2013].

DRC (Disability Rights Commission) (2006) *Equal Treatment: Closing the Gap, Part 2*. London: DRC.

DWP (Department for Work and Pensions) (2004) Estimate of the annual spending power of disabled adults, Press release 3 December.

DWP (2011a) *Personal Health Budgets Evaluation* (PHB), available at: https://www.phbe.org.uk/ [Accessed 8 January 2013].

DWP (2011b) 11 May 2011 – Government announces £3 m extra for disabled people's organizations, available at: http://www.dwp.gov.uk/newsroom/press-releases/2011/may-2011/dwp045-11.shtml [Accessed 8 January 2013].

EPP (Expert Patients Programme) (2002), available at: http://www.expertpatients.co.uk [Accessed 25 November 2012].

Fenton, W. (2011) *The Size and Structure of the Adult Social Care Sector and Workforce in England*. London: Skills for Care.

Finkelstein, V. (1981) Disability and professional attitudes, RADAR Conference Proceedings, NAIDEX '81, 21–24 October.

Finkelstein, V. (2001) *The Social Model of Disability Repossessed*. Manchester: Manchester Coalition of Disabled People, available at: http://www.leeds.ac.uk/disability-studies/archiveuk/ [Accessed 25 November 2012].

Fox, J. (2005) The role of the expert patient in the management of chronic illness, *British Journal of Nursing*, 14 (1): 25–8.

French, S. and Swain, J. (2001) The relationship between disabled people and health and welfare professionals, in G. L. Albrecht, K. D Seelman and M. Bury (eds) *Handbook of Disability Studies*. Thousand Oaks: Sage Publications.

Gill, M. (1966) No small miracle, in P. Hunt (ed.) *Stigma: The Experience of Disability*. London: Geoffrey Chapman.

Goffman, E. (1963) *Stigma*. Harmondsworth: Penguin.

Griffiths, C., Foster, G., Ramsay, J., Eldridge, S. and Taylor, S. (2007) How effective are expert patient (lay led) education programmes for chronic disease?, *British Medical Journal*, 334: 1254–6.

Holt-Lunstad, J., Smith, T. B. and Leyton, J. B. (2010) Social relationships and mortality risk: a meta-analytic review, *PLoS Medicine*, 7 (7).

Home Office (2010) Equality Act, available at: http://www.legislation.gov.uk/ukpga/2010/15/contents [Accessed 8 January 2013].

James, S. (2001) Social isolation kills: but how, and why?, *Psychosomatic Medicine, Journal of Biobehavioural Medicine*, 63: 2273–4.

Jolly, D. (2009) *Personal Assistance and Independent Living: Article 19 of the UN Convention on the Rights of Persons with Disabilities. Report Prepared for the European Network on Independent Living (ENIL)*, available at: http://www.leeds.ac.uk/disability-studies/archiveuk/jolly/Personal%20Assistance%20and%20Independent%20Living1.pdf [Accessed 8 January 2013].

Jones, K., Welch, E., Caiels, J. *et al.* (2010) Experiences of implementing personal health budgets: 2nd interim report. PSSRU Discussion Paper 2747/2, Personal Social Services Research Unit, University of Kent, available at: https://www.phbe.org.uk/documents/interim-report-nov-2010.pdf [Accessed 8 January 2013].

Kendrick, M. J. (2010) Historical contributors towards increasing respect for the voices of people with disabilities In western societies, in *Emmaus Welfare Centre Tribute to Father Noel O'Neil*, Hanuri Information Culture Centre, Seoul, available at: http://www.socialrolevalorization.com/articles/kendrick/respect-for-people-with-disabilities.html [Accessed 8 January 2013].

NHS (National Health Service) Executive (1999) *Doubly Disabled: Equality for Disabled People in the New NHS – Access to Services*. London: NHS Executive.

NHS (2009) *Health Survey for England 2009: Health and Lifestyles*. London: Department of Health and NHS Information Centre for Health and Social Care, available at: http://www.ic.nhs.uk/statistics-and-data-collections/health-and-lifestyles-related-surveys/health-survey-for-england/health-survey-for-england—2009-health-and-lifestyles [Accessed 8 January 2013].

NHS (2010) *Total Number of Recipients of Direct Payments in England 2001–2010*. London: Department of Health and NHS Information Centre for Health and Social Care.

NHS Information Centre (2011) *Percentage Distribution of Service Users Receiving Services by Gender, Age Group and Primary Client Group*, England 2009–10. NHS Information Centre,

Adult Social Care Statistics, Version 1.0., 20 April, available at: http://www.ic.nhs.uk/webfiles/publications/009_Social_Care/carestats0910asrfinal/Community_Care_Statistics_200910_Social_Services_Activity_Report_England.pdf [Accessed 8 January 2013].

ODI (Office for Disability Issues) (2012a) *UN Convention on the Rights of Disabled People: About the Language of the UN Convention*, available at: http://odi.dwp.gov.uk/disabled-people-and-legislation/un-convention-on-the-rights-of-disabled-people.php [Accessed 8 January 2013].

ODI (2012b) *Disability Prevalence Estimates 2009/10*. London: Department for Work and Pensions, available at: http://odi.dwp.gov.uk/involving-disabled-people/co-production.php [Accessed 8 January 2013].

ODI (2012c) *Co-production*, available at: http://odi.dwp.gov.uk/involving-disabled-people/co-production.php [Accessed 8 January 2013].

Oliver, M (1998) Theories of disability in health practice and research, *British Medical Journal*, 317: 1446–9.

ONS (Office for National Statistics) (2001) *The 2011 Census*, available at: http://2011.census.gov.uk [Accessed 8 January 2013].

Peacock, G. (1994) Riding for people with disability, Letters, *British Medical Journal*, 309: 340–1, available at: http://bmj.com/cgi/content/full/309/6950/340/a [Accessed 8 January 2013].

Phillips, J. and Cummings, P. (2008) The expert patient, *Healthcare Counselling and Psychotherapy Journal*, 8 (1): January.

Pitt, V. (2010) Wading into the sex, disability and direct payments minefield, Adult Care Blog for *Community Care*, 16 August, available at: http://www.communitycare.co.uk/blogs/adult-care-blog/2010/08/wading-into-the-sex-disability-and-direct-payments-minefield.html [Accessed 8 January 2013].

Riding for the Disabled (2003) *Positive and Unique Therapy UK*, available at: http://www.riding-for-disabled.org.uk/whatwedo.htm [Accessed 8 January 2013].

Seebohm, F. (1968) Report of the Committee on Local Authority and Allied Personal Social Services (Seebohm Report). London: HMSO, cited in Department of Health (2010) *Social Care: Capable Communities and Active Citizens*. London: Department of Health.

Shakespeare, T. (2006) *Disability Rights and Wrongs*. London: Routledge.

Shakespeare, T. and Watson, N. (2002) The social model of disability: an outdated ideology?, *Research in Social Science and Disability*, 2: 9–28.

Sibley, M. (2011) *The Disability Diamond Theory*, available at: http://martynsibley.com/wp-content/uploads/2011/06/The-Disability-Diamond-Theory1.pdf [Accessed 8 January 2013].

UN (United Nations) (2008) *United Nations Convention on the Rights of Persons with Disabilities*, available at: http://www.un.org/disabilities/index.asp [Accessed 8 January 2013].

Walker, P. (2012) Benefit cuts are fuelling abuse of disabled people, say charities, *Guardian* [Society Guardian online], 5 February, available at: http://www.guardian.co.uk/society/2012/feb/05/benefit-cuts-fuelling-abuse-disabled-people?INTCMP=ILCNETTXT3487 [Accessed 8 January 2013].

Warnock (1978) *Special Educational Needs: Report of the Committee of Enquiry into the Education of Handicapped Children and Young People*, Chairman: Mrs H. M. Warnock. London: Her Majesty's Stationery Office.

Welsh Office (1996) *Welsh Health Survey 1995*. Cardiff: Welsh Office.

Whitefield, M. L., Lagan, J. and Russell, O. (1996) Assessing general practitioners' care of adult patients with learning disability: case control study, *Quality in Health Care*, 5: 31–5.

Wilson, D. N. and Haire, A. (1990) Health care screening for people with mental handicap living in the community, *British Medical Journal*, 301: 1379–81.

Wolfensberger, W. (1980) The definition of normalisation: update, problems, disagreements and misunderstandings, in R. J. Flynn and K. E. Nitsch (eds) *Normalisation, Social Integration and Community Services*. Baltimore: University Park Press.

7 Issues affecting practitioners and service users in learning disability services

Julie Potten

I have chosen to work in the field of learning disability because work in this area provides the opportunity for me to challenge my practice, to be creative and recognize the range of options and choices open to individuals. It enables me to work with families, carers and individuals, supporting their increasing independence and helping them to develop roles in society and especially to become valued members of their local communities. The ability to work in a person-centred manner, recognizing the potential of each individual and appreciating the struggles and challenges that they face in pursuit of achieving their goals, makes this area of work for me particularly rewarding and inspiring.

Introduction

Working with individuals with a learning disability in a climate of change may offer unprecedented opportunities for individuals but it may also present professionals with a wealth of challenges and dilemmas in practice. In this chapter I will be using reflective exercises and case scenarios to consider issues in relation to a number of changes and developments in social work and social care engagement with people with learning disabilities. In particular the chapter will examine the impact of the personalization agenda and the legislative and policy drivers that have supported the personalization process in relation to people with learning disabilities.

Learning outcomes

By the end of this chapter readers should have developed their understanding and awareness of:

- the importance and challenges of collaborative working within integrated health and social care teams, such as the recognition and understanding of differing models of working and how these may complement or contradict each other;

- the importance of those professionals having clear, achievable targets for achieving outcomes of relevance to the individuals for whom they work;
- the challenge to practitioners to use and widen networks in areas such as mental health services for individuals who have a dual mental health and learning disability diagnosis;
- the importance of establishing a collaborative approach with colleagues, services and service users in order to empower individuals with learning disabilities and improve their standing in society.

This chapter will encourage the reader to consider what a learning disability is, the numbers of the population who experience a learning disability, how care for those with a learning disability has changed through history and the development of changes in approaches to providing care that attempt to involve individuals and place them at the centre of assessment, planning and managing their support. Case summaries will enable the reader to explore the challenges for practitioners in current approaches to care and hopefully lead to the development of greater understanding of some of the issues practitioners face in our society.

Individuals with a learning disability can lead fulfilling lives, but may also experience a range of social and health care needs; these may be exacerbated by issues such as poor housing or lack of housing, social exclusion, poverty or unemployment, in common with many other marginalized groups.

Reflective exercise

- What is a learning disability?
- What does it mean to have a 'diagnosis' of learning disability?
- What does having a learning disability mean for the service user and the practitioner?

Valuing People (DH 2001a: 14) defines learning disability as including the presence of:

- a significantly reduced ability to understand new or complex information, to learn new skills (impaired intelligence), with a reduced ability to cope independently (impaired social functioning which started before adulthood, with a lasting effect on development).

Valuing People (DH 2001a: 14) also identifies that 'Learning Disability does not include all those who have learning difficulties.'

The World Health Organization (WHO) defines learning disability as 'a state of arrested or incomplete development of the mind'. WHO also asserts that the person should be assessed for three fundamental criteria before a diagnosis of learning disability is made:

- assessing any intellectual impairment (IQ);
- assessing social dysfunction combined with IQ;
- identifying the early onset of the above.

What do these definitions mean? They suggest that rather than a diagnosis based on impaired intelligence a learning disability has to have been present from childhood and affect an individual's ability to function and adapt in all aspects of life including socially, learning and retaining new skills and being able to cope with day-to-day life independently. So individuals experiencing a learning disability will have had difficulties from birth or childhood. They may also have difficulty communicating their needs and wishes to others or may experience difficulty in forming and maintaining friendships. Delays in their development through childhood mean they may need support with many aspects of their daily life in areas where children without a learning disability will gradually learn to become independent.

Mencap (www.mencap.org.uk) identifies a lack of comprehensive information on prevalence of learning disability in the United Kingdom. *Valuing People* (DH 2001a) estimated the prevalence of learning disability to be 2 per cent, which would amount to a total of approximately 1.4 million in a UK population of 60.2 million. This figure was comprised of approximately 1.2 million with mild or moderate learning disability and 210,000 with a severe or profound learning disability. Further reading is available from Emerson and Hatton (2008) who conducted research on potential increases in numbers of individuals who are likely to become eligible for social care services.

Learning disability can range in severity and can be assessed by using the Wechsler Adult Intelligence Scale (WAIS). This tool was designed in 1955 by David Wechsler and identifies the Intelligence Quotient. Wechsler considered intelligence in terms of how individuals use their intelligence to adapt and constructively solve problems or how well they perform certain tasks. There is a problem in that intellectual capacity cannot be seen, therefore not reliably measured; however, performance can be seen and measured. Wechsler defined intelligence as the overall ability of individuals to think through their actions, carry out their planned actions and adapt to their environment.

In order to understand how current practice has developed it is useful to consider care for individuals with a learning disability through history.

Reflective exercise

- As you read how care has changed for individuals with a learning disability through history, consider whether the individuals in receipt of care would have been equal citizens in the society they lived in.
- Would the individuals be likely to have the opportunity to make choices about their lives?
- Consider this in the context of choices you make day to day, where you work or learn, where you live, who you choose to be friends with.

Duffy (2003: 1) identifies the following keys to citizenship:

- self-determination – the ability or authority to be able to get help to achieve self-determination;

- direction – a purpose, plan or idea of what we want to achieve;
- money to live or control one's life;
- a home or a base for life;
- support to achieve the things we need help to achieve;
- a community life – active engagement in the life of the community and our own network of relationships.

Care for individuals with a learning disability has changed immeasurably over the last three centuries; Mencap (2011) tracked how the lives of individuals have always been affected by intolerance and lack of understanding. However, the level of stigma would also be affected by the social conditions and medical knowledge of the time. Prior to the Industrial Revolution children with profound disabilities would have been unlikely to survive beyond early infancy and, due to lower levels of literacy, what we would now consider a mild learning disability may easily have gone unnoticed.

The Industrial Revolution changed communities and individuals who were unable to work came to be seen as either dangerous or a drain on society; many people with learning disabilities were moved to asylums. These individuals were not valued within society and had few choices.

In the twentieth century, such institutions were still present but with the emergence of the medical profession the medicalization of illness and impairment began to change the treatment of individuals with disabilities and a medical model of disability emerged. This was continued by the development of the National Health Service in 1946 and admission to hospital institutions continued until the 1980s. The medical model is characterized by professional expert-led practice where the practitioner holds the power and expertise in the relationship (Gabe *et al.* 1994: xiii; Shakespeare *et al.* 1999: 19).

Mencap (2011) identifies that the Mental Health Act (1959) began the process of questioning whether all 'mentally disordered' individuals actually needed to be cared for in hospital and began to distinguish individuals who had a learning disability from those experiencing difficulties with their mental health. Media publicity and ongoing concerns about conditions in 'mental handicap' hospitals (DHSS 1969, 1974) led to the paper *Better Services for the Mentally Handicapped* (DHSS 1971), and in turn to the expectation of care in the community.

With changes in government policy towards individuals with a learning disability, key writers began to develop theories and models of working that were an alternative to the expert-led medical model of disability. The concept of normalization (Wolfensberger 1983) began to influence the care of those with a learning disability in the 1980s.

Reflective exercise
• What is 'normal'? • What does the term normalization lead you to consider?

The term normalization may lead you to the assumption that this model was developed as individuals with a learning disability were not viewed as normal citizens. Let us consider what is viewed as 'normal' in today's society. Common general aspirations are to have employment, to find meaningful relationships, friendships and partners, marriage, to have a place in which to live independently, to be part of the local community, attending education, social and leisure activities, to make choices about lifestyle and to have families. Wolfensberger's (1983) normalization theory (which was also called social role valorization) has been particularly applied to individuals with a learning disability and focuses on the discrimination against individuals with disabilities and the need to concentrate attention on achieving valued social roles. Baxter *et al.* (1990) cited in Braye and Preston-Shoot (1995: 39) identify the process of normalization as having three major components:

- to enable people to lead normal and valued lives;
- to do this by valued means, using services used by the whole population;
- to change attitudes so that people with disabilities are respected and valued.

O'Brien's five accomplishments (1986), cited in Braye and Preston-Shoot (1995: 39) identified areas in which individuals should be empowered by services to achieve. These included:

- community presence, or experiencing a wide range of ordinary activities in the community rather than segregated provision;
- community participation, which considered the right of the individual to engage in a wide range of relationships with a wide range of people;
- choice, expecting services would maximize opportunity for choice, making use of information and advocacy;
- competence, where individuals have opportunities to develop strengths, skills and interests in a functional and meaningful context or in the ordinary communities in which they live;
- respect, in that services should work to enhance the reputation of individuals and contribute to promoting citizenship through presenting positive images.

Valuing People (DH 2001a) identified similar key principles for those working alongside individuals with a learning disability of rights, choice, independence and inclusion and focused on areas such as working with children and young people in transition to adult life, better health, housing, fulfilling lives and employment, partnership working, increasing choice and control including advocacy and Direct Payments to purchase services. Fundamentally, it stressed the importance of adopting an approach that placed individuals at the centre of any plans and processes involving them.

This progression from state to individual responsibility has a wider focus than simply within learning disability. The government paper *Our Health, Our Care, Our Say* (DH 2006) states that everyone using health and social care has a right to expect choice, control and personal dignity. *Putting People First* (DH 2007a) identified the need for health and social care services to be working in an integrated way to achieve agreed outcomes to support individuals, irrespective of illness or disability, to:

- live independently;
- stay healthy and recover quickly from illness;
- exercise maximum control over their own life and where appropriate the lives of their family members;
- sustain a family unit which avoids children being required to take on inappropriate caring roles;
- participate as active and equal citizens both economically and socially.

Policy is an essential component of changing practice but with people who have traditionally been disadvantaged it takes more than policy to change things; the commitment and energy of practitioners and other supporters is also vital for progress to be made. *Valuing People Now* (DH 2009) sought to look at the progress that had been made for individuals with a learning disability since 2001. While there was evidence of some improvement, it was limited. Further emphasis on housing, employment and community participation would be required in terms of making person-centred practice more of a reality.

Working with individuals with a learning disability now

Working with individuals with a learning disability in the current climate needs further focus on control for the individual and recognition that they will be, within their own lives, 'experts by experience'. However, in complex situations health and social care professionals need the ability to consider dilemmas and challenges to practise and balance the risks and rights of the individual. The requirements of legislation and guidance such as the Human Rights Act (1998), the duties of the local authority to safeguard vulnerable adults set out in *No Secrets* (DH 2000) and the principles of the Mental Capacity Act (DH 2005) need to be considered in practice with individuals. Professionals need to support individuals with whom they work in understanding the balance between their rights and the responsibilities of being a fully participating member of society. Practice must work towards acknowledging and developing the ability of individuals to make informed choices about day-to-day actions alongside developing understanding of the risks and consequences of actions they choose to take. Monk (2010) recognizes that alongside rights to choice and control there is increased responsibility, accountability, participation and obligation, which come as part of being a full member of the community.

Reflective exercise

- What does personalization really mean for individuals with a learning disability and practitioners working today in health and social care?

At its most basic level, individuals participate in a community care assessment where they are supported to identify their needs and strengths under the NHS and Community Care Act (1990). Once they have been assessed as eligible for a community care service (*Fair Access to Care Services*, LAC 2002), the shift towards personalization within community care takes the statutory duty to assess the needs of those who may require community care services (NHS and Community Care Act 1990) into a process of self-assessment and outcome-based assessment, encompassing the themes of recent legislation, white papers and guidance.

This approach presents an ideal of beginning with service users as the people best able to know what they need and how to meet these needs and identifying the outcomes they want to achieve, by the provision of personal budgets under the Community Care (Direct Payments) Act (1996), to manage their own packages of care and introduce greater choice and control over the way these outcomes are achieved. Self-directed support (DH 2007a) is the framework by which individuals are enabled to have more control over the services they receive.

The following case study (anonymized) looks at how a person-centred, outcome-based assessment may look in practice and considers where challenges may arise.

Case study

John is 34 and has a learning disability; he has attended a local day service since leaving school 15 years ago. John has a network of friends among his peers at the day service but other than this does not access the local community. John is highly skilled within the horticulture project run by the day service. John receives welfare benefits but these are absorbed into his family budget as his main carer is unable to work due to ill health. They live in an area of town where there is a significant level of crime and John has been targeted by local youths on a number of occasions when he walked to the local shop independently. John recently had a review meeting at the day service and is being asked to be involved in writing a support plan to identify outcomes for the future and has been informed he will be offered a personal budget to use to meet the outcomes he identifies.

- What issues need to be considered to ensure John can make choices and take control of how he will be supported?

John's experience is limited to school, day service and his family home. He has significant skills in horticulture developed at the day service and enjoys this; however, to date he has not had the opportunity to consider whether this may be an area that could lead to employment. John also has the skills to access the community independently and did so in the past, but has stopped doing this due to being targeted by local youths.

John has never managed his own finances or considered alternative living options to his family home. While John may have the ability to make choices about his future, at present he does not appear to have information on the options available to him, due to his limited experiences. John's power to take control of his support needs to be considered in the context of his social situation.

Thompson (2007) recognized that everyone has some power but some people in society are in stronger positions than others. Thompson's (2007) personal, cultural and structural (PCS) model of power as discussed in Chapter 2 can be considered in the context of John's situation.

John's personal power is affected by the level of knowledge he has about the choices available to him. He may be able to communicate the hopes he has but these will be limited to his experiences. Introducing opportunities to explore wider choices than are available in his current activities may begin to enable John to think about what he hopes for in the future. It has been identified that John is very skilled in his horticultural work within the day service but at present this is likely to have limited respect or status in his wider community. However, John may have a positive experience of the value and status of his workmanship within the day service which he can build on given opportunities. John's confidence and willingness to take risks may have been affected by his past experiences of discrimination and victimization. A practitioner will need to work with John to highlight his awareness that in going into the wider community and having wider experiences, there may be some risks. John may need support to consider whether the potential positive benefits outweigh those risks.

John's cultural power would appear to be limited, as the dominant concepts that construct power in western society, such as employment and financial independence, are not represented in his lifestyle. However, John has good physical health and he has skills that offer the potential to lead to employment and financial independence. The importance of support to enable individuals to move into work was identified as a priority in *Valuing People* (DH 2001a), and in the follow-up document *Valuing People Now* (DH 2009).

Structural power for John is affected by his limited financial resources. It was identified that his benefits are being absorbed into his family budget. John's level of choice may be further restricted by his life experience of discrimination in his local area and his limited knowledge of the options and opportunities open to him. The practitioners will need to engage with John's family as they are significant in providing the main care and support for John. In addition, due to their circumstances, John's ability to access his benefit entitlement is limited but John may need access to these finances in order to explore wider opportunities in the community. While a personal budget may be used to address some of the choices John can make, in a climate of limited resources other opportunities that may arise are likely to need to be funded individually.

It is important to consider the potential implications for all those involved in this process – service users, practitioners, carers and/or advocates. If we consider the difference in past practice, where professionals have led assessment and decisions on packages of care, the introduction of choice and control in decision-making for individuals may introduce a number of dilemmas in practice. As Fenge (2010) recognizes, power relationships are challenging and practitioners can experience tensions between service user empowerment, sharing of the assessment process and resource restrictions.

Case study

Jessica has attended a local school for individuals with special educational needs. She has a mild learning disability and had been a very quiet pupil, but during the post-16 years education programme Jessica began, with support from teaching staff, to work on a plan of what she hoped to achieve in the future. She had the opportunity to participate in a work experience placement; she had tried shop work and also catering, which she had really enjoyed. Once Jessica had become involved with adult services she had worked with a Care Manager who supported individuals through the transition from education. She had received a small package of support at this time from a support worker who also worked as an advocate and had encouraged Jessica to think about her plans for the future, helping her to consider how to make her hopes a reality.

Jessica is now 20 and left school a year ago. She accesses the local college on a catering course where she is developing her work skills; Jessica has clear ideas of working in a restaurant. After talking to a friend she met at the local youth club, of which she is an active member, she learned about the possibility of moving to her own flat. Jessica is developing her cooking skills at college, but has said she needs some help to learn about managing a home, paying bills, etc. Jessica receives welfare benefits which are paid into her bank account and she is learning to manage this money with the support of her parents. Jessica also had a review meeting at college and has asked to be supported to write a plan about her goals. She is being offered a personal budget to support her to meet these outcomes.

Reflective exercise

- How would you say Jessica's situation differs from John's?
- How could Thompson's PCS model help to analyse the difference?

Jessica has had the opportunity to consider her choices, such as what type of work interests her and what is available in the community to support her to achieve this, and has identified the goal of working in a restaurant. Jessica has had the opportunity to make wider networks locally at the club she attends and heard about different living options, and now hopes with the support of her parents and some purchased support to live independently. Jessica has the support and knowledge she needs to begin to take steps towards achieving the aspirations and goals she has for her life. She recognizes that there may be risks in that she will try experiences she has never had before but with the support and confidence to consider and tackle these risks.

In the context of Thompson's (2007) (PCS) model of power, Jessica would appear to have a high level of personal power. She is able to communicate her goals; she has positive parental support and has valued social roles as a student, a member of a club and with her work experience skills. She also has a confidence and belief in what she hopes to achieve. Jessica recognizes there are areas in which she may have to develop skills but has a willingness and awareness of the need to address these areas.

Cultural power for Jessica is attributed to her goals of employment which in her society is a desirable valued objective, as is her wish to live independently in her own home.

In terms of structural power Jessica may experience barriers (for example in the form of the attitudes and beliefs of others) relating to her disability, gender and, potentially, her reliance on welfare benefits. These may also impact on the power she could be perceived to have in the areas of personal and cultural power. In contemporary practice it could be considered that there have been developments which take steps to redressing the power balances for individuals with a learning disability. There are District Partnership Boards and Groups which have individuals with a learning disability as members alongside professionals and policy makers. The co-chairs of the Learning Disabilities Task Force are now individuals with a learning disability.

John and Jessica are being involved in outcome-based assessment in which they can if they choose manage a personal budget to purchase support to meet their needs. There appear to be clear disparities in each individual's opportunity to participate in the process. Parrot (2006: 26) recognizes the practitioner's responsibility to identify and counter such disadvantage. It could be argued that, as a key premise of personalization is the recognition of individuals as experts in their own situation, the importance of tackling disadvantage becomes even more significant. Many individuals may be able to engage with this process with a little support and have a range of life experiences and hopes and aspirations on which to develop plans. However, others may require much higher levels of support to be able to be involved in the process and to be able to experience real choice and control.

These dilemmas are not new in social care. However, in an environment which offers personalization and increased choice and control, rights must be balanced with individual responsibility and risk. Titterton (2005: 53) suggests that risk should form part of needs assessment, as risk is a need in itself. Person-centred approaches to practice (DH 2007a) may encourage and facilitate involvement in wider community facilities including employment and participation in integrated initiatives such as partnership boards or housing strategies (developed since *Valuing People*, DH 2001a). Social and leisure opportunities can broaden experience for people, but may also involve risks.

While choice and control are positive, this also has to be balanced with a greater expectation from society to be protected from risk (Cree and Wallace 2005). *Independence, Choice and Risk* (DH 2007b) recognized that risk is an unavoidable consequence of people making decisions about their lives.

Coverage of tragedies such as those of Victoria Climbié (Laming 2003), Steven Hoskin (Flynn 2007) and Kevin Davies (Carter 2007) identify the importance of person-centred work but also the critical need to adhere to the legislative and procedural frameworks within health and social care. All such enquiries have highlighted the need for good communication between professionals, the need for clear roles and responsibilities and collaboration between professionals ensuring effective direct work with individuals concerned (Koubel and Bungay 2009).

This may become clearer as we consider the next steps for Jessica.

Jessica wanted to live in her own flat, seek employment in catering and have some support to develop skills she lacks. Jessica has now achieved these goals and, in the process of becoming more involved in the wider community, has begun to form relationships. She has a boyfriend who is the same age and they enjoy an active social life. Jessica's family have become concerned that Jessica is spending increasing amounts of time with her boyfriend and that she is considering letting him stay at her flat overnight. Jessica's family have raised concerns that this is a 'serious' relationship and in conversation with the social worker express fears about Jessica becoming pregnant. They are also worried that Jessica is spending her money unwisely on going out and socializing, and demand that something is done to safeguard Jessica.

Let us consider how the social worker might work through the complex issues here. If we consider the expectations generally of many citizens in western society that we identified previously, among those were the right to form meaningful relationships and have a family.

Reflective exercise

- Are there concerns about whether Jessica is being treated as an equal citizen in society or is the 'learning disability' label having an impact on the way in which her rights are viewed by others?
- Do you think Jessica's parents would have the same concerns if Jessica did not have a learning disability? You could even question whether they would be so involved in her life as to even know that she was making these choices?

This is a potentially complex situation and many issues may need to be considered. The Mental Capacity Act (2005) provides a structure to empower and protect individuals who are vulnerable and may have difficulty in making decisions. It requires a presumption of capacity for adults and provides a statutory framework for assessing capacity as well as a framework for making decisions in the best interests of a person assessed as lacking capacity.

The social worker may need to give consideration to Jessica's capacity to make the decisions required to embark on this relationship and her ability to make decisions about managing her finances. If the assessment of capacity demonstrates that an individual is not able to make the decision required, the MCA provides a framework for Best Interests decision-making to be undertaken on behalf of the individual. In practice such decisions require excellent negotiating skills and consultation with all the relevant parties including family and professionals involved. An Independent Mental Capacity Advocate may be appointed where there is disagreement and there is recourse to the Court of Protection for particularly difficult situations.

Jessica was assessed as having capacity to make decisions about how she chooses to spend her money and also about her choice to start a relationship. Jessica explained she had attended a group session on relationships and sexual health held at her local youth club; she had then attended her GP surgery and discussed contraception and made choices in this area. Jessica recognized the relationship may not last for ever but she felt very positive about it and had got to know her partner over several months at the youth club as a good friend before they decided to start a relationship.

Jessica was also able to identify a week when she had the opportunity to go out several times and she had made a mistake with her finances, forgetting to set aside enough money for one of her utility bills, which she usually paid in at the bank. Jessica had realized this when going through the budget plan she had drawn up with her support worker and to cover the bill asked her parents for a short-term loan; she then arranged for this bill to be paid by direct debit in future. Jessica was able in discussion to explain the choices she had made and the actions she had taken, with reasons for those choices. She was able to demonstrate she had retained information and learned from experience.

Jessica may still require further support to gain the skills and knowledge to make decisions about her relationship in the future. The social worker also needs to recognize the concerns raised by the family and their view of the relationship needing to be stopped and consider how Jessica can be supported to express her choices and have her rights recognized. Jessica may need to be supported in explaining to her family what is important to her so they can understand her choices and her ability and rights to make choices. The importance of working with carers in partnership is recognized in legislation (Carers Recognition and Services Act 1995) and Twigg and Atkin (1994) identified models of how service providers may work with carers. However, Bungay and Walker (2009) recognize that some dilemmas practitioners encounter can raise uncertainty about who is in the centre of person-centred care – the carer or the service user.

In situations where risk is perceived, social care professionals will at times be faced with a 'something needs to be done' pressure from families and other professionals. This tension between rights and supporting individuals to take decisions and external pressure to remove the risk provides challenge and often complex dilemmas for practitioners. There may be a temptation to become 'defensive' in practice. Braye and Preston-Shoot (1995) observe that practitioners are often confronted by situations where there are risks that all the variables cannot be controlled and they suggest practitioners may be drawn into practising in an oppressive manner when they try to control the risks.

If Jessica had been unable to demonstrate her understanding and choices as described earlier, she may have been assessed as lacking capacity. The Mental Capacity Act (2005) requires individuals to be given the opportunity to demonstrate capacity and in order to facilitate this the social worker may need to involve wider professional support. The social worker may discuss with Jessica accessing support from other professionals to enable her to make an informed decision about the relationship. This may involve using mainstream services such as family planning clinics for advice. Access to mainstream services would require Jessica to be able to understand the information provided or there may be a need for support to assist with this understanding. Alternative support and the provision of more accessible information could be achieved through the involvement of specialist professionals such as Learning Disability Nurses, who could assess Jessica's understanding of relationships and her ability to maintain her own safety. Additional help may be sought from Speech and Language Therapy colleagues who can offer support in developing accessible information for individuals.

Ovretveit et al. (1997: 124) recognize the potential for professionals to lose sight of the significance of the viewpoints of individuals, carers and other networks. This highlights the importance of working in a multi-professional way, taking into account the range of skills various professionals can offer to support and promote individuals' rights to make choices. This process of collaborative working can itself bring challenges. In order to work effectively in an interprofessional manner practitioners need to develop their understanding of the roles of their multi-agency colleagues and appreciate that differing models of work may collide rather than gel seamlessly in their work with individuals. This presents a potential risk to the individual if professionals trying to work collaboratively become so engaged in the complexities of justifying their particular framework, policy or practice viewpoint, as the focus on the individual may become lost in the process.

In working together with other professionals to support Jessica in her decision-making about her relationship with her boyfriend, or understanding that although she is choosing to spend her money on her social life there are wider responsibilities, for example the payment of bills; there may be differences of view when assessing risks and her ability to take these decisions. The issues that have arisen give some insight into the importance of monitoring and review on a regular and ongoing basis. Each practitioner's experience, value base and skills in working in complex situations will impact on their decision-making. Milburn and Walker (2009) recognize that to work in a person-centred manner professionals working in a team need to have an understanding of each other's capabilities and roles.

When working collaboratively with Jessica and other professionals, the social worker may need to support Jessica to consider far wider issues than simply communicating the actions she wants to take. Alongside the right to take decisions about how an individual may wish to live comes a responsibility to understand the risks and the consequences of any decisions they make. Titterton (2005: 55) comments that:

> Voluntary risk taking can only occur when risks have been identified, enabling individuals to make personal choices about types and levels of risk which are appropriate in certain situations.'

For Jessica, understanding how and why her family are so anxious about her relationship may be difficult, as may be decision-making about how to spend her money. For her, each decision carries some risk; the risk of the previously close relationship with her parents being affected will unquestionably be a pressure in her making a decision about the possible loss of one or other of the relationships she wants to have. Risks associated with possible unwise decisions around budgeting may mean Jessica has some debts or has to experience some weeks where she finds she is short of money for essentials. However, while these are risks, Jessica's opportunity to learn and develop skills not only comes from support and advice but also from life experience. Koubel (2009) recognizes that within the social models of disability and vulnerability individuals need to decide what they want and practitioners then offer support with identifying how this can be achieved, recognizing the potential for individual learning and development, rather than relying on safe, systematic responses that protect organizations but may limit individuals.

For practitioners the challenge is balancing the desire and need at times to protect individuals with an awareness that positive risk-taking is equally important. Skills and knowledge can be developed by experience of the opportunities and situations encountered in day-to-day living. There needs to be recognition that many of the decisions practitioners have to take about how to act can be influenced by anxieties and fears about managing pressure from external sources, which at times may include the families of individuals with whom we work, in addition to wider fears about media attention and blame. Brown (2002), cited in Titterton 2005: 54, discussed the 'protection agenda' and tensions between protection and empowerment of individuals who are not traditionally powerful. Titterton recognizes the importance of keeping sight of positive risks and not only reducing the risk of significant harm, warning, however, that moves to promote a balance between minimizing risk and empowerment are subject to a wider agenda fuelled by media attention.

Specific targets for work with individuals with a learning disability were identified by *Valuing People* (DH 2001a) and *Valuing People Now* (DH 2009). Better health was also a key concept, in particular the importance of linking up local services especially around mental health and learning disability recognizing that each need is distinct. A further document, *About Learning Disabilities* (Debenham 2012) recognized that the needs of individuals with a learning disability who also have mental health problems are diverse and frequently complicated and this often causes difficulties in referring to other professionals and finding placements. Hardy *et al.* (2009) observed that in recent decades there has been great interest and progress in how mental health problems present and how they are assessed and treated in people with learning disabilities, but assert that little progress has been made in promoting mental health in this group.

It is of key importance to understand that mental health and learning disability are different. This was identified earlier in the chapter when the Mental Health Act (1959) began the consideration that experiencing difficulties with mental well-being should be distinguished from experiencing a learning disability. *About Learning Disabilities* (Debenham 2012) identified that mental health issues generally develop after childhood, can change over a period of time and may only be temporary, whereas a learning disability permanently affects intellectual function and is present from birth or before adulthood. People who have learning disabilities are vulnerable to suffering mental health issues due to the range of social, psychological and biological factors they may encounter throughout their lives, in the same way as the wider population. However, to add to the difficulty, individuals with a learning disability may also find it hard to communicate their problems and feelings. This may lead to difficulty in diagnosis and changes in behaviour can often be overlooked or misunderstood.

Case study

Joseph is 54 years of age. He has a learning disability and communication difficulties and he also finds it difficult to express emotions and has limited verbal communication skills. Over his life Joseph has been noted at times to withdraw from others, lose interest in activities and experience sleep disturbances. After some time Joseph appears to recover and return to what staff call 'his normal self'. Joseph lives in a small residential home with three other men who also have learning disabilities. Joseph's remaining parent, his father, passed away 18 months ago, and this was explained to him using a pictorial workbook designed specifically for this purpose, by staff familiar to him. Staff had described Joseph as appearing largely unaffected by his loss, although they had ensured he had photographs of family and opportunity to look at these with staff support.

Staff have reported to the social worker that over recent weeks Joseph has increasingly spent time in his room and has become reluctant to participate in activities he previously enjoyed. Joseph's appetite is poor and his sleep pattern is disturbed; he appears unable to sleep but also doesn't want to spend time with his friends or his keyworker. Staff are concerned that Joseph appears very low in mood and while they initially thought he might just be having one of his periods of feeling low in mood, and expected him to recover as usual, they are now concerned that he may be experiencing depression. A visit to the GP led to a referral to the local community mental health team. However, Joseph was unable to communicate how he was feeling and the historical pattern of Joseph's behaviour from which he has always previously recovered led to a conclusion that this is Joseph's way of coping due to his learning disability.

Consider the following issues:

- How could the practitioner support Joseph in accessing the support he needs?
- How could services for Joseph enable him to explore and express how he is feeling and work in partnership with professionals who can support him?

Joseph may be experiencing depression or not but clearly he appears to be significantly low in mood at present and will need additional support to be able to express to others how he is feeling, what is causing him to feel like this and how he can be supported through this. Ryan *et al.* (2012) identify the importance of individuals with a learning disability having the opportunity to explore their loss and grief after the death of parents, and how this is often unrecognized and unsupported.

Sines (1995) highlights the importance of recognizing the need to develop facilitative and empowering partnerships for individuals experiencing mental health problems. The usefulness of pictorial documentation was identified in supporting Joseph and involving other professionals with expertise could help him to explore and communicate his emotions. Joseph may be able to access wider support services such as speech and language therapy to develop his communication ability, psychologists and psychiatrists with expertise in learning disability may be available, or additional help in using effective communication might enable him to access mainstream mental health support. Individual or support group advocacy could help Joseph to communicate.

One way to help Joseph could be the use of communication tools such as cards indicating emotions and photographs to help him express how he was feeling. Alongside this, Joseph was encouraged to visit his GP again, where he was prescribed medication to treat his depression. Joseph's needs were able to be addressed through collaborative work; such an approach was required to ensure a positive outcome.

The social worker understood that many individuals with a learning disability experience grief that is not acknowledged or socially supported (Ryan *et al.* 2012) and recognized the need to act to ensure that Joseph was not disadvantaged by his communication difficulties. From a social model of disability perspective Joseph was experiencing discrimination due to his difficulty in expressing how he was feeling. In this situation the collaborative approach from a number of different professionals meant that he was able to be supported appropriately.

Conclusion

Provision of support and services for individuals with a learning disability has changed through history to the current day and this leads to new challenges and dilemmas. With rights and choices to make decisions come inevitable risks. The challenge for practitioners is how to enable the individuals with whom they work to recognize and understand risks so that those they choose to take are informed choices.

Practitioners also need to be aware, despite the move towards individual responsibility and choice, that many inequalities remain and in learning disability the work continues to ensure that people with learning disabilities are enabled to be active citizens in the community. The approach of collaborative working ensuring access to the skills of a range of professionals in promoting development of skills and communication brings opportunity but also further challenges for practitioners. To work with other professions in an open manner for the benefit of the individual requires practitioners to recognize the different models and frameworks of other professionals and seek ways of developing their working practices so that these diverse approaches become a benefit rather than a barrier to the service provided to the individuals.

In working with individuals with a learning disability many have identified positive changes and opportunities that have arisen over recent years but as a practitioner it is also clear to me that much needs to be done to develop further opportunities for inclusion, better access to mainstream services, ensuring accessible information and technology to enhance decision-making opportunities for all individuals with a learning disability. The personalization agenda, which encourages partnership working with colleagues, carers and disabled people themselves, provides the context in which these aspirations may be turned into reality.

References and further reading

Braye, S. and Preston-Shoot, M. (1995) *Empowering Practice in Social Care*. Buckingham: Open University Press.

Bungay, H. and Walker, P. (2009) *Care for the Carers*, in G. Koubel and H. Bungay (2009) *The Challenge of Person-centred Care: An Interprofessional Perspective*. Basingstoke: Palgrave Macmillan.

Carter, H. (2007) Three jailed over man's shed torture. *Guardian*, 9 July.

Cree, V. E. and Wallace, S. J. (2005) in R. Adams, L. Dominelli and M. Payne (2005) *Social Work Futures*. Basingstoke: Palgrave MacMillan.

DCSF (Department for Children, Schools and Families) (2004) *Every Child Matters*. London: DCSF.

Debenham, L. (2012) *Mental Health Issues*, available at http://www.aboutlearningdisabilities. co.uk/mental-health-issues [Accessed 1 January 2013].

DH (Department of Health) (1990) NHS and Community Care Act. London: HMSO.

DH (1995) Carers (Recognition and Services) Act. London: HMSO.

DH (1996) Community Care (Direct Payments) Act. London: HMSO.

DH (2000) *No Secrets: Guidance on Developing and Implementing Multi-agency Policies and Procedures to Protect Vulnerable Adults from Abuse*. London: Department of Health.

DH (2001a) *Valuing People: A New Strategy for Learning Disability for the Twenty-first Century*. London: Department of Health.

DH (2001b) *Working Together, Learning Together: A Framework for Lifelong Learning in the NHS*. London: Department of Health.

DH (2005) Mental Capacity Act. London: HMSO.

DH (2006) *Our Health, Our Care, Our Say: A New Direction for Community Services*. London: Department of Health.

DH (2007a) *Putting People First: A Shared Vision and Commitment to the Transformation of Social Care*. London: Department of Health.

DH (2007b) *Independence, Choice and Risk*. London: Department of Health.

DH (2008) Health and Social Care Act, s146. London: HMSO.

DH (2009) *Valuing People Now: From Progress to Transformation*. London: Department of Health.

DHSS (Department of Health and Social Security) (1969) *Report of the Committee of Inquiry of Ill-treatment of Patients and Other Irregularities at the Ely Hospital, Cardiff*. London: HMSO.

DHSS (1971) *Better Services for the Mentally Handicapped* (Command Paper 4683). London: HMSO.

DHSS (1974) *Report of the Committee of Inquiry into South Ockenden Hospital*. London: HMSO.

DHSS (1983) Mental Health Act. London: HMSO.

Duffy, S. (2003) *Keys to Citizenship: A Guide to Getting Good Support for People with Learning Disabilities*. Boulder, CO: Paradigm.

Emerson, E. and Hatton, C. (2008) *Estimating Future Needs for Adult Social Care for People with Learning Disabilities in England*, Project Report. Lancaster: Centre for Disability Research, Lancaster University.

Fenge, L. (2010) The changing face of community care: assessment, personalisation and outcomes, in K. Brown, *Vulnerable Adults and Community Care*. Exeter: Learning Matters.

Flynn, M. (2007) *The Murder of Steven Hoskin: A Serious Case Review*. Executive Summary. Truro: Cornwall Adult Protection Committee.

Gabe, J., Kelleher, D. and Williams, G. (1994) *Challenging Medicine*. London: Routledge.

Habermas, J. (1989) *The Theory of Communicative Action, Volume 2. Lifeworld and System: A Critique of Functionalist Reason*. Cambridge: Polity Press.

Hardy, S., Woodward, P., Halls, S. and Creet, B. (2009) *Mental Health Promotion for People with Learning Disabilities*. Brighton: OLM-Pavilion.

Koubel, G. (2009) A person-centred approach to safeguarding vulnerable adults, in G. Koubel and H. Bungay (2009) *The Challenge of Person-centred Care: An Interprofessional Perspective*. Basingstoke: Palgrave Macmillan.

Koubel, G. and Bungay, H. (2009) *The Challenge of Person-centred Care: An Interprofessional Perspective*. Basingstoke: Palgrave Macmillan.

LAC (Department of Health Local Authority Circular) (2002) *Fair Access to Care Services: Guidance on Eligibility Criteria for Adult Social Care*. London: Department of Health.

Laming, Lord (2003) *The Victoria Climbié Enquiry: A Report of an Enquiry by Lord Laming*. London: The Stationery Office.

Mandelstam, M. (2009) *Safeguarding Vulnerable Adults and the Law*. London: Jessica Kingsley.

Mencap (2011) *Changing Attitudes*, available at: http://www.mencap.org.uk/sites/defult/files/documents/changing-attitudes.pdf [Accessed 1 January 2013].

Milburn, P. and Walker, P. (2009) Beyond interprofessional education and towards collaborative person-centred practice, in G. Koubel and H. Bungay (2009) *The Challenge of Person-centred Care: An Interprofessional Perspective*. Basingstoke: Palgrave Macmillan.

Ministry of Health (1959) Mental Health Act. London: HMSO.

Monk, J. (2010) To what extent is selfdirected support- actually self-directed by people with learning disabilities?, in K. Brown, *Vulnerable Adults and Community Care*, 2nd revised edn. Exeter: Learning Matters.

Ovretveit, J., Mathias, P. and Thompson, T. (1997) *Interprofessional Working in Health and Social Care*. Bsaingstoke: Macmillan.

Ovretveit, J., Mathias, P. and Thompson, T. (2007) *Interprofessional Working in Health and Social Care*. Basingstoke: Palgrave.

Parrott, L. (2006) *Values and Ethics in Social Work Practice*. Exeter: Learning Matters.

Ryan, J., McCarthy, J. and Graham, M. (2012) How clients cope with the death of a parent, *Learning Disability Practice*, 15 (4): 14–18.

Sevenhuijsen, S. (2000) Caring in the third way: the relation between obligatory responsibility and care in the third way discourse. *Critical Social Policy* 20 (1): 5–37.

Shakespeare, T., Barnes, C. and Mercer, G. (1999) *Exploring Disability: A Sociological Introduction*. Cambridge: Polity Press.

Sines, D. (1995) *Community Health Care Nursing*. Oxford: Blackwell.

Smethurst, C. (2009) in A. Mantell and T. Scragg (2009) *Safeguarding Adults in Social Work*. Exeter: Learning Matters.

Thompson, N. (2007) *Power and Empowerment*. Lyme Regis: Russell House.

Titterton, M. (2005) Risk *and Risk Taking in Health and Social Welfare*. London: Jessica Kingsley.

Twigg, J. and Atkin, A. (1994) *Carers Perceived: Policy and Practice in Informal Care*. Buckingham: Open University Press.

UK Government (1998) Human Rights Act 1998. London: HMSO.

Wechsler, D. (1939) *The Measurement of Adult Intelligence*. Baltimore, MD: Williams and Witkins.

Wechsler, D. (1955) *The Range of Human Capacities*, 2nd edn. Baltimore: Williams and Wilkins.

WHO (World Health Organization) (1992) *The ICD-10 Classification of Mental and Behavioural Disorders: Clinical Descriptions and Diagnostic Guidelines*. Geneva: WHO.

WHO (1996) *ICD-10 Guide for Mental Retardation*. Geneva: World Health Organization.

Wolfensberger, W. (1983) Social role valorization: a proposed new term for the principle of normalization, *Mental Retardation*, 21 (6): 234–9.

8 Working with people with sensory disabilities

Keith French

My personal experiences in life as a deaf child and young person has led me to become interested in social work with D/deaf people to address oppression, discrimination, disadvantage and disempowerment and to be able to assist them to achieve a sense of well-being, self-fulfilment and self-control. This can be possible through social work intervention and support to enable positive change, empowerment, access to appropriate information and services, equal treatment and through addressing imbalances of power among other anti-discriminatory and anti-oppressive practices.

I have been a social worker for the Deaf since 1995 based within the sensory disability team for both deaf children and D/deaf adults. I have an interest around advocacy, empowerment and task-centred social work with D/deaf people as they are individuals with needs who happen to be on the margin of society and who have faced social and individual injustice. I am keen to enable them to develop life skills and confidence in using the language most appropriate for them, as well as assisting them by changing society's use of oppressive social relations. There is a constant focus on transforming power relationships between D/deaf people and mainstream society, and this chapter will in part explore the relationship between Deafness as a cultural identity and deafness and blindness as impairments. We will discuss the terminology around d/Deafness later in the chapter.

Introduction

As a Deaf person working in social work with Deaf people I have become aware of how my personal experiences and values have influenced my particular commitment to positive and proactive practice with service users with sensory disabilities.

This chapter will explore the nature of social work with people with sensory disabilities and look in particular at the changes that have developed more recently in this field. Using reflective exercises and case studies, the chapter will raise awareness of the challenges, dilemmas and conflicts in working with people with sensory disabilities, highlighting the traditional expectation that people with sensory impairments are likely to receive paternalistic services. Many people have other problems in addition to their sensory difficulties, such as other physical or learning disabilities. This will have an impact on the service area to which they are allocated and this in turn may affect the kind of service they are likely to receive. They may also be in different situations, such as prison or hospitals, where their communication needs are not addressed, exacerbating the impact of such an experience. The chapter will start by unpicking some relevant and important terms and principles that affect work with people with sensory disabilities.

- How do we understand the terms sensory loss and sensory disability?
- What is the scope of work for a social worker specializing in practice with people with sensory disabilities?
- How do models of disability relate to working with people with sensory disabilities?
- What are the most pressing challenges and dilemmas for those who undertake social work with adults with sensory disabilities?
- How has the nature of social work with people with sensory disabilities been affected by modernization and care management practice?
- How has social work with people with sensory disabilities changed and developed?
- What are the implications for people who are identified as being both deaf and blind?

This chapter will explore some of the challenges, political perspectives and ethical dilemmas that arise within the community care context of working with service users with sensory disabilities, and their carers and networks. It will look at the role of people with visual impairments as well as those with hearing disabilities and analyse the ways in which different groups have developed their cultural and political perspectives. Cultural differences and the recognition of communication needs are key elements of anti-discriminatory and anti-oppressive practice (Banks 2006; Thompson 2006), particularly in relation to people experiencing one or more sensory impairment.

The chapter will explore the ways in which society views people with sensory disabilities and analyse the need for greater awareness and understanding of the role of the social worker in relation to working in a meaningful way with people with sensory disabilities to challenge the discrimination and marginalization that many people in this group experience. In the wider context of social work with adults with sensory loss and disabilities, there is a need to trace some of the historical events that have shaped this relationship. The chapter will explore, for example, how people with sensory disabilities relate to the world of welfare, and the knowledge, skills and values required in promoting good practice in working in this area, taking account of recent changes due to the modernization/personalization agenda.

Complicated as it is in relation to the development and changes in use of language within disabilities generally, there are further complications within areas of sensory disability. In order to keep it simple, the term 'sensory disability' will be used unless referring to a specific issue in relation to hearing or visual impairment.

Learning outcomes

By the end of this chapter, readers should have developed their understanding and awareness of:

- the scope of sensory disabilities and the particular challenges facing this group of service users;
- the ethical, communicative and practical challenges that practitioners may experience when working with people with sensory disabilities and their networks;
- the scope and changing nature of the role of social work and its implications for practice with people within this group;
- the nature of the D/deaf community and the experience of exclusion of people with sensory disabilities as a minority group;
- the challenges for social work with adults in meeting the needs of people with sensory disabilities.

There is a need to be aware of the challenges, dilemmas and conflicts that arise as social work with adults moves towards a care management model which places personalization at the heart of social services' engagement with people who use services. This highlights issues for practitioners and service users alike in relation to the transition from the more prescriptive and paternalistic ways in which services have traditionally been provided to people with sensory disabilities.

The scope of social work with people with sensory disabilities

We have arrived at a point where it will be helpful to examine in greater depth the roles and duties of social workers who work with people with sensory disabilities. There are explicit main duties which include the provision of a specialist casework service, identifying communicative and other needs and assisting in developing a comprehensive social care service for people with sensory disabilities. It is clearly not possible for a single worker to undertake all the tasks effectively – they need to be shared between members of a team. If this only referred to D/deaf people, it would be daunting enough, but the inclusion of the whole diverse range of people with sensory disabilities such as auditory and visual impairment, and sometimes both, makes the task considerably more challenging. This work may also not be restricted to those people who normally use adult services such as older people, people with disabilities and those with mental health needs. People who use services because of some kind of sensory disability may include the following:

- people who are prelingually deaf (who were deaf before they could speak);
- people who are postlingually deaf (people who were speaking before they lost their hearing);
- people with a combination of mental health needs and sensory disabilities;

- people who have both hearing and visual impairments (known as deaf/blind);
- people with sensory disabilities who experience additional physical impairments or who also have learning disabilities;
- people with sensory disabilities who come from an ethnic minority;
- children with sensory disabilities who may or may not have parents who experience sensory disabilities themselves;
- people with sensory disabilities who have other problems such as homelessness, drug or alcohol misuse, placement in prison, etc.;
- older people who experience sensory loss as they age.

This list is not exhaustive, but gives an indication of the breadth of demand likely to face services. The response to the largest group, older people with measurable deafness as well as blindness, has at best been inadequate, at worst scandalous as many departments assume that this group and their needs will be met by general provision for older people, but this is rarely the case. The needs of those who are both deaf and blind have only been recently addressed by social services within the Social Care for Deaf/Blind Children and Adults LAC (2001) 8 under section 7 of the Local Authorities Social Services Act 1970. This is a statutory guidance outlining the rights of deaf/blind people and the duties placed on local authorities to provide appropriate services (Roberts *et al.* 2007).

Reflective exercise

The following are some questions to help you think through the role of social workers in relation to people with sensory disabilities, and to raise awareness about your own attitudes and understanding of the issues that arise when people experience sensory disabilities.

- What do you think of when you hear about people who are blind or D/deaf? Or both?
- What words and images come to mind when you think about people who have problems with their hearing, vision or speech?
- What are the specific issues that you think a social worker would have to think about in relation to working with people who have sensory disabilities?

Social workers who work with people with sensory disabilities are likely to have different roles in relation to those whose primary issue is visual impairment and those who have problems hearing. In the past, a typical job description of a social worker with D/deaf people had two tasks that consumed the greatest amount of time and resources – to act as an interpreter and to make recommendations for adaptations or aids. These were not social work tasks in other settings. Interpreting was and still is a major plank in the provision of services to D/deaf people and is given a high priority by D/deaf people themselves.

Blindness as a concept causes a great deal of fear and anxiety (De Leo *et al.* 1999) and can lead to psychological as well as practical difficulties for the individual concerned. There are several well-established programmes (often provided by the private or voluntary sector) that can help to promote independence and enhance people's ability to interact with other people, but people with visual impairments have identi-fied a number of issues that they feel have not been addressed from their particular perspective. Research has highlighted issues of independence for individuals and their families and the crucial value for people with visual impairments of the 'emancipatory and empowering paradigms' that inform the social model of disability. Duckett and Pratt (2001: 820) identified the key areas for research, as highlighted by people with visual impairments themselves, as:

- access to the environment;
- access to information (including socio-medical terms);
- attitudes, stigma and its impact on education/employment opportunities;
- civil rights (collective action and relationship to the disability movement, organizational and political issues, allocation of resources, etc.);
- support (social and financial).

Despite the real disadvantages of visual impairments, unless there are other prob-lems such as learning or other physical disabilities, people with visual impairments do not necessarily see themselves as part of a B/blind collective or culture in the same way as, for example, many people with hearing impairments do (Duckett and Pratt 2001).

Deafness is seen by most people as one of a group of disabilities that can create communication and relationship difficulties and presented as a physical problem that needs to be remedied, particularly within the medical model of disability. In recent years, people from the deaf community have rethought of themselves as Deaf (as a dis-tinct minority group) rather than deaf (as an impairment). As a result of this, the way that Deaf people are seen with regard to state services has largely changed. The social model of disability and recent legislation such as the Disability Discrimination Act 1996 and the Equality Act 2010 has framed a positive shift for social care professionals to see the needs of Deaf people as a cultural group with a distinct language, i.e. British Sign Language. It is now recognized that Deaf people have different needs to those of other client groups relating to their unique communication and cultural requirements (Ladd 2003).

Terminology of D/deaf

You may have noticed in this chapter that sometimes deaf is spelt with an upper case 'D' (Deaf) and at other times with a lower case 'd' (deaf) and that this does not follow the usual conventions of written English. The use of the upper case 'D' indicates those Deaf people who identify themselves as part of a cultural and linguistic minority group, the Deaf community, and who have a distinct and unique identity and language. The convention of the use of the upper case is one that has been increasingly adopted by Deaf people. It is similar to the way that an upper case 'J' would be appropriate when referring to a Jewish person, or an upper case 'B' for a Brazilian and also when there is a discourse about the Black community.

Therefore, the use of the upper case 'Deaf' refers to a group of deaf people who share a common language – British Sign Language (BSL) – and culture. Deaf people use BSL as a primary means of communication among themselves and hold a set of beliefs about themselves and their connection to the larger society. This is similar to other cultures, in the traditional sense of the term, that have historically been created and actively transmitted across generations.

However, this distinction is not entirely clear-cut as we need to consider deaf children from hearing families who encounter Deaf people and their culture outside the family arena. Therefore, the challenging question is at what point are they said to have adopted the conventions of the culture and become Deaf? One way of thinking about social work with people would be to apply various theoretical models of disability as they may be applied to sensory disabilities, particularly deafness and deaf/blindness. Adapting a model relating to disability in general (Swain and French 2008), these would include:

- the *spectrum model*, which refers to the range of visibility and audibility functions;
- the *moral model*, which refers to people being morally responsible for their own disability;
- the *expert model*, which is a traditional offshoot of the medical model response to disability issues that treats the doctor or social worker as the expert;
- the *tragedy model*, which people with disabilities are seen as victims of circumstance and deserving of pity; this model is often used in fundraising;
- the *social* or *social adapted model* of disability, which recognizes that society and the environment is often more limiting than the disability itself;
- the *empowering model*, which highlights the need for people with disabilities to set their own goals and decide what help and support they need to achieve these goals;
- finally there is the *market model* which focuses on minority rights and a consumerist model of disability and economic empowerment.

Legal imperatives and drivers for change

The provision of aids to daily living is an important service both in terms of the quality of life for the client and in terms of high demand for specialist equipment. Such aids have been acknowledged as important in a range of legislation, beginning with the National Assistance Act (NAA) 1948 through to the Chronically Sick and Disabled Persons Act (CSDPA) 1970 and the Disabled Persons Act (DPA) 1996. The Blind Person's Act in 1920 attempted to respond to the large numbers of disabled people returning from the First World War by establishing sheltered workplaces for people with a range of sensory disabilities and the National Assistance Act in 1948 empowered local authorities to register blind, deaf and physically disabled people who lived in their areas with a view to determining what services would be required (Harris and Roulstone 2011), but most legislation refers to people with disabilities in general.

Despite the impetus created by the legislation and policy drivers that have been promoting the process of independence and personalization, comments from Deaf people make the process of service provision sound more like a reflection of the Poor Law, with its attitude towards the 'deserving' and the 'undeserving', than a rights-based service as intended by the legislation. This may be partly due to the fact that the deaf element of services has only recently been looked at and may have retained some outmoded attitudes, but it is probably partly the response to disability in general which may have been reactive rather than proactive, and carried low status. This picture is complicated by the inclusion of all disabled groups as one entity, making sensible management decisions impossible as details about assessment criteria, budgets and workload are hidden. I think it is too early to assess whether improvements will be made through personalization, as it is in the embryonic stage when applied to sensory disabilities, but present indications are that there are considerable difficulties to be overcome in meeting the sensory needs of Deaf and deaf/blind people in a creative and flexible way.

Since the inception of social work, there have been debates about the nature of social work with Deaf people and others with sensory disabilities. Throughout the chapter there will be opportunities to think about some of these, concentrating on questions such as:

- Is it real social work and is it similar to other forms of social work?
- Is it a specialism and is it necessary to have specialist workers?
- Is there still specialist social work and is the specialist nature of practice with people with sensory disabilities lost or enhanced within mainstream care management?

Looking at the first question, we have already seen the definition of social work. A related conception from the Barclay Report, *Social Workers: Their Roles and Tasks* (DH 1982), identified two major components – counselling and social care planning. Definitions of social work have often been confused because of the many contexts in which it can be practised and the concentration on the individuality of service users rather on common groups or strands.

In addition to the two major components of social work as mentioned in the Barclay Report, there are other essential tasks to social work. These include assessments, advice giving, provision of practical services and acting as an intermediary or advocate. All of these feature in the day-to-day work of social workers with people with hearing and visual impairments. Due to lack of comparative studies, it is difficult to tell whether the emphasis and the time spent on individual tasks is different for social workers with people with sensory disabilities compared with workers in other sectors of social work and social care.

Communication is often viewed as important and is the key to undertaking effective social work, but such communication is not as simple as it seems. The areas of specialization in social work had always been defined as (a) setting, (b) method of work and (c) client groups. It has been suggested that the method of work has not been a major focus in the UK and that in relation to setting, the distinctive nature lies in the agency context. Work with Deaf people has mostly been described as specialist in relation to particular skills such as interpreting and understanding their needs and ways of perceiving the world. Specialist knowledge in one area allows expertise to build and when any of us are in difficulty we would like to consult with those who have the expertise that we do not possess ourselves. This may be problematic within flexible and mobile working when practising in isolation. Some people are of the belief that division into specialist client groups is an efficient way to deliver appropriate services and on these grounds, social work with Deaf and visually impaired people would seem to qualify as a specialist area. However, there are some concerns that recent merging with mainstream care management within self-directed support (SDS) would result in the reduction and eventual loss of specialism of social work with Deaf and deaf/blind people. The following case studies illustrate some of the perspectives discussed so far and highlight opportunities to critically evaluate the role and purpose of specialist social workers with people with sensory disabilities.

Case study

Gregor is a 45-year-old man with profound hearing loss, some visual impairment and mild learning disabilities. He spends most of his time at home and has limited speech and, his mother says, understanding. His mother, Daria, who is in her late seventies, has cared for Gregor on her own for the past 30 years or so as her husband left them when Gregor was a teenager, soon after the family migrated to England. Daria has never asked for help with Gregor before but is now finding it difficult to manage as she says that her son is becoming 'very naughty and defiant' and that as Daria is herself becoming less mobile and having problems with her sight, she is not sure whether she can look after Gregor any longer. She thinks Gregor might be better off in a 'hospital' where they'll be able to address his particular needs.

- What do you think are the main issues in this situation?
- Who is the main 'client' in this situation?
- What particular knowledge and skills would be helpful in trying to understand what's going on and to seek out possible ways to resolve this situation?

Looking at this case scenario, it is essential first to recognize that while Gregor's and his mother's lives are intrinsically intertwined, their needs and wishes may not be the same and yet both of them may be eligible for assessment and services within the NHS and Community Care Act definition. For a social worker working within care or case management services, theories around systems and relationships will need to be at the heart of any hypothesis that may be drawn up to understand the individual and joint requirements.

There may also be cultural issues informing Daria's attitudes towards her son, both in terms of the possible shame and stigma she may have experienced at having a disabled son but also in terms of her belief that it was her duty to care for Gregor alone and that the only alternative if she cannot manage is for him to go into hospital. It will take some sensitive interviewing skills to elicit Daria's attitudes and beliefs without being insensitive to the fact that these may be very different from what we might believe would be the options for a man in Gregor's position today. There is also likely to be some ambivalence about letting Gregor go, and a sense of loss as well as relief at giving up her 'child'. The situation regarding Gregor's father may be a further area that the social worker could explore if it seems relevant.

A social worker can apply theory, judgement and practice experiences that have been amassed over many years (Oko 2009) but in this case the prime difficulty was to find a way of speaking with Gregor himself rather than his mother speaking on his behalf. At this stage a specialist social worker with experience of working with people with hearing impairment was introduced into the situation. As a result, Gregor was able to express his frustration and anger at being kept as a 'child' for so long and finally given his voice. Far from being upset that his mother wanted him to leave, Gregor was excited at the possibility of his own accommodation and social life. The specialist worker was also able to introduce Gregor to specialist groups where he could relate to other people nearer his own age, and where he learned fairly quickly to communicate with them.

At the same time it was possible for the social worker working with older people to concentrate on Daria's own needs and to support her in separating from Gregor in a way that meant she was still able to maintain contact with him. This enabled the two to form a more adult-to-adult relationship which both could appreciate.

The discussions created by the separation of interpreting from social work have led some people (DH 1982) to suggest that social services should be provided by a social worker with an interpreter. There are difficulties in conducting interviews through a third party and Deaf people's strong preferences for workers with a knowledge and understanding of Deaf culture points to the need for specialist social workers with BSL skills. These specialists can also modify their communication methods to suit Deaf people by developing new approaches.

Scott Gibson (1991) traces the slow and sometimes painful process of the separation of the symbiotic relationship which developed between social work and interpreting. Initially social work with deaf people was invested in the early missioners who had a combined role of interpreting and providing for the needs of the deaf community. The state inherited this multiplicity of roles, which was made more complicated by the dual responsibilities of statutory social work to provide both care and control. This put social workers into an uncomfortable position as well as raising the need for interpreters to explain to D/deaf people the benefits of separating the two functions. Therefore, it may be incompatible for social workers with Deaf people to act as interpreters due to their being agents of the department with clear conflicts of interests. The clear divisive roles can actually uphold the rights of Deaf people and avoid either profession being placed in an invidious position. Moorhead, in his article 'Social work and interpreting' (cited in Gregory and Hartley 1991), suggests that the continued use of social workers and members of the family as interpreters prolongs bad practice, which denies Deaf people control over their own lives.

Case study

This case study looks at the situation of Sarah, a 22-year-old woman with both hearing and some visual difficulties. As you read through it, think about the questions below not just in terms of skills but in particular around the specific areas of knowledge that a social worker with experience of working with people from a specialist background can bring to the situation.

A request was received from the police for a specialist social worker to accompany Sarah as an 'appropriate adult' as they intended to arrest her and charge her with sending threatening and abusive text messages, as alleged by her previous partner, Roger, and his wife. Sarah is profoundly deaf and uses British Sign Language as her form of communication. She was very calm despite the stressful situation in which she was placed, and this appeared to convince the police that Sarah was used to the experience of being in police custody, although they had no evidence of this. However, they had identified the need to involve someone who could understand Sarah's communication needs and interpret between Sarah and themselves so they could be sure that she was clear about the process that was happening to her. During the interview process, Sarah denied sending any threatening or abusive text messages and she was not aware that any other members of her family were involved.

- What is the role of the 'appropriate adult' in this situation?
- What are the legal and ethical implications for the social worker working at the interface between welfare services and criminal justice systems?
- What are the key issues that could arise for Sarah if she had not had the support of a specialist worker who could understand her communication needs?

The role of the appropriate adult in this situation is to ensure that Sarah does not receive treatment that would be to her disadvantage as a result of her specific communication needs. While Sarah cannot and should not be given particular advantages because of her sensory impairments, the 'appropriate adult' would need to be sufficiently familiar with her specific needs to ensure that she is not treated in a manner that discriminates against her because of lack of expertise, or because of the assumptions of those unfamiliar with her situation.

This links with the concept of the multiple theories of vulnerability and disability (Swain and French 2008 ; Koubel and Bungay 2009). If there is evidence of a lack of understanding and capacity by Sarah, she meets the eligibility criteria for support and advocacy but not necessarily intervention by a social worker within the 'appropriate adult' role. Without such support in the police station, Sarah could have experienced abuse by being placed or left in a situation which may put her at risk through a failure to protect and challenge discrimination, or been seen as 'difficult' and not perceived as part of a minority linguistic cultural group with dual sensory communication needs.

Looking at the second question, the referral was made to assist a young vulnerable person with dual sensory needs as a profoundly Deaf British Sign Language (BSL) user with a sight impairment within the National Health Service and Community Care Act 1990 s6, Chronically Sick and Disabled Persons Act 1970 s2 and the National Assistance Act 1948 s29. In terms of the ethical framework of the social worker, the prime concern must be to influence the police to make them more aware of the needs of Deaf and Deaf/blind people and to realign in some way the imbalances of power due to disinformation that may be experienced by Sarah in this situation. Dominelli (2002) states that anti-discriminatory practice can be seen as reformist social work with a remit to challenge situations deemed to be unfair and unequal. The role of the social worker therefore involves a commitment to using their power within practice with service users to remove barriers and seek change.

At this point, within the role of appropriate adult, the social worker has to be mindful to be non-judgemental, to attempt a level of rationale and only consider the evidence and facts, and any social worker could carry out these functions appropriately according to the knowledge and values that have been discussed.

However, on closer examination of the texts that Sarah was alleged to have sent it would be apparent to a specialist social worker with expertise in this area that, because of the high literacy content and grammatical use of English within the text messages, Sarah could not possibly have done this task herself, nor was it likely that she could have asked someone else to do this on her behalf. The social worker would have to bring to the attention of the police and to the solicitor in the case the linguistic differences between BSL and English as well as cognition and language issues from a psychological perspective. Quigley and Paul (1984) examine both the quantitative and qualitative differences that exist between deaf and hearing people in terms of cognitive functioning and acquisition of language.

There are also some interesting theories that help us to think about the specific situation of an individual like Sarah with sensory disabilities becoming involved in the criminal justice system. Classical and entrenched theories suggest that crime is a result of rational thinking: weighing up the relative risks and benefits of committing a crime and acting accordingly. In the case of D/deaf people, and also those with learning disabilities, there are other instances of why offenders are less able to make rational thoughts, decisions and consequences of their actions. Therefore, it can be argued that there is a small population of criminal offenders whose behaviour cannot be explained by current theories (Twersky-Glasner 2006).

Twersky-Glasner makes the assertion that such criminological theories have been applied to 'hearing' offenders, but none have demonstrated much relevance when describing or explaining criminality within the Deaf community. This raises questions about the difference in the psychological, sociological and biological functioning of a D/deaf offender. Hirschi (1969, cited in Twersky-Glasner 2006) presents the 'social disorganization' theory to explain crime as a product of uneven development in society, with change and conflict affecting people's behaviour, which may have blocked linguistic, literacy, attachment, socialization and academic competences.

A social worker would therefore need to consider how Sarah's life experience and her family upbringing could have affected her in terms of possible lack of attachment and relationship opportunities due to linguistic differences, cultures and barriers. Ninety per cent of deaf children are born with hearing parents and siblings and are therefore more likely to experience communication barriers within family life and upbringing; this potentially could affect their opportunities to learn positive morals, values and mores at some of the informal, unconscious levels that operate within the family. If Sarah had attended a deaf boarding school, this could also have exacerbated the communication and attachment problems with her family as she would have seen them only during weekends and school breaks.

Twersky-Glasner recommends further development programmes and research to look at criminality in the Deaf community and to apply new theories in relation to Deaf offenders in order to make better comparisons and understanding of this linguistic and cultural minority group, particularly those with dual sensory needs.

Personalization in working with people with sensory disabilities

This shift in orientation of social work in general was accompanied by a critique and review of the role of social work with people with sensory disabilities. These professionals are now seen more as agents of integration and enablement to encourage service users to function without a protective and restrictive system of care and to become part of wider society. The DPA 1986 provides opportunities for all groups of disabled people to make comments on the types of services that local authorities offer and provide. Recent key transformational documents such as *Our Health, Our Care, Our Say* (DH 2006), *Putting People First* (ADASS 2007) and *Transforming Adult Social Care* LAC (DH 2009) promote recurring themes of choice and control, participation, empowerment, addressing inequality, partnership working and enablement within the new personalization agenda. The aim is to provide person-centred support planning to meet identified needs through the provision of personal budgets in a more creative, flexible and proactive way.

The personalization philosophy (Leadbetter 2004) seeks to enhance people's rights, freedom, choice and control over the way their needs are met. It emanates from two sometimes conflicting sources. The first seeks to emphasize personal responsibility for an individual's own personal welfare while at the same time looking for ways to reduce the size and scope of publicly financed collective provision and to think about the needs of all taxpayers as well as the creation of markets for goods and services. The other affirms the requirement for social responsibility for the promotion of personal welfare in developing a needs-led welfare service with greater flexibility in providing different ways of meeting needs as opposed to previous arrangements of a service-led framework based on public prescription. This looks at the needs of such people and the need to reinforce social structures for the benefit of individuals.

Both of these sources are evident and give rise to policies that highlight user involvement and consumer choice, an expansion of services, the monitoring of the quality of services, cost-effectiveness and a more effective targeting of resources.

The challenges that face social workers with adult service users with sensory disabilities is that their roles have changed to care management (see Chapter 2), which is having a major impact on practice in the separation of assessment and provision, representation and information giving. Due to the lack of current appropriate brokerage support for people with sensory and communicative difficulties in some authorities and the likelihood that some of these workers may be operating in small teams or on their own, this could adversely affect the rights and interests of clients. It may be problematic if one individual carries out all the assessment, enablement, coordination and brokerage processes as well as being the provider of services to meet the service user's needs.

Care managers with people with sensory disabilities have seen a recent rise in safeguarding and abuse cases in relation to situations which have involved the provision of personal assistants via allocations of Direct Payments. There is a complex involvement of family, professionals and other agencies as well as confusion over clear clarification of rights, risk and responsibilities for Deaf people. Tensions arise between the emphasis on user empowerment and rights and the increasing demand on professional and local authority accountability that some people with sensory disabilities may find difficult to grasp.

Case study

Brian is profoundly Deaf and acquired Ushers, which resulted in gradual complete blindness in his twenties. Ushers is a congenital disability that can affect some Deaf people in later life and leads to an increasing visual impairment (Sacks 1991). This had an effect on his ability to communicate and diminished his contacts with his family and with friends in the Deaf community. Brian received training to develop hands-on signing skills and with doing everyday tasks to achieve independence and self-worth. He was given specialist computer equipment from a sensory communications aid budget to enable him to continue his contacts with his family and friends and to gain access to information and services.

Following the development of personalization and allocation of personal budgets, Brian had a reassessment to identify his current needs. His predominant wish was to increase his social life and this was met by provision of a personal assistant skilled in hands-on signing communication who was also Deaf. Initially this appeared to be a step forward for Brian and it was considered very lucky that a hands-on signer had been available to take on this role. However, at a later stage, Brian disclosed concerns over his financial situation in the belief that his personal assistant was defrauding him. An investigation was conducted and it was discovered that the personal assistant abused his position of trust by encouraging Brian to spend his money on fishing equipment and on a boat which he, Brian, did not need or use but which actually benefited the personal assistant. It was noticed that this personal assistant had been quite controlling in Brian's life for some time and that one of the reasons Brian had been reluctant to complain had been his fear of losing this specialist sensory service.

- What are the social work policies and procedures that are relevant to this situation?
- What are the priorities for social work intervention in this situation?
- What do you think should need to happen next?

Subsequently, adult protection procedures were put in place and disciplinary action was taken to dismiss the personal assistant. Although it took some time, Brian was eventually able to find another personal assistant with the same level of hands-on signing skills to meet his communication needs. However, as the personal assistant was female and Deaf, this has caused considerable friction and tension between her and Brian's wife who believed that a relationship had developed between them beyond the client and professional roles.

It is interesting to note the change that has happened for Brian in terms of being provided with personal assistants and its impact on him in being financially abused and in being caught up in the middle as a result of tension between his wife and the female personal assistant. While recognizing that a personal budget and provision of a personal assistant would meet Brian's communication and social needs, this opportunity created unexpected and unfortunate events for him. The lesson for social work practitioners is to constantly aim to weigh up the balance between advantages and disadvantages.

Conclusion

In my opinion, current legislation and service provision within the personalization and self-directed support (SDS) agenda still fails to acknowledge a distinct group of people with sensory disabilities, as deafness is seen to be dealt with within the wider context of disability. This may change substantially in the foreseeable future.

In some cases, personal budgets are being considered to purchase sensory-specific equipment or to fund social inclusion opportunities such as access to a local gym to offset social isolation experiences. Difficulties have arisen in locating skilled communicators in BSL as personal assistants and specialist services.

Local authorities are attempting to address issues in relation to information for people with disabilities (Davis and Woodward 1981). They need to avoid disadvantage as a result of the restriction or withholding of information, which may constrain opportunities for full participation in the mainstream of social life as well as is isolating or excluding D/deaf and deaf blind people from the processes of production (Swain 2004). Local authorities are having to consider adapting their information about SDS in British Sign Language (BSL), and this can be achieved either by newly designed and accessible websites or face-to-face with a skilled signer.

Local authorities that employ specialist sensory disabilities teams view self-directed support as a positive step that gives Deaf BSL users more support to access mainstream services, and thus anticipate that new providers will be created and services can be commissioned on behalf of service users up to the limit of their indicative budget. The market will need to be stimulated and developed over time to support increased choice and control for this client group. However, there is a risk that the powers of social workers with people with sensory disabilities could potentially be reduced to the level of their generic care management colleagues and result in the loss of their specialism as there appears to be an increase in other mainstream professionals making their information and services more accessible. There will be a minority of people who will still require social work in the purest sense, but the question remains of how will this be provided within the care management role.

Innovative ways of using personal budgets for Deaf BSL users are being discussed, such as the potential to employ personal assistants with signing skills up to 16 hours per week without adverse effects on their benefits. Other creative solutions are being put forward, for example community support, life skills trainers and specialized computer programs for deaf/blind people.

Within the new concept of the government's 'Big Society' proposals to change the relationship between the state and broader civil society and its Localism Bill, as well as public sector reform, it will be interesting to see how this will work for Deaf people and others with sensory disabilities. There is no guarantee that these policies will in themselves lead to the changes that will enable people with sensory disabilities to engage with and be fully accepted by mainstream society. Some people may still seek support from social workers and from specialist organizations which have a clear role in looking at issues relating to marginalized people and communities who may find it difficult to be active citizens, particularly in situations where communication is a substantial barrier. This may lead to the risk of failing to engage with equalities issues due to current and proposed policies that might exacerbate established inequalities for Deaf and deaf/blind people. Therefore, practitioners will need to continue to promote the needs, aspirations, responsibilities, rights, representation and participation of people with sensory disabilities, helping them to achieve what they want for themselves and reach their goals.

References and further reading

ADASS (Association of Directors of Adult Social Services) (2007) *Putting People First: A Shared Vision and Commitment to the Transformation of Adult Social Care*. London: ADASS.

Banks, S. (2006) *Ethics and Values in Social Work*. Basingstoke: Palgrave Macmillan.

Davis, K. and Woodward, J. (1981) Dial UK: Development of the National Association of Disablement Information and Advice Services, in A. Brechin, P. Liddiard and J. Swain (eds) *Handicap in a Social World*. London: Hodder and Stoughton in association with the Open University, pp. 328–34.

De Leo, D., Hickey, P. A., Meneghel, G. and Cantor, C. H. (1999) Blindness, fear of sight loss, and suicide, *Psychosomatics*, 40 (4): 339–44.

DH (Department of Health) (1982) *Social Workers: Their Roles and Tasks*. Report of a Working Party Set Up by the National Institute of Social Work at the Request of the Secretary of State for Social Services (Chairman: Peter Barclay). London: Bedford Square Press.

DH (2006) *Our Health, Our Care, Our Say: A New Direction for Community Services*. London: Department of Health.

DH (2009) *Transforming Adult Social Care*. London: DH.

Dominelli, L. (2002) *Anti-oppressive Social Work*. Basingstoke: Palgrave Macmillan.

Duckett, P. and Pratt, R. (2001) The researched opinions on research: visually impaired people and visual impairment research, *Disability and Society*, 16 (6): 815–35.

Gregory, S. and Hartley, G. (1991) *Constructing Deafness*. Buckingham: Open University Press.

Harris, J. and Roulstone, A. (2011) *Disability, Policy and Professional Practice*. London: Sage Publications.

Koubel, G. and Bungay, H. (eds) (2009) *The Challenge of Person Centred Care*. Basingstoke: Palgrave Macmillan.

Ladd, P. (2003) *Understanding Deaf Culture: In Search of Deafhood*. Clevedon: Multilingual Matters.

Leadbetter, C. (2004) *Personalisation Through Participation: A New Script for Public Services*, available at: http://www.demos.co.uk/publications/personalisation [Accessed 1 January 2013].

Oko, J. (2009) *Understanding and Using Theory in Social Work*. Exeter: Learning Matters.

Quigley, S. and Paul, P. (1984) *Language and Deafness*. London: Coombe Hill.

Roberts, D., Scharf, T., Bernard, M. and Crone, P. (2007) *Identification of Deafblind Dual Sensory Impairment in Older People*. London: Social Care Institute for Excellence.

Sacks (1991) *Seeing Voices: A Journey Into the World of the Deaf*. London: Pan Books.

Scott Gibson, L. (1991) Sign language interpreting: an emerging profession, in S. Gregory and G. Hartley, *Constructing Deafness*. London: Continuum.

Swain, J. (2004) *Disabling Barriers, Enabling Environments*. London: Sage Publications.

Swain, J. and French, S. (2008) *Disability on Equal Terms*. London: Sage Publications.

Thompson, N. (2006) *Anti Discriminatory Practice*, 4th edn. Basingstoke: Palgrave Macmillan.

Twersky-Glasner, A. (2006) Cultural dissonance of deaf criminal offenders: antecedents of linguistic and cultural dissonance, *Journal of Knowledge and Best Practice in Juvenile Justice and Psychology*, 1 (1): 11–24.

9 Social work with older adults: working with older people and people living with dementia

Mark Wiles

Thinking about how I came to social work with older adults has taken me on a very personal journey. I have had a wonderful relationship with all of my grandparents. As I grew up they cared for me between them, told me stories about their lives and the world, taught me how to make things, how to paint with oil colours, how to grow flowers and vegetables, and gave me a powerful sense of my family and cultural identity. I have seen each of them in turn retire from work and witnessed their image and role within the family and society changing as they aged. They in turn became increasingly frail and I saw them at various times in hospital and needing care from myself and others.

My love and respect for them, allied with my lifelong interest and formal studies in social science and social work, led me at various times in my life and studies to reflect upon the human life course and how older people are seen in our society. As a result, I learned of the need to see beyond the cultural stereotypes of older people. It may sound rather sentimental, but feels very straightforward that this experience, allied with my education and the values my grandparents helped shape, led me to social work with older people.

Introduction

As you are reading this, you will be getting older. Despite worries about the process of ageing, becoming an older adult is something most of us will be hoping to experience. Thanks to achievements in health and social care, it is also one that we are much more likely to experience than our ancestors. However, it is also a time in life about which there can be a great deal of anxiety and uncertainty. This anxiety is likely to have increased for some as a result of the debates currently taking place in the United Kingdom (UK) about the future of health and social care services for older adults, and how these may be structured and funded. As a key element of such services, social workers, particularly those working for local authorities, are also facing a period of significant change and anxiety that is questioning not only the role of social work within services for older adults, but whether it has a role at all in the future of social and health care services for adults (Galpin 2009a).

This chapter will explore some of the key issues facing social work with older people today. It will begin by briefly examining the social and political context in which social work with older people is currently being developed and practised. It will then explore some of the different ways in which ageing can be viewed and understood and how an awareness of age discrimination can help those working with older people better understand and challenge the often negative attitudes that exist about ageing and older people. Providing along the way a brief overview of key policy, legislation and guidance in this area, the chapter will include a number of case studies to illustrate how one might best approach social work with older people today.

Learning outcomes

By the end of the chapter, readers should have increased their awareness and understanding of:

- ageism and its relation to social work and care/case management practice, particularly in relation to working with older people, their networks and carers;
- the key demographic changes that are informing policy and practice developments in social work and social care with older people, as well as those for people living with dementia;
- the nature of social work with older people and the development of expertise in working with people with dementia, their carers and networks in the inter-professional context;
- the meaning of person-centred perspectives and their significance in terms of using this approach to improve practice with older people in general and people with dementia in particular.

Current debates about the future of social work with older people have to a large extent been brought about by the significant demographic changes we are currently experiencing and are projected to undergo in the United Kingdom (UK) over the next 30 years. Consequently, it seems the best place for us to begin is by looking briefly at some of these demographic changes that are driving debate and social policy for social work and social care with older adults at this time.

UK demographic changes

The single most significant factor in such debates is the growing proportion of older people now living within the population of the UK. In the past 40 years there has been a 24 per cent increase in the number of people aged 50 and over, and by the year 2033 it is predicted that 23 per cent of the population of the UK will be aged 65 or over (ONS 2009).

Not only is there projected to be an increase in the number of us living into older age, but as the population ages it is the numbers in the oldest age groups that will increase the fastest. In 2008, there were 1.3 million people in the UK aged 85 and over. This number is projected to increase to 1.8 million by 2018 and to 3.3 million by 2033, doubling the number of people aged 85 in the UK population in the next 25 years. This trend continues into the older age groups, with the number of centenarians projected to rise from 11,000 in 2008 to 80,000 in 2033, a more than sevenfold increase (ONS 2009).

Significantly, at the same time as this increase in the number of older people is taking place, the number of people of working age in the UK is set to reduce significantly. In 2008, there were 3.23 people of working age for every person of pensionable age. By 2033, allowing for the change in women's state pension age, this ratio is projected to decline to 2.78. Among other responses, this has prompted government and policy-makers to seek to increase the age at which people will in future be entitled to receive a state pension and for those working in the public sector to be able to claim their employment pension (ONS 2009).

Reflective exercise

- What effect do you think these demographic changes will have upon the way in which services for vulnerable older people will need to be organized and funded in future?
- What are the key considerations governments and services (and society) will need to address?

It is important to consider that as people get older research demonstrates that they are more likely to experience an increase in their health and social care needs, and in significantly greater numbers as people pass the age of 80 (Johns 2011). This means that as people age they are correspondingly more likely to need support from others to assist them in managing their daily living and in meeting their health and social care needs. Furthermore, as it is the numbers in the oldest age groups in our society that are set to increase the fastest, the increase in the group of people potentially needing such support is set to increase significantly in the next 20 to 30 years, with fewer people of working age to support them physically and through the payment of pay-related taxation.

The nature of those health and social care needs will, of course, vary greatly depending upon the individual, their personal circumstances and many other variables, including lifestyle and social class, but overall such increases as those outlined above will have a significant bearing upon the ways in which services for older adults will need to be organized and funded in the future and, therefore, upon the way in which social workers will have to approach their work with older people.

One can see from the statistics and population projections above that there are some common factors associated with growing older in UK society. People are on average going to be living longer lives, but are correspondingly more likely to experience an increase in their health and social care needs as they age.

This raises an important point for consideration here about social work with older people: why is it that older adults are seen as a specific service user group at all? For example, in many areas prior to turning 65 years of age, those adults needing health or social care service are most likely to be seen by a service defined by its specialism in dealing with the primary presenting need/s of the individual at the time, such as services specializing in mental health, physical disability or learning disability. Those aged 65 and over may be referred to generic adult teams, dealing with a cross-section of younger adults who do not meet the criteria for one of these specialist services. This can lead to a service that is charged with meeting an increasingly broad range of complex needs associated with an increasingly large number of health conditions and social circumstances, including physical disability, long-term health conditions, brain injury, drug and/or alcohol dependence, degenerative conditions, end of life support, functional and organic mental health conditions and learning disability, with the only common factor often being that the service user is over a certain age.

Reflective exercise

- Do you think that we can talk of older adults as a distinctive service user group for social work?
- Consider some of the arguments for and against such an approach and write these down to reflect upon as you continue to read the chapter.

One influential factor, whatever your views and answers to this question, is our own and society's attitude to ageing and growing older. Consequently, any serious attempt to understand and answer this question needs to consider the human life course and the differing approaches to both defining and approaching the subject. An understanding of this theoretical framework can be seen as essential to social work with groups or individuals of any age.

The ageing process

There are numerous theoretical models of the human life course, most of which belong to one or more of three main academic disciplines: sociology, psychology and biology. While offering distinctive perspectives on the human life course they are often used in combination.

- biology, or more specifically, physiology, is concerned with the biological changes that take place throughout the life course;
- sociology is concerned with the social context for the individual and how this is affected by group attitudes and responses to ageing; and finally,
- cognitive/psychological perspectives are concerned with individuals in that society, their ideas, thoughts, feelings and behaviours and how these might change through the course of a person's life.

Thinking about this in relation to the subject of older adults, we can briefly explore some common themes that arise for older people that are informed by the perspectives offered by biology, sociology and psychology. As we look at these alternative models, think about which most nearly approaches your own views and attitudes towards older people.

Physiological/biological changes

With regards to ageing, this approach is concerned with the physiological changes associated with older adulthood. It is clear to us all that we change physically as we age. Such changes are associated with changes within the cells of which we are all made and in older adults these changes become increasingly degenerative. Research shows us (Johns 2011) that the physiological changes associated with ageing make us more susceptible to certain health conditions, ranging from increasing sight impairment and/or hearing impairment, osteoporosis, respiratory difficulties and to dementia and other long-term progressive conditions, such as Parkinson's disease and multiple sclerosis.

It is this view of ageing that appears most influential in British society. The majority of older people using social care services will be doing so as a result of difficulties associated with physical ageing, such as health conditions that they have developed as they have reached older age. As a result, old age is sometimes seen as a medical condition in itself, the prognosis for which is general decline and a growing dependence upon others (Thompson 2005). As there is currently no medical treatment to reverse or stop the physical effects of ageing, this model often leads to a negative view of growing old. This view may well play its part in the well-reported poor treatment and neglect of older people in the health and social care system. This is often referred to as the medical model and leads to the medicalization of ageing (Thompson 2005).

Social/cultural changes

While the physiological changes associated with ageing may be, for the time being at least, unavoidable, societal responses to them are not. Attitudes towards ageing and older people have changed through history and between different societies and cultures, demonstrating that our own attitudes and beliefs about ageing and older people are not universal or timeless, but specific to our place and time. Sociological perspectives start from this understanding and help us to explore and understand why these differences might exist. By so doing, sociological approaches help us to think more openly about the cultural influences and responses to ageing. It is by using a sociological perspective that one can begin to see how thinking in the UK is strongly influenced by the medical model of ageing discussed above.

Cognitive/psychological changes

The psychological/cognitive perspective is concerned with how older adults see themselves and the impact that biological changes and social responses have upon individuals. It is also concerned with the impact of age-related health conditions, such as dementia, and their impact on the cognitive functioning of people living with such conditions. Research also suggests that there is a high level of undiagnosed depression experienced among older adults (Commission for Healthcare Audit and Inspection 2009; Royal College of Psychiatrists 2009), which may be a significant issue for social workers and other practitioners working with older people.

Research and our own experience of living in the UK at this time demonstrate to us that as people age they are more likely to encounter the impact of dementia, whether as relatives, carers or through developing it themselves (Alzheimer's Society 2007). Alongside this, and it would appear influenced by such age-related associations between ageing and dementia, many assumptions are made about the cognitive functioning and mental capacity of people as they age. Most of these are negative associations that assume severe cognitive decline is an unavoidable part of ageing, rather than a symptom of a long-term health condition such as dementia.

One can see here how these differing perspectives may overlap and inform each other. Sociologically influenced studies have highlighted the high levels of social isolation experienced by older people in UK society and its negative impact upon the health and well-being of older people (Hawton *et al.* 2011). Medical studies have highlighted how the risks of certain long-term health conditions increase with age. Add this to the view of ageing as a medical condition itself and the psychological impact of high rates of depression among older people living in the UK is made more understandable.

Reflective exercise

- As you think about your own ageing using these three perspectives, what feelings does this conjure up for you?
- What do you think will change for you as you get older?

It is likely that, either consciously or unconsciously, while you were reflecting upon these models of ageing, you will have drawn upon the representations given in the media and society more generally through jokes and anecdotes about older people. When you next see or hear a representation of an older person in the media or in a joke it is useful to consider what image of ageing and older people they reflect and help to create or reinforce. If we want to understand where a group stands in society, one could argue that there are few better ways of getting this information than by watching television or reading newspapers. One can immediately think of comedic characters such as Godfrey in *Dad's Army*, a bumbling, gentle man who often needs the lavatory and raises his hand like a child to ask for permission, or Victor Meldrew, the bitter old man, with 'one foot in the grave', angry at the world. While such representations of ageing offer less than positive images of older people, and are still fairly rare, the representation of older women in any guise is far more difficult to find, with many female actors publicly criticizing the lack of roles for older women. Cohen (2002) provides an example of research that examines the representation of older women in the media and uses her findings to argue for more positive programming to challenge the negative images she found.

As we have briefly explored, it is rare in our modern culture, which places such a high value on youth, beauty, change and economic productivity, to see positive representations of ageing and older age. News reports concerning older people often focus on the health and care services and how badly older people are treated when using them. Television programmes, when they do portray older people, tend to do so using commonly held stereotypes that reduce older people to passive and burdensome people who are good sources for jokes and mockery or victims of abuse.

Such negative views of growing older can only increase our own anxiety at the thought of growing old ourselves. Our society places, quite literally in terms of resources for care and support, less value on older people. This appears to be based upon a view that we somehow become less complicated and our needs less complex as we age. The effect this has on older people living in our society is first to characterize or 'stereotype' them in a certain way, which then informs and justifies certain standard responses and attitudes towards them. As argued by Barber *et al.* (2009), we all use such stereotype-based thinking in our daily lives and practice as social workers, but we need to have an awareness of their use and their potential to prevent us seeing and treating people as individuals. If the characterization of older people is overwhelmingly one of dependency, illness, foolishness and burden then the attitudes and responses are more likely to lead to discrimination against older adults, with such views providing the justification. This being the case, it is important to understand the collective force that such views, or 'ageism', can have in discriminating against and disempowering older people.

Ageism

Ageism is the idea that it is acceptable to discriminate on the grounds of a person's age. This can exist for any age group, but we are here concerned with the particular form of ageism associated with older people. That is not to say that older people are only subjected to this form of discrimination, as that would itself offer a discriminatory view of older people, and ignore the other forms of discrimination and oppression that exist in our society, including sexism, racism and homophobia, but ageism is central to our subject and an exploration of this in more detail should not only help us to understand this form of discrimination better, but also encourage a deeper exploration of our own attitudes and prejudices in relation to older adults. It is hoped that having gained such an understanding you will be better equipped to practise in an anti-discriminatory way when working with older adults.

Reflective exercise
• What words, jokes, stereotypes and images come to your mind when you think about older people?   • Where do you think these attitudes towards older people come from?   • Is this how you think about yourself getting older?

Thompson (2005) provides a comprehensive introduction to this topic and offers a model for how one might better understand and challenge ageism. Thompson states that key to helping us to understand age-related discrimination is the concept of ideology. Put simply, an ideology is a set of ideas and beliefs that are formed into a way of seeing the world and how it works. These ideologies then inform how groups define themselves and think about others.

Thompson (2005) describes how the discrimination that derives from such ideologies operates at three different yet interrelated levels of society. At the personal level this may lead to negative comments, exploitation or even physical assaults upon older people based upon the negative ideologies that exist. When you hear the term 'old' being used in everyday language, is it used mostly in a positive or negative context? Such discrimination on this personal level is what the older adult, with whom social workers may be working, will experience most obviously. One can see here how such an approach might help us to make links with the ways of viewing ageing that were outlined earlier in this chapter, and so better understand the ideology that associates older age with an inevitable loss of cognitive functioning and memory and leads to terms like 'silly old fool'.

The cultural level would include how old age is talked about, portrayed and represented through the media, in jokes and comedy and social norms and behaviour. These offer subtle, yet extremely powerful ways to oppress others. The stereotypes that are common in society about older adults are often influenced and powerfully realized and reinforced at the cultural level. Think of the representations of older people that you have seen in the media as discussed above. Do you think they provide a positive view of older people?

The structural level refers to the level at which discrimination is institutionalized by organizations, societies, policy and law. An example of this, very close to those working in social work, is the discrimination experienced by older people in terms of the resources allocated to them to meet their social care and mental health needs (Forder 2008; Royal College of Psychiatry 2009). Research by Forder (2008) concluded that support provided by local authorities for older adults was markedly lower on average than that provided for younger people with similar needs. It discovered that if these imbalances were to be 'levelled up', it would take on average a 25 per cent increase in the level of support provided to older adults. The research found similar evidence of discrimination in access to social work support, with younger adults having greater access than their older counterparts.

The discrimination that stems from ageism appears in many different forms, some very clear to see and others more subtle and difficult to detect without an awareness of age-related discrimination and its effects. To help identify these, Thompson (2005) provides some specific examples of how age-related discrimination manifests itself. These include the following:

- Infantilization – treating the older person as if they are a child. Examples are the use of patronizing terms like 'darling' or 'sweetie', and behaviour such as patronizing nods, tones of voice and exaggerated smiles from those engaging with an older person. This is based upon the idea that older people are so foolish and unable to understand what's being discussed, they merely need to be humoured and treated like children.

- Marginalization – this refers to the impact of discrimination in excluding older people from decision-making and mainstream activities. An example common for older people is the reliance in society upon residential forms of care for older adults as this very often creates a life apart from mainstream society and activities. It can also be argued that the current moves towards personal budgets and self-directed support appear to have ignored the voice of older service users, who in research (Glendinning *et al.* 2008) have expressed lower psychological well-being than other groups when using personal budgets.
- Medicalization – this has already been touched upon earlier in the chapter when we looked at the biological/physiological view of ageing. It is the biological view that leads to the medicalization of ageing and the linking of symptoms, otherwise associated with particular health conditions, as rather symptoms of old age, a primary example being memory loss.

It is important to note, however, that such discrimination may not always be conscious on the part of the person doing it. He or she may love and care about the person to whom they are directing such behaviour, but the effects on the older person remain discriminatory. At its worst, as we will explore later when looking at age-related discrimination, such thinking and discrimination can lead to older adults losing their right to have a say in, let alone in determining, the nature of their own care or where they should live.

Armed with a greater self-awareness of age-related stereotypes and discrimination, practitioners are better placed to consider the ways in which such attitudes can be challenged. To do so effectively, practitioners in social work and social care must develop models of thinking and acting in practice that take this self-awareness and apply it to avoid falling victim to such stereotypical thinking and so focus attention better on the specific individual needs of the individual with whom they are working. One such example is that offered by person-centred approaches to social and health care work.

Person-centred approaches to work with older people

Elliot and Koubel (2009) provide a brief history of person-centred perspectives in social and health care work, which highlights the various strands that have contributed through history to the current thinking that informs the person-centred approaches we see today. These can all be characterized as humanistic in their outlook, placing value on human life and the quality of life lived. Consequently, person-centred approaches in social and health care work seek to challenge attempts to stereotype and dehumanize older people, recognizing the uniqueness of each individual service user and placing them at the centre of the assessment and support planning process. Such approaches are closely aligned with anti-oppressive practice (Thompson 2006) aimed at supporting individuals to challenge discriminatory views and behaviours that seek to undermine and prevent them from achieving their desired outcomes and potential.

There is not one model of person-centred practice, but rather a closely related number of models stemming from a common value base, but providing differing structures to help direct practice. While not wishing here to reinforce stereotypes of older people by focusing on work with people living with dementia, it is now increasing likely, due to the demographic changes taking place in our society, that if you choose to work with older adults you will find yourself working with many people living with or affected by dementia. As the condition causes the gradual loss of memory and general cognitive decline, both central to personality and self-determination, person-centred approaches in this area are critical in maintaining the focus on the individual. For this reason, the chapter will now look at person-centred approaches that can be used when working with people living with dementia.

The principles of person-centred approaches to dementia care are well defined by guidance issued by the National Institute for Health and Clinical Excellence (2006):

- the human value of people with dementia, regardless of age or cognitive impairment, and those who care for them;
- the individuality of people with dementia, with their unique personality and life experiences among the influences on their response to the dementia;
- the importance of the perspective of the person with dementia;
- the importance of relationships and interactions with others to the person with dementia, and their potential for promoting well-being.

A key figure in promoting person-centred work for people living with dementia is Tom Kitwood (1997), and his model, although concerned with improving the treatment and care of those living with dementia, also offers a more general value base and approach that arguably could be applied when working with people living with any long-term health condition and/or disability. Kitwood was a psychologist who through personal circumstances came to question what he saw as the medicalization and dehumanization of people living with dementia. In his work *Dementia Reconsidered*: *The Person Comes First* (1997), Kitwood proposes a psycho-social model of care which challenges fundamentally the focus of assessment, care planning and approach for those living with the condition. Central to this approach is Kitwood's notion of 'personhood', which he describes as 'a standing or status that is bestowed upon one human being, by others, in the context of relationship and social being. It implies recognition, respect and trust' (Kitwood 1997: 8).

Using Kitwood's approach, the practitioner seeks to enhance the opportunities for supporting the 'personhood' of the individual, and of removing factors which Kitwood termed 'malignant social psychology' (MSP), which reflect the general discrimination faced by older people generally, and more specifically, by those living with dementia. One can see here how the approach is related to the discussions about discrimination explored earlier in the chapter when looking at ageism. For Kitwood the behaviours stemming from such discrimination include mockery, intimidation, outpacing, infantilization, labelling, treachery and ignoring. The cumulative effect of such MSP upon a person's sense of well-being is to undermine the personhood of that individual, leading to their alienation and disempowerment. Using this model, behaviour is no longer seen as symptomatic of the person's health condition, but rather as forms of communication which need to be understood in order to understand the individual better and so plan the support they need in a person-centred way.

Kitwood proposes the use of what he terms the 'enriched model of dementia' that, if applied, promotes a holistic and person-centred approach to the individual. This model suggests five key areas for consideration:

- neurological impairment: understanding the neurological symptoms for the individual;
- health and physical fitness: the examination and promotion of physical well-being;
- biography (life history): understanding of the individual's life and experiences;
- personality: an understanding of the individual's strengths and vulnerabilities ;
- social psychology: the social and psychological environment in which the individual finds himself or herself.

Kitwood's approach to person-centred care is firmly placed within the context of human relationships. This has influenced current thinking, which often now talks of the importance of 'relationship-centred care' (National Institute for Health and Clinical Excellence 2006) for those living with dementia.

The model not only provides a theoretical and philosophical model that places the person at the centre of the process but also a clear purpose for assessment and practice, which is aimed at gaining a thorough understanding of the person and reducing his or her exposure to and experience of MSP. Opportunities are then sought to enhance the individual's sense of well-being and 'personhood' through what Kitwood termed 'Positive Person Work'. In short this means being fully present and psychologically available to the individual with whom one is working.

As one can see, there is a close relationship between age-related stereotypes and discrimination (Thompson 2005, 2006) and what Kitwood termed 'malignant social psychology', with the negative stereotypes that exist for older people leading to them being marginalized, alienated and disempowered. Such potentially damaging implications mean that practitioners working with older adults need a sound understanding of age-related discrimination, its negative impact upon the lives of older people and the legislation available to help challenge such behaviour and promote self-determination and autonomy in a person-centred way.

Key policy and legislation

We have already seen in this chapter how important it is to have an understanding of the demographic, social and cultural context in which social work with older people takes place. It is equally important that social workers have an effective understanding of the political, legal and policy framework that exists for them and the older adults with whom they are working. This is important not only because it directs and guides social work practice with older people, but also because it reflects and influences the social, political and cultural ideologies and attitudes towards older people in our society.

Strongly influenced by the atrocities committed by the Nazi Party in Germany in the Second World War, thinkers and politicians sought ways to try and ensure that such a gross dehumanization of people based upon negative stereotypes and ideologies could never happen again. The political moves following the Second World War gave rise to the United Nations and in 1948 to the Universal Declaration of Human Rights (UDHR) that was adopted by the 56 members of the United Nations and gave rise to the European Convention of Human Rights 1950, later adopted in British Law through the introduction of the Human Rights Act 1998. The Articles within the Human Rights Act protect the rights of the individual and seek to promote, barring harm to others, the right to self-determination. The Human Rights Act can be seen as a legal embodiment of the values of person-centred approaches with its focus on the worth of individuals and their inalienable right to self-determination. Consequently, some now argue that human rights-based practice within social work offers a distinctive approach in its own right (Galpin 2009b).

The National Service Framework for Older People (2001) was introduced with the express aim of challenging and removing age-related discrimination from health and social care services. It remains important for those wishing to challenge ageism and promote person-centred care for older adults.

At the time of writing, social work with adults is undergoing a significant period of change, often referred to as the 'transformation' or 'modernization' agenda (DH 2005, 2006, 2007b, 2008). This has seen the introduction of practices and procedures within local authority social services departments aimed at promoting and encouraging the increased 'personalization' of services for those eligible for local authority assessment and support. This is supported by the provision of 'personal budgets', regular payments paid to people by the local authority to allow them to organize and plan their own support and care in the way they choose to meet their needs. Originating from a Demos report, *Personalisation Through Participation: A New Script for Public Services* (Leadbeater 2004), personalization was introduced by the government in the form of 'self-directed support' as defined in *Putting People First: A Shared Vision and Commitment to the Transformation of Adult Social Care* (DH 2007b). It is based upon the premise that people needing and using local authority services find better and cheaper solutions to their needs when they are given greater choice and control through the allocation of personal budgets which they can use to organize and plan their own support. The coalition government has continued with the personalization agenda. It has also recently introduced the Health and Social Care Act 2012, which seeks to bring health and social care services closer together in terms of both commissioning services and frontline service provision. It is too early at the time of writing to say with any certainty what this will mean for social workers working within the statutory adult social care system.

Personalization is seen by some to reflect the growing individualization seen more broadly in UK society and by some as a manifestation of the growing marketization and commodification of social care (Galpin 2009b). While such an approach can be argued to encourage creativity and self-determination, or greater choice and control, in those with the ability and desire to take control of their own support, some argue that for those who are most vulnerable, and who may lack the mental capacity to make informed decisions about and manage their own budgets and support, there are considerable risks associated with such an approach (Burrow 2009).

Research by Glendinning *et al.* (2008) found that older people using personal budgets and their carers reported lower psychological well-being than their younger counterparts. This may be due to the fact that many older adults come into contact with social services under very different circumstances to those of younger people, who are more likely to be living with a lifelong physical or mental disability. The older adult who becomes unwell in later life is more likely to have come to services following a lifetime of having made decisions and of having taken responsibility for their and their family's needs (Galpin 2009a, 2009b). It may be, therefore, that as older adults are more likely to be arriving at services in ill health and with the associated crises and sense of loss and powerlessness that so often accompanies such events, they are not best placed to take advantage of the potential choice and control offered by self-directed support and to manage and plan their own care. It may be that they require a more traditional response than 'personalization' on the surface appears to offer, and may prefer an option that seeks to reduce the stress such added responsibility of managing budgets and directing care may cause at a time of crises and ill health. The fact that older people appear to have gone largely unheard through this process of 'transformation' may itself be further evidence of their continued marginalization.

Reflective exercise

- What do you think about the role of personalization in the support of older people?
- If you imagine yourself becoming unwell with a long-term illness, what kind of service would you want from a social worker or social care services?
- Do you think there is a distinction to be made between older people and younger people when offering care services, and why?
- Or do you think it is the image of older adults as dependent and powerless that encourages such thinking?
- Alternatively, consider whether you think this could be further evidence of the marginalization of older people in society and that their voice is being ignored in debates about the future of social and health care services?

Older people and the Mental Capacity Act 2005

Mental capacity is a concept introduced and legally defined by the Mental Capacity Act 2005 (MCA). This legislation is now central to social work with adults and its presumption of capacity informs and influences all areas of social work with adults, young and old. For this reason, it is important here to look briefly at the philosophy and key principles of the MCA. A working knowledge of the MCA and its associated code of practice (DH 2007a) is now central to good social work practice and readers are encouraged to use this as an introduction to go on and read on the subject in more detail themselves. The MCA Code of Practice (DH 2007a) offers a very good, practical guide for those needing to refer to and use the MCA.

The MCA states that adults (aged 16 or over) have full legal capacity to make decisions for themselves (the right to autonomy), unless it can be shown that due to a mental disorder or impairment they lack the capacity to make a decision for themselves at the time that the decision needs to be made (DH 2007a). The Mental Capacity Act and its associated Code of Practice provide the legal structure and practice guidance for how one must approach the assessment of a person's mental capacity and any associated best interest decision stemming from this. It sets out clear principles that help promote the right of people with the mental capacity to do so to make their own decisions. Equally, it provides important safeguards to help ensure that where a decision does need to be made on behalf of another person it is done so in their best interests.

A study commissioned in 2007 by the Alzheimer's Society, entitled *Dementia UK* ((Alzheimer's Society 2007), estimated that there were then 683,597 people with dementia in the UK. It went on to forecast that the number of people with dementia is set to increase to 940,000 by 2021, and 1,735,087 by 2051 – a massive 154 per cent increase over the next 45 years. This statistic alone demonstrates the need for social workers working with older adults to have a sound working knowledge of the Mental Capacity Act. There are a number of different types of dementia that may be of medical interest but for the social worker/case manager working with someone with dementia, the issues around professional judgement and decision-making and a strong commitment to person-centred values are most significant, for dementia by its very nature gradually reduces the ability of the person living with the condition to retain the information necessary to weigh up and make informed decisions themselves.

Case study

Mrs Stone is an 85-year-old woman who has a diagnosis of vascular dementia. This has greatly reduced her short-term memory and leads to her becoming very agitated and anxious about the medication she is prescribed when being prompted by others to take it. Thinking that people are trying to poison her, Mrs Stone becomes very distressed and angry and very often refuses all of her medication. As a result, Mrs Stone's GP was contacted by a social worker aware of the problem to ask if she might consider using the MCA to complete a capacity test to assess Mrs Stone's ability to decide whether or not she should take her medication. The GP responded by saying that there was no need for a test of Mrs Stone's mental capacity, as she had been diagnosed with dementia and had lacked capacity for many years, but that she would review her medication.

- What do you think this response says about the GP's attitude towards Mrs Stone?
- Do you think it respects the assumption of capacity and autonomy enshrined in the MCA? The MCA clearly states that an assessment of capacity must relate to a particular decision and be recorded when addressing complex decisions.
- Do you think there is any discrimination evident here in such an attitude towards Mrs Stone and her ability (inability) to make her own decisions about whether or not she should take her medicines? How else might it have been dealt with?

The GP could have assessed Mrs Stone's mental capacity to make such a decision and, had she concluded that Mrs Stone lacked the mental capacity to do so, could then make a best interest decision to either remove certain medications from her prescription, change them or disguise them in food or drinks. The key here is that the assessment takes place, for if it were found that Mrs Stone had the mental capacity to make such a decision, she has a right, however unwise others may view her decision, to refuse to take the medicines prescribed to her. This brief scenario provides an example of how the medicalization of Mrs Stone led to her being the victim of what Tom Kitwood termed malignant social psychology. She was defined by her health condition, which led to her being marginalized and ignored.

For older adults, the role of mental capacity assessor and best interest decision-maker is one that very often falls to the social worker/case manager within the local authority adult services team. Decisions often need to be made about the level and type of care and support that is required by service users who have *a mental disorder that may be impacting upon their ability to make such decisions for themselves* (DH 2005). This can become a contentious and challenging area in which to work. The values of personalization are compromised by the need for the local authority through the social worker to take a more paternal role and make decisions in the best interests of service users.

Some of the most contentious decisions that social workers with adults will have to be involved in are where consideration needs to be given to the possibility of a person moving from his or her home to accommodation that can provide higher levels of support, such as a residential home. Such situations call upon all of the knowledge, skill and values of the social worker involved and therefore provide a good example on which to base the next case study. To provide a contrast, the following case study will look at the use of personalization, self-directed support and personal budgets in enabling a man leaving hospital to plan his own support and care.

Case study

Mr Arnott is 78 years old. He has peripheral vascular disease which has resulted in him having both legs amputated below the knee. He lives alone. The amputations mean that he now has to think about the support he will need before returning home when discharged from hospital. Mr Arnott has a neighbour who has helped him in the past and during meetings about his future support needs she has said that she would be willing to assist him in a formal way.

An assessment completed by the hospital social worker identified Mr Arnott's eligibility for support from the local authority (DH 2002), particularly in the areas of his personal care needs and management of his home environment. Having discussed the option of a direct payment, Mr Arnott expressed a preference for his neighbour, whom he had known for some time and trusted, to provide the bulk of his care needs. This was something that his neighbour was willing to do and support was provided to help Mr Arnott and his neighbour/carer arrange for her to take on the role of his personal assistant. The budget allocated by the local authority to Mr Arnott included funds for training for his personal assistant and for contingency plans for when his personal assistant was taking leave or unwell.

The role of the social worker in this situation had been in the assessment of Mr Arnott's needs (DH 1990) and eligibility (DH 2002) and in then advising him of the options available for the provision of the support he needed. Important here was the expert advice and support provided to both Mr Arnott and his personal assistant in setting up the systems and safeguards required for them both in entering into such a relationship. The social worker also called and chaired a multi-agency meeting at the hospital prior to his discharge to ensure that the services he required were provided. In addition an occupational therapy visit was completed prior to discharge in order to ensure that any equipment and adaptations needed by Mr Arnott were provided before he went home.

Case study

Mrs Markham is 85 years old. She has short-term memory loss and lives alone in a remote rural location. She has no family, and has relied upon an informal network of community support for many years. However, neighbours and friends are now finding that they are no longer able to meet Mrs Markham's increasing care and support needs, and are finding her resistance to help and behaviour increasingly concerning. They have called the local authority and asked for an assessment, stating that they think she now needs to be moved to a residential home.

Mrs Markham is assessed (under section 47 of the National Health Service and Community Care Act 1990) and is found to have marked short-term memory loss with little or no insight into her condition or the impact it is having upon her ability to live independently. The social worker contacts the local GP and community mental health team for older people and discovers that Mrs Markham has a diagnosis of vascular dementia from some years earlier. This provides evidence of 'a disorder of the mind' that can prompt the need to consider Mrs Markham's mental capacity (DH 2005) to make decisions about her care and accommodation needs and how these should best be met.

A Mental Capacity Act assessment is completed and finds that Mrs Markham is unable to retain the information necessary for her to make an informed decision about her care and accommodation needs. Aware of the local community's interest and support of Mrs Markham, the social worker arranges a 'Best Interest' meeting to which Mrs Markham's key informal carers and friends are invited, along with the community mental health team and GP. On hearing the opinions and gaining the evidence from those in attendance, it is decided, using the principle of least intrusive/restrictive intervention as required by the Mental Capacity Act guidance, that the social worker acting as best interest decision maker and the mental health professional should create a support plan and package of care services for Mrs Markham that can attempt to support her to remain in her own home. The plan is to be reviewed in three months.

It is also found that Mrs Markham has considerable financial resources that friends have been accessing to buy her food and pay essential bills. However, this has all been arranged informally. Consequently, the social worker also assessed Mrs Markham's mental capacity with regard to the decisions needed to manage her finances. Finding that she lacked this, the social worker makes a best interest decision that a solicitor needs to be employed to make an application to the Court of Protection to become Mrs Markham's Deputy and manage her finances in her best interest.

Reflective exercise

Consider the two case study examples provided above and think how the approaches required by the social worker in each differs.

*   Are the values, skills and knowledge required by the social worker the same for both Mrs Markham and Mr Arnott?
*   If not, what do you think are the differences here?

Reflections on the case studies

Although Mrs Markham could not make these decisions, the values of personalization are consistent with the action taken here. Using the principles of person-centred care and the model of dementia care proposed by Kitwood, Mrs Markham was supported to remain living in her own home and, by so doing, maintain her close and very positive association with her home environment and the relationships she has with those living around her.

If you wanted to support Mrs Markham to remain in her own home, how could she self-direct her care when she lacks insight and denies the need for care and support? The practice that is required for Mrs Markham needs to be more assertive and directive than that needed for Mr Arnott, as we cannot rely upon Mrs Markham to self-direct her care safely and appropriately. Somebody else is required to make judgements, using values of empowerment, but also using relevant legislation to balance this with the need to consider her mental capacity (DH 2005, 2007a) and need for collaborative working in planning the support and care she will need to remain in her own home.

Mrs Markham is not going to be able to manage a Direct Payment – services have to be provided, but the principles applied in so doing must be based upon person-centred approaches, here using Kitwood's enriched model of dementia to guide the assessment and support planning for her. By so doing, her personality and life story, both reinforcing her close and positive association with her community and environment, are used to inform her support plan.

Mr Arnott's situation differed in that he has the mental capacity to make decisions about his support needs. Advice, brokerage and help in facilitating his support needs were the primary roles for those assisting him. Person-centred values here are interpreted in a way that needs to defer to Mr Arnott, but also with a responsibility to ensure that he is well-informed about his options and is supported where necessary to make the choices and plans needed to direct his future support.

Person-centred practice relies upon the practitioner being aware of the role that social workers and social care professionals play in the care system. These roles, as we have seen, may differ depending upon the intervention required. Claiming to be 'experts' on service users' needs and situations has led to many service users, particularly within the disabilities movement, seeing social work as a major obstacle to people taking control of their care and lives. However, as we have touched on above, there remain a large number of service users, many older adults, for whom this approach may not be appropriate. The important thing for social workers is that the real and diverse needs of each person are considered in each situation without making blanket decisions about older people as a group whose needs are similar just because they are all of a certain age.

Conclusion

Demographic changes in our society mean that the demand for and pressure upon services for vulnerable older people are increasing. An understanding of the ageing process and the different ways of defining and understanding it can help increase our awareness of the experience of individual older people and better understand some of the attitudes towards older people more generally in our society.

There are many negative stereotypes of older people in our society that influence age-related discrimination or ageism. Such ideologies of old age and older people undermine the individual by contributing to behaviour in others that denies the complexity of older people and treats them as if they are unable to make decisions for themselves. Person-centred approaches to working with older people, whatever their circumstances, seek to break such stereotypes and encourage those working with older people to see them as individuals and to challenge behaviours that prevent older people from achieving their desired outcomes and potential.

Person-centred values have informed the transformation of social and health care currently under way in most parts of the UK. This seeks to replace the direct provision of services with individual budgets that individuals can then use to personalize the care and support they need. However, research and anecdotal evidence from practitioners suggest that this can be problematic for some older people, whose experiences and situation when arriving at a need for health and social care services are very different from that of many other service user groups.

The number of older people experiencing health conditions that may lead to dementia and cognitive impairment is set to increase. The Mental Capacity Act 2005 has become a central element of practice for social workers and can help support individual service users to make decisions for themselves. This legislation and guidance can also assist practitioners to make decisions in the service user's best interests where mental capacity is lacking. This process requires a more assertive and traditional approach than a single self-directed model of social and health care can promote.

Older people are not a homogeneous group, but while it cannot be assumed that all older people do not want, or could not manage, to self-direct their support and care using an individual budget, many clearly can and do. However, it does also seem clear that many older people come to services as a result of illness, later in their lives, which leads to crises and dramatic changes for them following a lifetime of making choices and having responsibility. Thinking that services can only be personalized and person-centred through the provision of individual budgets may marginalize older people and be evidence itself of age-related discrimination.

Social work has a clear role to play both in supporting people who are able to self-direct their own care and support and in using legislation allied with person-centred approaches to intervene more assertively to promote well-being and protect vulnerable older people who may lack the capacity to make important decisions about their lives and care needs.

References and further reading

Alzheimer's Society (2007) *Dementia UK: A Report into the Prevalence and Cost of Dementia,* prepared by the Personal Social Services Research Unit (PSSRU) at the London School of Economics and the Institute of Psychiatry at King's College London. London: LSE/King's College London.

Barber, C., McLaughlin, N. and Wood, J. (2009) Self-awareness: the key to person-centred care?, in G. Koubel and H. Bungay (eds) *The Challenge of Person-centred Care: An Interprofessional Perspective.* Basingstoke: Palgrave Macmillan.

Burrow, E. (2009) Direct payments and older people: developing a framework for practice, in D. Galpin and N. Bates (eds) *Social Work Practice with Adults.* Exeter: Learning Matters.

Cohen, H. (2002) Developing media literacy skills to challenge television's portrayal of older women, *Educational Gerontology,* 28 (7): 599–620.

Commission for Healthcare Audit and Inspection (2009) *Equality in Later Life: A National Study of Older People's Mental Health Services.* London: Commission for Healthcare Audit and Inspection.

DH (Department of Health) (1990) The National Health Service and Community Care Act. London: HMSO.

DH (2001) *National Service Framework for Older People*. London: Department of Health.

DH (2002) *Fair Access to Care Services: Guidance on Eligibility for Adult Social Care*. London: HMSO.

DH (2005) Mental Capacity Act. London: HMSO.

DH (2006) *Our Health, Our Care, Our Say: A New Direction for Community Services*. London: HMSO.

DH (2007a) Mental Capacity Act Code of Practice. London: HMSO.

DH (2007b) *Putting People First: A Shared Vision and Commitment to the Transformation of Adult Social Care*. London: HMSO.

DH (2008) *Transforming Social Care*. London: HMSO.

Elliot, P. and Koubel, G. (2009) What is person-centred care?, in G. Koubel and H. Bungay (eds) *The Challenge of Person-centred Care: An Interprofessional Perspective*. Basingstoke: Palgrave Macmillan.

Forder, J. (2008) *The Costs of Addressing Age Discrimination in Social Care*. Canterbury: Personal Social Services Research Unit, University of Kent at Canterbury.

Galpin, D. (2009a) Transformation: a future for social work practice?, in D. Galpin and N. Bates (eds) *Social Work Practice with Adults*. Exeter: Learning Matters.

Galpin, D. (2009b) Personalisation: from consumer rights to human rights, in D. Galpin and N. Bates (eds) *Social Work Practice with Adults*. Exeter: Learning Matters.

Galpin, D. and Bates, N. (2009) *Social Work Practice with Adults*. Exeter: Learning Matters.

Garner, A. (2011) *Personalisation in Social Work*. Exeter: Learning Matters.

Glendinning, C., Challis, D., Fernandez, J. *et al.* (2008) *Evaluation of the Individual Budgets Pilot Programme: Final Report*. York: Social Policy Research Unit, University of York.

Hawton, A., Green, C., Dickens, A. P. *et al.* (2011) The impact of social isolation on the health status and health-related quality of life of older people, *Quality of Life Research*, 20 (1): 57–67.

Johns, R. (2011) *Social Work, Social Policy and Older People*. Exeter: Learning Matters.

Kitwood, T. (1997) *Dementia Reconsidered: The Person Comes First*. Buckingham: Open University Press.

Leadbeater, C. (2004) *Personalisation Through Participation: A New Script for Public Services*. London: Demos.

Leadbeater, C., Bartlett, B. and Gallagher, N. (2008) *Making it Personal*. London: Demos.

NICE (National Institute for Health and Clinical Excellence) (2006) *Dementia: Supporting People with Dementia and their Carers in Health and Social Care*, available at: http://publications.nice.org.uk/dementia-cg42/person-centred-care [Accessed 20 July 2012].

ONS (Office for National Statistics) (2009) National population projections, 2008-based projections, available at: http://www.ons.gov.uk/ons/rel/npp/national-population-projections/2008-based-projections/index.html [Accessed 22 July 2012].

Parrott, L. (2006) *Values and Ethics in Social Work*. Exeter: Learning Matters.

Royal College of Psychiatrists (2009) *The Need to Tackle Age Discrimination in Mental Health: A Compendium Of Evidence*. London: Royal College of Psychiatrists.

Thompson, N. (2006) *Anti-discriminatory Practice*, 4th edn. Basingstoke: Palgrave Macmillan.

Thompson, S. (2005) *Age Discrimination*. Lyme Regis: Russell House Publishing.

10 Working as a social worker in community mental health services

Charley Melville-Wiseman

I am a Senior Practitioner Social Worker in a community mental health team which is predominantly health-led. I also work as an approved mental health professional, a role which can cover all age groups. I have an MSc in Mental Health Social Work with Children and Adults, which included research into the relational needs of women with mental health difficulties, an ongoing area of particular interest to me. I have worked in a variety of settings, including in countries and communities where there is no welfare state and where people are marginalized due to colour, poverty or disability. This made a deep impression on me and empowering people to regain control and confidence in their own lives is a driving force in my everyday social work. Promoting the social model comes with challenges in my workplace but identifying how a person's social environment and relationships impact on and shape their lives and mental well-being is essential to recovery. Although as a team we work to the recovery approach, as a social worker it is important to me to use strengths-led models of working to enhance equality and achieve this goal.

'If you take an interest in what people are good at then you will find the best in them' (Bramble 2004: 4).

Introduction

Social workers have a complex and challenging role working within mental health services in the UK. The provision of services is an ever-changing and dynamic process, constantly affected and moulded by both central government imperatives and local direction and distribution of resources. Changes have been made in more recent years, with mental health needs being incorporated into overall health needs. However, the stigma and social exclusion that is associated with having mental health needs will be slow to change as it has not been a priority with policy-makers in the past and is deeply entrenched. More recently policy initiatives (DH 2008a) have begun to promote and advocate more choice and control for all, including significant changes in mental health services. The primary focus is with a preventative approach to mental illness and a more proactive approach to holistic wellness, where all aspects of life that affect a person's health and well-being are incorporated. Fawcett *et al.* (2012: 111) describe the 'well-being agenda' as a model that:

... relates both to the ways in which a government can promote the well-being of its citizens as well as to a citizen's responsibility, to themselves and to their community and society, to promote their own well-being.

Aspects of mental health needs that are rooted in social inequality and power imbalances are likely to be exacerbated by the current economic climate, public sector cutbacks and subsequent economic pressures on the private and voluntary sector. In addition the improved regulation of mental health professionals and mental health services has presented new challenges and new safeguards but with greater central control. In contrast, the personalization agenda and self-directed support gives greater responsibility as well as autonomy to individuals to manage their own support and budgets.

Learning outcomes

This chapter aims to explore some of the key dimensions affecting mental health care from a social work practitioner perspective. At the end of the chapter readers will be able to:

- identify the role of a social worker within multi-disciplinary mental health teams and consider the challenges of interprofessional working;
- identify key areas of recent policy developments affecting people with mental health needs and the challenges these present for mental health social workers;
- explore the role of social workers in promoting the understanding of social dimensions such as the importance of relational needs and risks;
- understand the need to adopt integrated theoretical models relating to mental health needs;
- use the case vignettes to explore and reflect on the dilemmas of complex decision-making for social work practitioners with people who are vulnerable through mental health needs.

A brief introduction to mental health social work

Social work in a multidisciplinary mental health service can provide excellent outcomes. Multidisciplinary teams can produce an effective service if they are well organized with clear role identification and expectations, with staff feeling valued and fulfilled as they work in a variety of settings and with a diverse client group. Social workers have worked with individuals, couples, parents, families, extended families and children, building relationships as a vital characteristic of promoting and enabling change. Interventions and support are carried out with people within their own social contexts, for example their families, neighbourhoods or communities. When different professions work side by side it provides the opportunity for a balanced and holistic service to be provided where professionals can consult each other's expertise and offer alternative explanations for mental health needs.

In recent times there has been a greater awareness of the effect the media has on how people view mental health needs. The Broadcasting and Creative Industries Disability Network produced a report dealing with how people with mental health difficulties are portrayed in the media. Examples in soap operas such as EastEnders, Hollyoaks and Emmerdale were identified, in which a character was suffering from a mental illness. They then demonstrated how these characters are often portrayed in a negative, discriminatory and often dangerous way both on the television and in the press (www.shift.org.uk). Derogatory comments that refer to people with mental health needs continue to be commonplace on the television and in general conversation. However, if social workers are to work according to the code of practice (COP) of their regulatory body (General Social Care Council), it is not enough to ensure this does not discriminate against others. The COP provides guidance that social workers must challenge discrimination and promote equal opportunities and so have a responsibility to raise and confront negative and derogatory language or actions.

The exercise below will help you begin to think about the way in which individuals who have mental health needs are often marginalized in society. You are encouraged to think about and reflect on how you may use derogatory or negative language during this exercise while trying to consider ways in which you as an individual are an important part of challenging stigma and discrimination.

Reflective exercise

Write down as many words or expressions you can think of from the media, adverts and phrases used in schools, at work and on the street to describe people with mental health problems.

- What alternative language could be used that would be respectful to a person with mental health needs, thereby reducing stigma?
- What would you do if you heard someone use such derogatory words? Would it make a difference if they were:
  - A member of your family?
  - A stranger?
  - A work colleague?

The term mental health is thought about in different ways and with different meanings. How do we think about our own mental health, or do we think about our own mental health? Do we only think about these issues when we, or someone we know, is suffering from a mental illness or mental distress? It is surprising how many people use the term 'mental health' when they actually mean mental ill health, but the term appears to have become a catch-all for mental health problems or difficulties. It is not unusual to hear someone describe a person as having 'mental health' when in fact they mean 'mental health problems'.

The role of social workers in community mental health teams

Social workers in community mental health teams have complex and diverse roles. These services are provided within legislative and policy frameworks, parts of which vary from area to area. The Care Programme Approach (CPA) (DH 2008b) was introduced in 1991 as the government's framework for providing mental health services. It has been updated and revised and continues to be used by secondary and tertiary (more specialist services, for example Personality Disorder Units or Eating Disorder Units). However, further changes include Care Pathways, which are used for more straightforward cases with less complex needs. These frameworks have been introduced to ensure that adults with mental health needs requiring at least a secondary service receive appropriate treatment and support. Interventions provided must be evidence-based using the National Institute for Health and Clinical Excellence (NICE) guidelines, which provide information for both professionals and service users about the condition and what interventions and treatments can be provided. Listening to and involving service users is vital as they are the experts of their condition (Watkins 2007) and can provide professionals with key knowledge that would otherwise be ignored. Although some people will require the help of secondary mental health services, many are cared for by their GP with additional support if needed from a voluntary organization such as a resource centre or employment support agency. Mental health services for people in psychiatric hospitals or in prisons with complex mental health needs are also provided under the CPA as it is a framework for providing for complex mental health needs in the UK, ensuring that no matter where individuals might be, their needs should be assessed and care provided in an equitable and commonly understood way.

Within mental health services there are a variety of teams that have specialist roles. These include Access Teams or First Response Teams (names may vary for teams from area to area). This team would usually be the first point of contact with secondary services where a person would be assessed according to specific criteria and, if it was needed, a care plan drawn up with treatment or intervention offered. Although the recovery approach focuses on empowerment, negotiation and choice, Tew (2011: 116) takes this further by promoting action planning rather than care planning, stating, 'It places the person with mental distress at the heart of decision making so that they can retain as much control over their life as they are able.' Should longer-term treatment be needed they would be transferred to another longer-term team such as a Recovery Team where more agencies may be involved or the needs are more complex. A Care Coordinator would then manage the treatment provided and ensure that regular reviews take place, at the very least annually, to identify changes needed and progress and outcomes made. Teams have been further developed specifically to meet government policies on, for example, early treatment and preventative measures (Mind 2012). An example of this is the Early Intervention in Psychosis Team. There is some evidence that early intervention can prevent psychosis and can also help to mitigate some of the social consequences of mental ill health such as unemployment, misuse of drugs or alcohol, or getting into difficulties with the criminal justice system.

Evidence and research indicates that these specialist teams have positive outcomes and other examples include a dedicated team available to provide treatment for people in crisis. Treatment may, if appropriate, be offered within a person's home with the aim of trying to keep people within their own social setting and avoid admission to an in-patient psychiatric ward. Keeping a person within their own personal social system is often less traumatic than admission to hospital although at times this is not appropriate when there is risk to others, for example. Another example is a team that provides services to people who are often more difficult to engage in services, which may be due to 'negative past experiences of mental health services, mistrust of mental health professionals or feeling that services have little to offer' (Mind 2012). This team is often referred to as an Assertive Outreach Team. By accessing a variety of teams and approaches, service users are more likely to receive a service that is suited to them.

The following case vignette will provide an example of a person who may be treated and supported in a community mental health team.

Case study

Sadie is a 22-year-old woman who returned to her home town from university a year ago, having completed her degree. She has been applying for jobs but has been feeling increasingly anxious about interviews and has been expressing little hope for her future. Her mother was supportive while Sadie was at university but her father has always believed that women should be in the home caring for their family so cannot see the point of higher education. He repeatedly reminds her of this and over the past few weeks she has been feeling very panicky about leaving the house and has been avoiding going out. Sadie thinks her friends are giving up on her as she makes excuses for not wanting to go out and this makes her feel more alone and isolated. Sadie's GP has treated her for depression for the last eight months but has been increasingly worried about some of her thoughts and hopeless feelings. He has referred her to the community mental health team (CMHT).

Although many people with depression and anxiety can be successfully supported by their GP, Sadie was experiencing thoughts of harming herself which increased risk. Her needs had become more complex as she was also becoming very isolated and having suicidal thoughts. With intervention, possibly in the form of access to psychological services for talking therapy, attending a group for anxiety management, the support of a vocational adviser and medication prescribed by a psychiatrist, Sadie may only need short-term help from the CMHT. She may be seen by a social worker who could help her to address her home situation and explore the possibility of moving into her own home. The social worker would also assist in challenging the discrimination from her father, which could support the work of her talking therapy. A mental health social worker can offer far more than the term 'care coordinator' would seem to suggest. Many will have had training and developed skills in psychosocial interventions and may have developed specialist interest areas such as working with people with personality disorders, family solution-based therapy or working with survivors of abuse.

Although Sadie would be allocated to a staff member as her care coordinator, she may require longer-term intervention and treatment. In that situation Sadie may be allocated to a care coordinator in a longer-term team such as a Recovery Team, rather than having her needs met in an initial assessment team (DH 2008b). The care coordinator would manage her care and liaise with other professionals or services and ensure she had regular reviews and that her needs were being met. In all cases a risk assessment is taken and a care plan produced. The social worker will need to:

- identify the range of treatment and support that might be available to Sadie;
- explore whether there are any resources outside a community mental health team that might assist Sadie;
- consider the strengths Sadie has developed that she may be able to use in her care plan to help herself;
- think critically about Sadie's situation to understand how gender has played a part in her mental health needs; and
- consider what strengths and resources Sadie could draw on to overcome some of these particular issues.

Social workers are able to provide a significant amount of social and therapeutic support and have many skills and the knowledge to work with complex difficulties. They are also skilled in identifying and addressing social inequalities that affect many people's mental health. In Sadie's case she was receiving mixed messages from her parents about what she should expect in her life, with her mother supporting her desire to further her education while her father was treating her in a discriminatory manner. This had left Sadie confused and lacking confidence and self-esteem. By identifying inequality and oppression it becomes possible to support Sadie to believe in herself. This would then enable her to take control of her life. In this way Sadie would own her care and recovery plan and be able to use it to make necessary changes in her life. Had her depression and anxiety been treated solely as a medical problem the underlying causes may have remained unaddressed.

The social work role begins with social justice and this is a significant contribution that social workers bring to multidisciplinary teams. Day-to-day mental health social work includes helping people to secure changes and resources in their lives that they have a right to. Social inclusion is not a new concept as may be mistakenly thought, and social workers have expertise in addressing this already. Working alongside vulnerable people in order to assist and enable them to bring about their own changes is a key role.

A further important role for social workers is that of safeguarding. The government document *No Secrets* (DH 2000) was provided to give guidance to agencies involved in safeguarding. Local authorities have the lead on safeguarding but other agencies and professionals are expected to be involved (Pritchard 2008: 14). Although all professionals are expected to report any concerns regarding safeguarding issues it could be argued that, as social workers have historically had more direct contact with families, additional social contacts or relatives, they may be more likely to identify safeguarding concerns, whether those of vulnerable adults or children. Safeguarding may also include the need to detain a person under the Mental Health Act 2007 in order to ensure, for example, that a mother or child is safe, or to report that a child is not safe with its parents who are suffering from mental health problems and are unable to care well enough for that child. A further example may be identifying financial abuse by a carer or domestic violence.

This second case vignette is used to explore these issues further. While reading, consider as many explanations as you can for Laura's mental health needs.

Case study

Laura and Jack have lived in a rented flat for four years but Jack has left, recently saying he wants their relationship to end. Laura has suffered from mental health needs for the last year and finds it difficult to manage on her own. She does not feel able to go out of the flat alone. She has been prescribed medication by her psychiatrist, which she takes. As the allocated worker it is your responsibility to assess her needs and any potential risk. You will need to identify and assist her to develop a plan for her recovery. You remember, however, that women have been saying for some time 'that too much attention is focused on their problems and not enough importance placed on the positive aspects of their lives'. You also remember the importance of thinking about women's 'strengths, abilities and potential for recovery' (DH 2002). This could then make up a significant part of the recovery plan.

Laura feels she has been dependent on others all her life. Although this new situation presents an opportunity for change, she is understandably nervous. Laura has described how she would like to meet other people and have the chance to find a job. However, she also wants to talk with Jack to see if they could try again with their relationship. She described how he used to do the shopping and pay bills and other things she found very difficult due to her mental health needs. This raises a dilemma for you as you know Laura wants to move on in her recovery but Jack also has anger issues and has subjected Laura to episodes of violence.

- In what ways could you help Laura to identify a plan for recovery and then take ownership of it?
- What potential support networks and opportunities would enhance Laura's mental health?
- Taking into account the effect of domestic violence on a woman, how may her relationship with Jack affect her mental health and what are the resulting complexities and dilemmas?
- Alternatives to the medical model are the possible explanations for Laura's mental health needs. Reading the document *Women's Mental Health Strategy: Into the Mainstream* (DH 2002) may be helpful in understanding what support women may need or be asking for.
- Consider the social inequalities that are impacting on Laura's mental well-being.

By using a social model of intervention and addressing the inequalities present in Laura's life, necessary changes can be achieved. If issues such as domestic violence remain unaddressed the cycle of pain, fear, distress, feelings of low self-worth and anxiety continue. Had Laura not been asked about any abuse she had experienced in her life, this could have hindered or prevented her recovery. Women want to be asked about such issues (DH 2002). Social workers are trained to visit people in their own homes and use interview techniques and skills of observation, non-verbal communication and sensitive questioning to identify alternative explanations for mental health needs.

Rowett (cited in Gilbert *et al.* 2010: 11) encapsulates the above situation:

> Mental distress may be caused or compounded by poor living conditions and difficult personal circumstances. The role played by social workers can therefore be crucial to recovery from mental illness precisely because their focus is personal, giving practical support and help to resolve problems of living that might otherwise appear insurmountable to someone who is also trying to deal with his/her mental distress. This type of support not only contributes to recovery from a period of illness, it can also help reduce the likelihood of a further episode recurring.

There is substantial evidence of the impact of domestic and sexual violence in childhood and adulthood on the mental well-being of women (Read *et al.* 2003). However, this impact can be varied in its nature and extent. For example, women who have experienced violence have an increased chance of acquiring a diagnosis of mental illness; one survivor stated: 'I don't call it mental health; I call it "symptoms of abuse", because to me that's what it is' (Humphreys and Thiara 2003: 213).

Changes in policy and legislation and the challenges this presents for social workers

The mental health system has been at the forefront of the development of multidisciplinary working. In the 1960s psychiatric nurses began working with their patients in the community as well as in hospital settings and this was followed in 1975 by the White Paper *Better Services for the Mentally Ill* (DHSS 1975). This set out a plan for an integrated local approach to mental health care involving the health service, local authorities and the voluntary sector. The Care Programme Approach was introduced in 1991 and in 1995 *Building Bridges* added to this (DH 1995). The CPA was reviewed again in 2008 with *Refocusing the Care Programme Approach* (DH 2008b).

The government is now pushing new approaches to commissioning of services, with the personalization agenda and payments by results being key changes. Although social services have historically charged for services, mental health services have been excluded until now. Government policy is directing an increase in the number of people who manage their own budget and support and, again, mental health services have been slower in the uptake and promotion of this than other client groups. The personalization agenda is the government's 'cornerstone of public services' and will provide choice and control for individuals needing care and support (DH 2008c).

The document *No Health Without Mental Health* (DH 2011) also presents the broader picture. It highlights the length to which good mental health affects the ability to live a fulfilling life. Good mental health enables us to engage in social relationships and employment, access community resources including housing and health services, and live a fulfilling life. It is vital to living a full life and yet when mental ill health or distress is experienced it is often associated with stigma and shame. For women this can be a further disadvantage as they are already more likely to have had life experiences which are associated with mental health difficulties and are also likely to have less access to mental health-enhancing resources. These may include being able to meet with friends, using the gym or joining clubs or groups.

The government's ten-year strategy for mental health, *New Horizons* (DH 2009), focuses on causes of mental ill health and the need to intervene at an early stage. It identifies the impact of social inequalities and the social context of mental distress. There is abundant evidence that environment affects well-being and good housing, employment, access to leisure and health services enhance mental health. There is also evidence of the detrimental effect of poor living conditions, social isolation, poverty and unemployment on a person's mental well-being, but these are all areas with which social workers are very familiar (Repper and Perkins 2006). Tew (2011: 36) comments that:

> Both wider social environment and particular life events, such as trauma or abuse, can play a major part in influencing whether we come to experience mental distress at some point in our lives. It is not only our current situation that makes a difference; it is also the cumulative impact of our previous social experience.

This cumulative impact indicates the necessity of addressing social aspects and mental health needs of children early, as given in the document *No Health Without Mental Health* (DH 2011). A preventative approach to mental well-being is the key to this strategy. A further issue relates to the mental health needs of older people. A myth that is often an obstacle is that depression is normal in ageing, when this is not the case. Historically the mental health needs of older people have not been prioritized and have been overlooked due to physical symptoms that are similar, for example lack of sleep due to arthritis (Age Concern 2007). In older age a person has had much longer to accumulate previous social experiences which may affect mental health needs. Addressing these needs of older people is also included in this strategy.

These new strategies and approaches are in fact not new for social workers because core values and competencies have been generating anti-discriminatory practice and the empowerment and independence of individuals to make changes in their lives with some assistance rather than being 'done to'. Social workers are, however, reported to have mixed feelings about these recent changes. BASW (2010) point out that this is a vital and perfect time to raise the profile and importance of social work. Social workers often feel that their knowledge and skills are marginalized and not valued but there is an individual responsibility now to change this. Bamford (2011: 1) states that 'If the traditional ambivalence of social work towards medicine and the medical model can be overcome social workers can improve the overall effectiveness of team functioning'.

Social workers have a key role to play in the recovery approach to mental health needs, which is now the focus of treatment and intervention in mental health services. As social work core values include empowerment and enablement this approach is one that social workers already know a considerable amount about and to which they are making a significant contribution in multidisciplinary teams. Social work is already underpinned by advocating social inclusion, a key factor in recovery, and in order for this to be realized oppression and social inequality must be challenged and rectified. A challenge facing social workers is to recognize their existing skills and knowledge and to pair this up with current terminology, thereby increasing their confidence and belief in themselves to play a valued part within the multidisciplinary team. This will also address the negative experiences social workers have described as they themselves are clear about their role and know the importance of it. Translating evidence and theory into practice is another challenge. It is well known that power imbalance and lack of control over one's own life can result in mental distress. When a person eventually comes into contact with secondary mental health services there is an opportunity to explore changes that could be made in that person's circumstances. However, there is always a danger that the result is explored in order to aid recovery without looking into the cause. In these circumstances recovery is not possible as this is like sticking on a plaster, which will possibly help in the short term but will not prevent a return of the mental distress.

Changes in legislation have had a further impact on the social work role and threaten to dilute social work intervention, with its intrinsic values and skills in assessments under the Mental Health Act 1983, updated in 2007. Under the 1983 Mental Health Act, approved social workers (ASWs) were introduced to enable information on the significant social aspects of a person's mental health needs to be identified and explored. Comprehensive training had been developed for social workers to qualify as ASWs and to carry out this statutory role. During assessments under the Mental Health Act 1983, where individuals may be detained in a psychiatric hospital against their will the ASW would identify the impact of social aspects of their lives and also their strengths and the resources available to them which may be utilized as an alternative to admission. These would then be presented as part of a detailed discussion and consultation in order to make decisions as to whether individuals would lose their liberty. It brought a balance between the medical and social models, ensuring that social aspects of mental health needs were taken into account. In 2007, amendments to the Mental Health Act meant that social workers are no longer the only profession to train for this role and it can now be undertaken by other professionals within the mental health service. These may include community psychiatric nurses, psychologists and occupational therapists. Although they have access to the same training, social workers have always listened to carers, have good knowledge about other social factors and the impact of these. Social workers are not trained using the medical model and may be more able to challenge doctors.

It is helpful to consider and reflect on your own thoughts and ideas when looking at changes in policy and legislation. The next exercise is provided to help you with this.

Reflective exercise

- What do you think is meant by the terms health and well-being? In what ways would you assess this?
- How would you describe your own health and well-being?
- Make a list of resources that you think add to your health and well-being.
- What may negatively affect your health and well-being?
- What are the differences between the rights of a person and protecting the public from that person?
- How often do you stop to think about your health and well-being?
- Does this include consideration of your mental health and well-being or do you mostly focus on your physical health and well-being?
- How would you feel if an assessment of your mental health was biased towards protecting the public from you rather than your human rights?

With the changes in policy and legislation it is envisaged that service users will be able to take more control of their health and well-being and care needed. This will also enable people to move on with their lives with the notion of wellness rather than mental ill health. Rather than remaining under a psychiatrist for many years, individuals will be able to return to the care of their GP for their ongoing mental health difficulties while they are stable, thus reducing the possible feeling of stigma and shame they may experience otherwise. This may also provide more possibilities for accessing employment and leisure facilities and other mental health-enhancing opportunities such as going to the pub with friends, feeling the same as others who go to the GP when needed.

However, the important change highlighted in the amendments to the Mental Health Act in 2007 was the shift in focus to protecting the public. This could infer that mental illness is identified more recently as dangerous and that, rather than service users living as equal citizens in the community, the mentally ill need to be contained and controlled. This is inconsistent with other policies that promote equality and anti-discrimination such as the Equality Act 2010. This is an important reason for social workers to continue to promote equality, to challenge discrimination and promote the rights of individuals. This also appears to be in conflict with the closure of psychiatric beds and more people being cared for in their own homes. However, it is vital that community mental health services are able to meet the needs of these individuals. Davies (2008: 60) states:

> The fundamental question arises, if people are no longer cared for in large institutions, or in psychiatric units in general hospitals, how can we be sure that community services provide them with a better quality of life and greater recovery opportunities?

There have been different experiences of treatment in the community and at home and still further improvements are needed in order to meet the aims of the recovery model. Ensuring that social workers are part of all teams in mental health services is important so that services are able to address all aspects of life that impact on our mental health.

Further issues for professionals include the significant number of changes to legislation, policies and services that need to be incorporated and learned. As already stated, services are ever changing and this additional work is at times stressful but essential to enable practitioners to keep up with these changes. Professionals must be supported to keep up with changes that affect the way they work, otherwise they will be unable to work effectively and with confidence. However, practitioners are limited in the time they have available to read and reflect on changes and adapt to new ways of working, often leading them to feel confused and dissatisfied and therefore challenged in their ability to provide the level of service needed.

Although professionals have mixed feelings about this new strategy, there may be different causes for this. While it is positive for people to be discharged from secondary mental health services when they are stable and able to access resources in the community, there may be concerns that people will become unwell again and need help but that this may go unnoticed. Yet if this approach continues to be thought of as the best way, people with mental health needs may be inadvertently hindered or prevented from their recovery and from accessing social benefits again, including secure housing, education and employment. Services may unintentionally exacerbate the feelings of despair rather than promoting feelings of hope, which are vital to recovery (Repper and Perkins 2006: 11). However, the initiatives of early intervention services have recognized the research that '"getting in early" can pay dividends in minimising the social losses that may attach to mental distress, thereby making it easier for people to recover' (Tew 2011: 109).

There have been different experiences of treatment in the community and at home and still further improvements are needed in order to meet the aims of the recovery model. Providing a seamless service where individuals are transferred to and from a Crisis Resolution and Home Treatment Team and Recovery Team (there may be alternative names for these teams in different areas) for this treatment at home is vital. Excellent communication and collaborative working are crucial to ensure effective multidisciplinary working. It is essential to value other professionals' knowledge and skills and vice versa, coupled with open communication, for this process to work successfully.

The Department of Health's *Women's Mental Health Strategy: Into the Mainstream* (DH 2002) illustrates how women have been asking for a number of years for mental health professionals to 'place importance on the underlying causes and context of their distress in addition to their symptoms' (DH 2002: 10). Women also say that 'they want recognition that their psychological vulnerability is not rooted in their "biology" but in the context of their lives'.

Social workers are well placed to listen and take into account the various causes of mental health needs. Women have demonstrated in the above research that they want change in their lives in order to experience a sense of well-being. For the social worker it provides a perfect opportunity to address the complex area of relational need during interventions.

A way of exploring this would be to ensure that during assessments people are given the opportunity to express areas of concern such as domestic violence or a history of childhood sexual abuse. Some professionals or service users may find this difficult but by including this question for all assessments it will provide the vital opportunity for those who wish to or need to accept help. It is also crucial that service users are recognized as part of family groups and that intervention is offered at appropriate times and places. For example, if the Crisis Resolution and Home Treatment team came to visit a mother when her family was having their meal this could cause conflict. It may not be right for children to be present during treatment, or the service user may want more privacy, but it is also vital for the family to continue to function in their usual way as much as possible. Pressure of time and shortages of staff can make it more difficult to provide the time needed but it is essential if social workers are to support people in making a recovery and living with a sense of well-being and quality of life. Some aspects of intervention may be more challenging, for example taking away a person's liberty, but if it is to ensure the safety of another or others it may be vital.

Sir William Utting, former Chief Social Worker Officer, DHSS states:

> I do not expect social work to be popular. It deals with people society would usually prefer to forget: unwanted, stigmatized, dependent. It does not do so quietly, but acts as an irritant by standing up for their rights and needs.
>
> (cited in Gilbert *et al.* 2010: 153)

As social workers strive to treat people equally and to work with a sense of social justice, this presents its own challenges. There will be occasions when helping a service user to sustain or develop relationships is vital to recovery. Being aware of our own discrimination against others is the beginning of the journey which continues as a long and, at times, difficult learning process. In order to practise in a non-discriminatory and anti-oppressive manner we have to examine and reflect on ourselves and our attitudes on a regular basis. It would be foolish to think otherwise as there are times when power imbalance is inevitable, from the simple example of a person needing your help to when a person has plans to harm himself or herself or others. Reflecting regularly on this power imbalance and how we view ourselves is essential.

Although recent models of working may appear to be in conflict with traditional social work roles, this is not the case. Social work has always promoted recovery and for people then to be able to move on with their lives without the support of services.

The Sainsbury Centre for Mental Health highlights that although the recovery approach has been criticized there are many positive aspects that should be embraced.

> Recovery ideas have not been without their critics. There is already a significant consumer 'backlash' against recovery ideas: which are seen by some as simply a rationale for cutting services, reducing benefits and forcing people back to work. These are understandable fears but, in our view, they should not be allowed to obscure the value of recovery ideas and their potential to transform mental health services for the better.
>
> (Shepherd *et al.* 2008)

There continues to be a culture of 'them and us'. Repper and Perkins state that a way of challenging this would be for those with mental health needs and those who are not currently experiencing mental health needs to be brought together under an equal setting and conditions, for example working together. Research already indicates that there are a number of professionals already working in mental health services who themselves have had, or continue to experience, mental health needs (Shepherd *et al.* 2008: 12).

The Sainsbury Centre for Mental Health acknowledges that there are already professionals with mental health needs but also suggests the following possibility:

> A more radical way of transforming mental health services may be to change recruitment practices so as to involve many more people with 'lived experience' as paid staff, including as managers and practitioners.
>
> (Shepherd *et al.* 2008: 15)

Additionally, social workers have a responsibility to be willing to accept changes in their ways of working and both embrace and support those around them, both colleagues and service users with mental health needs, while taking responsibility for their own mental health.

> Either way, achieving 'recovery-oriented practice' will mean a significant change in the culture, as well as to the organization, of services. It means the whole organization accepting the reality that 'mental illness' is all around us and that people with 'mental health problems' are already involved in delivering mental health services: it's just that they are encouraged to keep this identity secret.
>
> (Shepherd *et al.* 2008: 15)

Challenges for professionals

In mental health services professionals are expected to act as care coordinators for individual clients. This may include safeguarding issues, benefits, family work, being required to do general health care checks or referring to others. Professionals have indicated that this raised challenges, with lack of specific training, learning on the job and lack of knowledge and confidence being key factors. There is a need to attend extra training, for example social workers and occupational therapists need to understand about medication, nurses and occupational therapists need to know about benefits and self-directed support. However, a further challenge is often feeling a lack of in-depth knowledge and perhaps lack of support. It may be possible to undertake particular practical functions, for example taking a person's blood pressure, but would a social worker know when there is cause to be concerned? This situation will be exacerbated with the introduction or furthering of mobile working, of not being office-based other than for meetings. Staff will be unable to offer each other unplanned informal support and sharing of information and knowledge. Stress levels could increase and people may feel more isolated and out of their depth in what is a difficult and very demanding job.

Further challenges arise for professionals working with vulnerable people and their carers. Carers may not be supported in their vital role, which is essential to the recovery of the person they care for. Carers 'often feel ill-informed and unsupported'. (Shepherd *et al.* 2008: 5). Practitioners are often involved in situations where people are no longer able to reside in their family home due to their complex mental health needs and possibly the addition of a learning disability or old age. Social workers involved in placing a person in a residential care home will be aware of the importance of maintaining contact with family and other social networks in order to maintain well-being. However, with the competing demands of the current economic climate and so many changes with closures of beds and residential care homes, placing people within their home area can be challenging. This poses ethical dilemmas of preventing the ongoing contact with a people's social system and those who have known them and who can provide vital information when necessary. Isolating a vulnerable person can also raise the possibility of poor or unacceptable care being overlooked or ignored. Changes in people's presentation may also go unnoticed as there is not regular contact with friends and family who have known them prior to their current situation. The right to private and family life (Article 8, Human Rights Act 1998) is challenged in so many ways for vulnerable people and social workers are well placed to confront and address oppression and discrimination.

Conclusion

Social workers are skilled to assist, enable and manage change but the current climate, with extensive financial savings and cuts set to continue, presents significant challenges for social workers. In mental health services many areas are undergoing significant changes with, for example, some local authorities withdrawing their employees from partnership trusts with health. One example of how changes will affect professionals is the introduction of social enterprises to meet social care needs. Charities are also calling for changes in services to include a more joined-up approach in meeting the complex needs of people with a dual diagnosis (Centre for Mental Health 2012). These are very challenging and uncertain times for individual social workers. It is crucial that as a professional body we continue to drive forward the emphasis on the social model of intervention when addressing mental health needs and give sufficient prominence to the effects of social aspects of life on recovery from mental ill health.

References and further reading

Age Concern (2007) *Improving Services and Support for Older People with Mental Health Problems: The Second Report from the UK Inquiry into Mental Health and Well-being in Later Life,* available at: http://www.ageuk.org.uk/health-wellbeing/conditions-illnesses/depression/ [Accessed 5 January 2013].

Bamford, T. (2011) The team approach in person-centred health care: the social work perspective, *International Journal of Person Centred Medicine,* 1 (1): 23–6.

BASW (British Association of Social Work) (2010) *Policy on Social Work in Multi-Disciplinary Mental Health Teams.* Birmingham: BASW.

Bramble, R. (2004) *The Nameless Social Worker.* London: Janus Publishing.

Centre for Mental Health (2012) Available at: http://www.centerformentalhealth.org.uk/news/2012_dual_diagnosis.aspx [Accessed 5 January 2013].

Davies, M. (2008) *The Blackwell Encyclopaedia of Social Work.* Oxford: Blackwell.

DH (Department of Health) (1995) *Building Bridges: A Guide to Arrangements for Inter-agency Working for the Care and Protection of Severely Mentally Ill People.* London: The Statonery Office.

DH (2000) *No Secrets: Guidance on Developing and Implementing Multi-agency Policies and Procedures to Project Vulnerable Adults from Abuse.* London: Department of Health.

DH (2002) *Women's Mental Health Strategy: Into the Mainstream.* London: Department of Health.

DH (2008a) *Putting People First: Transforming Adult Social Care.* London: Department of Health.

DH (2008b) *Refocusing the Care Programme Approach: Policy and Postive Practice Guidance.* London: Department of Health.

DH (2008c) *Service Users and Carers and the Care Programme Approach: Making the CPA Work for You.* London: Department of Health.

DH (2009) *New Horizons: A Shared Vision for Mental Health.* London: The Stationery Office.

DH (2011) *No Health Without Mental Health.* London: Department of Health.

DHSS (Department of Health and Social Security) (1975) *Better Services for the Mentally Ill.* London: The Stationery Office.

Fawcett, B., Weber, Z. and Wilson, S. (2012) *International Perspectives on Mental Health: Critical Issues Across the Lifespan.* Basingstoke: Palgrave Macmillan.

Gilbert, P., Bates, P., Carr, S. *et al.* (2010) *Social Work and Mental Health: The Value of Everything.* Lyme Regis: Russell House Publishing.

Humphreys, C. and Thiara, R. (2003) Mental health and domestic violence – 'I call it symptoms of abuse', *British Journal of Social Work,* 33: 209–26.

Mind (2012) How We Can Help You, available at: http://www.mind.org.uk/help/community-care/community-based_mental_health_and_social_care [Accessed 5 January 2012].

Pritchard, J. (ed.) (2008) *Good Practice in Safeguarding Adults: Working Effectively in Adult Protection.* London: Jessica Kingsley.

Read, J., Agar, K., Argyle, N. and Aderhold, V. (2003) Sexual and physical abuse during childhood and adulthood as predictors of hallucinations, delusions and thought disorder, *Psychology and Psychotherapy: Theory, Research and Practice,* 76: 1–22.

Repper, J. and Perkins, R. (2006) *Social Inclusion and Recovery: A Model for Mental Health Practice.* London: Balliere Tindall.

Shepherd, G., Boardman, J. and Slade, M. (2008) *Making Recovery a Reality.* London: Sainsbury Centre for Mental Health, available at: http//www.centreformentalhealth.org.uk/pdfs/Making-recovery-a-reality-policy-paper.pdf [Accessed 5 January 2013].

Tew, J. (2011) *Social Approaches to Mental Distress.* London: Palgrave Macmillan.

Watkins, P. (2007) *Recovery: A Guide for Mental Health Practitioners.* London: Churchill Livingstone Elsevier.

11 Working in palliative and end-of-life care

Marilyn Russell

Prior to my role in the hospice I had worked for 13 years as a probation officer, both in the community and latterly in the probation department of a women's prison; I had also completed counselling training to Advanced Certificate level. While working in the prison my interest developed in working therapeutically with those experiencing grief, loss, anger, separation and isolation; I was drawn to hospice work for the opportunity it offered to continue complex work with individuals and families affected by death and dying. While working at the hospice I have qualified as a couples' counsellor with Relate, which has been invaluable for the therapeutic work I complete with couples and families. Social work in end-of-life and palliative care is continually varied and challenging. The benefits and rewards of working in a multidisciplinary setting are enormous, particularly with regard to the provision of specialized holistic care for those who are dying, their families and carers.

Introduction

This chapter will begin with a brief historical overview of the origins, development and guiding principles of hospice care. An outline will follow of the current government policy on improving the health and social care provision of end-of-life and specialist palliative care to service users, their families and carers; this will also highlight the recognition of the importance of skilled social work practitioners working in palliative care.

In addressing the learning outcomes (listed below) the chapter will continue by exploring death, dying and society and the importance of effective communication and listening skills; social work and working with loss and bereavement; spirituality, use of narrative; effective multi-professional working and the necessity of supervision, reflection and harnessing support from colleagues.

Reflective exercises will be used to encourage consideration of personal attitudes, values and beliefs regarding chronic and incurable illness. Case studies are provided to highlight the multitude of complexities and challenges for the social worker in palliative care.

Learning outcomes

By the end of this chapter, readers should have developed their awareness and understanding of:

- the definition, scope and understanding of the role of the specialist social work practitioner working with people facing palliative and end-of-life care;
- the knowledge, skills and values which inform work with people facing the end of their lives, and work to support their families and networks;
- how to apply holistic models of intervention using practice-based case scenarios which highlight values-based intervention and ethical challenges;
- the importance of support, supervision and collaborative working in managing emotionally demanding practice situations.

All case studies are based on service users known to me or my colleagues professionally. Identifying features have been changed to ensure confidentiality.

For the purposes of this chapter, I will use the term 'service user' to describe those receiving end-of-life and palliative care. Within a health care setting, particularly a hospice or hospital palliative care team, people will usually be referred to as the 'patient'. In some hospital settings there has been a change to describing someone as receiving a service, i.e. a 'service user' or a 'client' of the organization. With regard to life-threatening and life-limiting illness there has also been a move away from referring to 'terminal' illness as the focus has moved to emphasize living with incurable illness rather than dying with terminal illness.

Caring for the dying

Larkin (2011) considers that the roots of palliative and hospice care date back to the work of eighteenth- and nineteenth-century religious orders; he details the work of two religious orders (the Irish Sisters of Charity and the Sisters of Charity in Montreal) in caring for the chronically sick and dying, noting their influence on the founders of the hospice movement worldwide. Larkin discusses compassionate care in the early development of the provision of institutional care for the dying. He notes the significance of the religious foundation of health care in understanding why compassion is essential to palliative care, citing Sevensky's (1983) suggested core religious ideals underpinning the work of religion in health care, including human dignity, justice, compassion, finitude, stewardship and the sanctity of life. These core ideals link to social work values and ethics '... a compassionate response to suffering is through action and not merely an empathic feeling towards others' misfortune' (Larkin 2011). Randall and Downie (2006, cited in Larkin 2011) posit: 'These ideals echo ethical values which are ascribed to good medical practice and upon which the "principalist" model of ethics in health care is built.'

Dame Cicely Saunders set up St Christopher's Hospice in Sydenham in 1967, which began the development of the modern hospice movement worldwide. Dame Cicely trained as a nurse, medical social worker and, while working part-time at St Luke's Home for the Dying Poor in Bayswater, began training at St Thomas's Hospital Medical School to become a physician. She was committed to the provision of holistic care that recognized and responded to psychological, spiritual and social needs in order to address the 'total pain' experienced by service users suffering with cancer. Her strong Christian faith was a driving force in her approach to caring for the dying. St Christopher's Hospice has been a beacon of excellence in the provision of clinical care and education and research – the Education Centre of St Christopher's Hospice offers an extensive range of training courses attended yearly by 7000 health and social care professionals (www.stchristophers.org.uk).

End-of-life and palliative care – the end-of-life care strategy

'End of life care' is given the following definition by the Department of Health:

> 'End of life care is care that helps all those with advanced, progressive, incurable illness to live as well as possible until they die. It enables the supportive and palliative care needs of both patients and family to be identified and met throughout the last phase of life and into bereavement. It includes management of pain and other symptoms, and provision of psychological, social, spiritual and practical support.

The World Health Organization (WHO) defines palliative care as follows:

> 'Palliative care is an approach that improves the quality of life of patients and their families facing the problems associated with life-threatening illness, through the prevention and relief of suffering by means of early identification and impeccable assessment and treatment of pain and other problems, physical, psychological and spiritual.
>
> (World Health Organization 2011)

The publication, in July 2008, of the *End of Life Care Strategy for England and Wales* (DH 2008) outlined an extensive programme to improve and transform the care given to people nearing the end of life, as well as support for their families and carers.

The report of the Social Advisory Group of the National End of Life Care Programme, *Supporting People to Live and Die Well: A Framework for Social Care at the End of Life* (NHS 2010), sets out key objectives and recommendations to enable skilled social care workers to improve the quality of services to support people needing end-of-life care. These include:

- Strengthen the specialism of palliative care social work
- Promote understanding and best practice in holistic assessment of individuals, their carers and families at the end of life
- Create a supportive work environment that enables social care workers to maximize their contribution to quality end of life care
- Apply social work and social care assessment models to end-of-life care and integrate these with specialist health assessments

(NHS 2010: 4,5)

These objectives and recommendations highlight the role of the skilled social worker, and the value of social work skills and experience is emphasized in the document (NHS 2010: 19). The case studies within this chapter will evidence the value of social work skills.

The College of Social Work guide, *The Route to Success in End-of-life Care: Achieving Quality for Social Work* (NHS 2012) highlights the historical involvement of social work in supporting the dying and bereaved but notes the dwindling numbers of specialist palliative care social workers, raising concerns that the specialism is under threat. The National End of Life Care Programme responded to the absence of social work and social care support in end-of-life care by establishing its social care workstream in 2009 (NHS 2012: 5).

The guide notes the importance of social work's core values and skills for end-of-life care:

> Their professional role is based on a clear framework of values and ethical standards, a thorough understanding of diversity and social inequality, ... and a repertoire of knowledge and skills that are of direct relevance to good end of life care (NHS 2012: 6).

Social workers work with those who are marginalized, isolated and financially disadvantaged – 'these are the people whose mortality rates are highest' (NHS 2012: 6). Examples of social work practice across the six steps of the End of Life Care Pathway are provided:

- discussion as the end of life approaches;
- assessment, care planning and review;
- coordination of care;
- delivering high-quality care in different settings;
- care in the last days of life; and
- care after death.

Key messages of the guide include the particular contribution of social workers 'in maintaining a focus on the dying person in their family, community and cultural context' (NHS 2012: 36).

Financial challenges

The *Supporting People to Live and Die Well Framework* emphasizes the challenges ahead – particularly the expected 17 per cent annual rise in deaths between 2012 and 2030 (NHS 2010: 3) and that fewer than one in ten of these people will die at home. A recent World Health Organization (WHO) report, *Palliative Care for Older People: Better Practices* (2011), highlights the fact that although the preferred place of care and death is home, the majority of people in the European Region die elsewhere.

The work of the Palliative Care Funding Review highlights the financial challenges in meeting the vision of the Strategy's programme for England and Wales to transform end-of-life care needs: in its report to the government (July 2011) it estimates 'that around 90,000 people have an unmet palliative care need. The report further estimates that 'between 70 per cent and 80 per cent of all deaths are likely to need palliative care input' (Palliative Care Funding Review 2011).

This comes at a time of continued extensive financial cutbacks to local services, which in turn may well impinge on the training needs and provision of skilled social work practitioners within end-of-life and palliative care settings. In addition, financial restrictions, resultant necessary changes to service delivery and concerns relating to job security can impact on positive interprofessional working.

Death, dying and society

In discussing death, dying and society the Strategy highlights evidence indicating that death is felt to be a taboo subject for many people and notes that 'promoting a better understanding of death and dying will therefore be an important part of delivering this strategy' (DH 2008: 37). Michael Wenham, in his autobiography on living with motor neurone disease, comments: 'The art of dying – we need to think and talk more about it. Death is the last enemy. It's also the last taboo' (Wenham 2008: 154).

The Dying Matters Coalition (www.dyingmatters.org) was set up in 2009 by the National Council for Palliative Care to examine issues related to talking about dying matters; one of the findings was the avoidance of using the terms 'dying' and 'death', with 'passed away' the most frequently used euphemism. The use of euphemisms can create difficulties and misunderstandings, particularly for children. Health and social care professionals have a role to play in using clear language when encouraging more open discussion between service users and their families and carers.

Reflective exercise

- Consider your own experiences of situations in which end-of-life care, death and dying have been discussed.
- How have those within your close networks responded?
- Have you, or those around you, been reluctant, or avoided, in-depth discussion of these issues? Consider the impact for service users with palliative or end-of life care needs in this situation.

Many people with serious illness and end-of-life care needs experience avoidance with regard to the preparedness of (some) family and friends to discuss their illness; this can increase further the emotional and psychological impact for service users and limit their opportunity to share feelings and to discuss end-of-life wishes with those close to them. People can be left feeling that they are carrying the emotional burden of their illness both for themselves and those close to them.

Lack of open communication will impact on the grieving process, particularly for children and young adults. Worden (1996: 140–1) highlights the difficulties that can arise if children are not given adequate information that is clear and comprehensible – both before and following the death of a close family member. Kissane and Bloch (2002: 18) note the importance of 'information being effectively disseminated throughout the whole family'. A key role for the social worker will be to encourage and enable, where possible, more open discussion between couples, families and carers.

Good communication and listening skills are crucial, as is the ability to 'sit' with silence where appropriate, which can enable the service user to reflect and raise subjects that may be difficult. The skill of actively listening and sitting with the expressed sadness, fear and uncertainty can feel daunting. Rogers's (1967) core conditions of congruence, unconditional positive regard and empathy are very relevant. Service users with life-limiting illness will usually have become very observant at noting the visual signals and tone and content of verbal responses of health professionals:

> There is a kind of hush in the room that doesn't bode well. I am swaddled in bandages, and I feel soft and wounded, filleted, oozing … Doctors say a few things to me but I am aware of some kind of avoidance, of averted eyes, hasty retreats.
>
> (Hobhouse 2004: 289)

Rogers (1979: 66) comments on the importance of the therapeutic relationship 'as experienced by the client' and Mearns and Thorne (1988: 82) note that a congruent response 'must be one which is relevant to the immediate concerns of the client'.

A social worker needs to be prepared for direct and difficult questions relating to how a service user is feeling and the physical impact of disease progression. Working with congruence and honesty may present challenges in situations where it is known that the person prefers to manage their situation day to day and is frightened of the implications of feeling less well, but nevertheless is querying 'Does this mean I am going to die soon?' This necessitates the importance of preparation when working therapeutically and drawing on social work values of working respectfully and empathically while affirming strengths of the service user.

Social work and working with loss

Most social work practitioners will at some stage work in situations (both in health and non-health settings) where adults, children or families are living with life-limiting or chronic conditions, facing issues relating to loss, death or bereavement.

Weinstein (2008: 2) gives a working definition of loss:

> Loss is wider than a response to a death, important as that is. It is any separation from someone or something whose significance is such that it impacts on our physical or emotional well-being, role and status. The experience

and manifestation of loss can be more or less difficult depending on other important variables.

McGoldrick (1997: 126) explores generational patterns of families and the striking recurring themes and, with regard to loss, death and bereavement comments: 'More than any other human experience, loss puts us in touch with what matters in our own lives. Coming to terms with death is the most difficult experience we face in life.'

Reith and Payne (2009: 6) highlight that 'social work in end-of-life care focuses on losses of identify and expectation' and consider how identity defines us. Serious illness and disability will impact on relationships and how we view ourselves and how our hopes and expectations will change. The loss of close intimacy and a sexual relationship can be very distressing and, for some service users, heighten their sense of isolation and separation. Palm and Friedrichsen (2008) explore the importance of closeness for partners of service users with advanced cancer. A social worker providing therapeutic support can enable the discussion, where appropriate, of the impact of loss of closeness and the exploration of maximizing quality time with partners.

Weinstein (2008: 9–10) outlines some of the key themes of assessing loss and the impact for those bereaved, including 'the nature of the attachment, personality of the bereaved, sudden or anticipated death, unsupportive families or communities and issues of diversity, disadvantage and discrimination such as race and gender'.

It is important to remain alert to the impact of physical and psychological changes associated with life-threatening illness and loss. Physical changes may include increasing levels of pain, digestive changes, tiredness and insomnia, while psychological changes may include emotional, cognitive and behavioural changes. Feelings of isolation, exclusion, helplessness, anger, sadness, depression and exhaustion are all key factors for service users, their families and carers with end-of-life needs.

Reflective exercise

Reflect on your personal experiences of loss.

- What has been the impact for you?
- How might your personal experiences of loss (or lack of personal experience) impact on your ability or desire to work in an end-of-life or palliative care setting?
- On the other hand, how could they make it difficult for you to work in such situations?

The shock of diagnosis and consequential changes of expected future plans for service users and their families will be devastating. As illness and disease progresses there will be constant changes and adjustments for service users and those close to them: 'When dying people are least adaptable they are called on to be more so. No healthy person has to make such sharp adjustments in such short order' (Young and

Cullen 1996, in Currer 2001: 44). Families frequently articulate the distress associated with all areas of their lives being 'taken over' by cancer (or their particular illness). Physical symptoms will increasingly encroach on the ability of service users and families to live in the way they had been used to or had envisaged for themselves in the future. Key roles for the social worker are to engage with and support service users and those close to them, while promoting, wherever possible, the expressed needs and wishes of service users to maintain (within their limitations) their independence and some control over what is happening to them.

Reith and Payne (2009: 8) identify that ... 'end of life is a process of social change for individuals as they become aware that death is close to them; this change is part of a family's journey through community, society and culture'. They further highlight the skills needed to work in supporting people and the necessity for practitioners to 'understand, influence and react to how death is seen in the culture of society and the policies that govern how services are provided'.

In considering the impact of loss it is helpful to read some of the written accounts by people who have detailed their experience of facing death. Reading the stories of others can assist in uncovering emotions, values and beliefs related to death and dying that we have not previously considered.

Hobhouse (1993: 281) gives a vivid and passionate personal account of her thoughts and feelings from her initial faltering realization of the potential seriousness of her diagnosis: 'It wasn't until she said goodbye and "good luck to you" that I began to be apprehensive.' Gradually she realized the impact on those around her (both health professionals and family and friends) and became aware of her own fears around the process of dying: 'Sometimes I was afraid because I did not know how to die ... I was unlearned, untutored. How give up strength, will, surrender body functions piece by piece? I was afraid I was going to blow it, this dying' (Hobhouse 2004: 292).

Currer, in her chapter on facing death (2001), provides an overview of individual and research accounts. Her chapter highlights the emotions and turmoil for those trying to manage acceptance of increasingly limited life expectancy, while trying to retain hope and resilience and humour. This is particularly significant as health and social care professionals can, at times, struggle with their perception of an individual's continuing 'denial' or 'unrealistic attitude' regarding their disease progression.

The value of reading personal accounts is the power of the written word in conveying the turmoil and challenges for those trying to reach an acceptance of their impending death. The personal account of Hobhouse and those that Currer details highlight the impact for people of 'abandoning the future', including working through processes of denial, realization and wanting 'to lengthen the odds'. Separation, loneliness and the social bond are also explored and, again, the quotes powerfully portray the impact of declining health and changes in personal relationships. There is extensive writing on grief and bereavement and stage theories for understanding grief; recommendations for further reading are noted at the end of the chapter.

Working with narrative and family stories

As with all areas of social work, practitioners working in end-of-life and palliative care settings will be engaged with service users, their families and carers across all age ranges and cultures with unique life experiences. Using narrative and stories can be a starting point for dialogue and assist social workers in opening channels of communication.

'When we participate as listeners in the narrative of others, we recognize the plight of others in all the plots and counterplots of life stories' (Bruner 2002: 9). Weinstein (2008: 16) highlights the importance of disenfranchized grief and narrative in informing understanding of anti-discriminatory practice, highlighting that narrative:

> ... builds on the conventional strengths of social work, namely to hear the story that the service user brings but develops this to make it a more active process where the individual is helped to see that they do not just have a voice but that it is equally, or even more, important than that of the professionals whose views are normally given more prominence. It seeks to help the individual become the subject, not the object, of their story.

This is particularly significant for service users with end-of-life care needs. Many will feel it has been a struggle to have concerns regarding symptoms taken seriously. Diagnosis and subsequent health appointments and palliative treatment can be overwhelming, with little opportunity for service users to tell their story of the impact for themselves and their family.

> Narrative approaches have the potential to be anti-discriminatory once the power dynamics within these dialogues are fully recognised and the individuals experiencing loss are allowed to tell their own story rather than be swamped by what is called the dominant narrative, the language of 'oughts' and 'shoulds' representing the world view of professionals, including social workers.
>
> (Weinstein 2008: 46)

Reflective exercise

As you read the case studies, reflect on the narrative and stories for those involved and consider the possible longer-term narrative and impact on family stories following death and bereavement – particularly in the case study of Mark. As McGoldrick (1997: 127) highlights: 'Death ends a life, but not a relationship, which struggles on in the survivor's mind, seeking some resolution which it may never find.' Reflect on the impact for yourself of working with the service users and their families and carers depending on your relationships, expectations and hopes and wishes for the future.

Case study

Mark is a 20-year-old white male recently diagnosed with an aggressive carcinoma following visits to his doctor for a few months complaining of lethargy, nausea and vomiting. He lives at home with his parents and a younger sister (Charlotte) and brother (Toby) aged 15 and 11 respectively. Surgery is not possible due to the spread of the cancer. Chemotherapy was commenced but Mark experienced nausea and vomiting following chemotherapy and felt isolated and embarrassed. He had a break from chemotherapy treatment for a period during which his energy levels started to pick up. Chemotherapy was recommenced but quickly had to be stopped due to the side effects for Mark and his disease progression. Mark's mother Mary is struggling with her emotions and feels that her husband Ian tries to be cheerful. Ian and Mark have previously had a fiery relationship. His sister Charlotte holds her feelings in while Toby is more open. Mark wants to see himself as the same as others and is upset by people being overly nice (including his dad); at times he feels angry and frustrated. Mark has been admitted to the hospice for symptom control but his condition is continuing to deteriorate. Mark is adamant that he wants to return home to die and he is also determined that he will go out with friends to celebrate his twenty-first birthday. There is some concern in the medical team that the process of transferring home may be risky for Mark with regard to further accelerating his condition. Mary also wants Mark to return home to die and feels the family will be able to manage.

From a social work perspective you are a keen advocate for the family and support Mark in his wish to go home. Consider how you can work with health professional colleagues to advocate on the family's behalf regarding the emotional and spiritual importance of Mark going home for the final stages of palliative care.

Two practitioners from the social work team worked closely with ward staff and the family – one meeting on one occasion with Mark and the other meeting with Charlotte for listening support and also with Mary. Mary later asked for support in advising Charlotte and Toby that Chris was dying and one of the social workers facilitated this discussion prior to Mark returning home and liaised closely with the district nurse team to advise of the family discussions before Mark was discharged home. Mark's condition improved slightly on his return home and he was able to go out with friends (with a syringe driver in place) to celebrate his twenty-first birthday. Mark talked about his concerns and fears relating to dying at a young age – questioning whether he would be remembered and wanting his room to be kept as it was. He died approximately three weeks after his twenty-first birthday and four weeks after returning home.

Full discussion with the ward team of the emotional needs of Mark and the family gave the opportunity to highlight the importance not only of Mark being at home to die but also with regard to the bereavement grieving process for the family. It allowed Mark's parents and siblings to have more quality time to say their goodbyes. The parents of Mark had had great anxiety regarding telling Charlotte and Toby that Mark was close to dying. Support from one of the social workers eased the opening of the discussion and enabled the family to share their distress. Charlotte and Toby were encouraged to take the opportunity to ask questions of their parents relating to disease progression and the family had the opportunity to reflect on making the most of the remaining time together as a family. Good liaison from the social worker and the hospice clinical nurse specialist with the community district nurses supported the district nurses in their management of Mark's symptom control and the impact of witnessing his quick deterioration and the distress for the family. A debriefing/reflection meeting was held with the community nurses following Mark's death; they were aware that Mary was visiting the grave daily and had concerns for her and Mark's siblings. Overall, the management and response to Mark's needs and those of his family was a good example of multidisciplinary working. The family were offered bereavement counselling.

Multidisciplinary working

Working with people with life-limiting illness and their families requires the ability to engage positively with colleagues and work proactively within a multidisciplinary setting. Multidisciplinary working will include all health and social care professionals in varying settings who will have involvement with the service user and their family and carers.

Professionals often have preconceived beliefs about other professionals (Okitikpi and Aymer 2008: 132) which can hinder effective interdisciplinary working. Good interprofessional working is paramount in providing care that improves the quality of life of service users and their families facing the difficulties related to life-threatening and end-of-life care.

Reflective exercise

- Consider whether you have established stereotypes of other professions.
- If yes, where do these stereotypes stem from – are they related to media influence, your own experience or that of close family or friends?
- How might preconceived ideas impact on your interprofessional working? What has been your experience of working with other professions?
- What do you see as the strengths of the Social Work Codes of Practice and British Association of Social Workers (BASW) values and ethics that you can bring to multidisciplinary working in end-of-life and palliative care?

Participation in multidisciplinary meetings in a health care setting can initially present a new set of challenges, particularly for a lone social worker. A key role of the social worker in a hospice or hospital setting will be to assess the psychosocial needs of the service user and to highlight and promote these needs within the wider teams, and liaise with other professionals.

> Psychosocial care addresses the psychological experiences of loss and facing death for the patients and their impact on those close to them. It involves the spiritual beliefs, culture and values of those concerned and the social factors

which influence the experience. Psychosocial care includes the practical aspects of care such as financial, housing and aids to daily living and overlaps with spiritual care.

(MacLeod 2008: 8)

Clear assessment skills and the ability to maintain a balanced view of the service user's needs and concerns will be vital, particularly in situations where complicated medical issues may concentrate the focus on a medical model of caring to the detriment of the psychological and social models of care – and related need(s) – that may also be causing distress. Social work theory addresses concepts of difference (Trevillion 2004, cited in Okitikpi and Aymer 2008: 132), which is beneficial in partnership working with regard to the skills social workers have in negotiating barriers and boundaries.

Following referral to a palliative care team, the initial assessment of the service user will usually be carried out by a clinical nurse specialist. This will be a holistic in-depth assessment of relevant medical history and current nursing needs and will also take account of any presenting psychological needs, both for the service user and his or her carers. The time and approach devoted to this first assessment can be critical in establishing a positive working relationship between service users and professionals (MacLeod 2008).

Within the hospice and hospital setting the presentation at multidisciplinary meetings of new referrals to the service provides crucial indicators of psychosocial needs; the potential for complicated bereavement patterns may also be indicated.

Genograms (family diagrams) are widely used as a presenting feature of new referrals. Genograms 'were originally used for identifying genetic conditions and may be simplified when used as a social work assessment tool' (Reith and Payne 2009: 80).

Reflective exercise

- Complete a family genogram for yourself.
- Reflect on significant family or close relationships and, if relevant, any distant or broken relationships.
- How might you view your attachments, or distant and broken attachments, if serious illness suddenly became a factor for yourself or a close family member?
- Would this lead to a reassessment or desire to build on or improve a particular relationship?

New referrals often detail a service user who has had a late diagnosis of incurable illness. Delayed diagnosis can cause increased emotional distress, frustration and anger, both for service users and those caring for them. Treatment options may be more limited due to advanced disease progression and resultant limited tolerance to the side effects of (palliative) chemotherapy and radiotherapy. However, the service user will often be determined to commence treatment as soon as possible. Hospital and hospice palliative care medical professionals can feel thwarted in providing a realistic view of the limitations (and indeed qualitative value of what the treatment can offer) particularly where the person may have been given a vague prognosis by the consultant of treatment outcomes. In this situation the social worker will need to remain alert to the continuing and changing psychological and spiritual needs for the service user and his or her family.

Safeguarding, deprivation of liberty and end-of-life care

For many service users with life-limiting disease or chronic illness, confusion and lack of mental capacity may also be an issue. The burden of full-time care for partners and family members can be overwhelming and, as disease progresses, can also cause great anxiety and distress in trying to manage care at home. Full-time care is particularly difficult for older carers who may themselves have health needs and/or be resistant to having care services going into the home. Health and social care professionals working in end-of-life care are increasingly involved in monitoring and responding to safeguarding concerns, which can range from older carers with increasing confusion and dementia to family financial abuse or partner abuse in a long-standing abusive relationship. The following case study highlights some of the relevant issues.

Case study

Betty is a 74-year-old white woman with cancer of the pancreas. Her husband Jack has increasingly struggled to manage her care at home but has been resistant to a Care Manager assessment taking place to provide some care for Betty. Betty and Jack have three children living locally who are all busy and unable to help with physical and emotional support. Jack appears to struggle with accepting that Betty should not be left alone during the day due to her confusion. Additionally he becomes anxious if it appears that Betty is in pain. Betty has previously been into the hospice for respite care and symptom control. Following a brief period at home she has been readmitted to the hospice as Jack is again struggling to manage her care. Betty is increasingly confused but is very clear in stating her wish to be at home. She became disorientated and confused following Jack leaving on the first day of readmission, insisting that she wanted to leave the building. A Deprivation of Liberty Safeguards Authority (DOLS) was raised, a 'Best Interests' meeting arranged and an Independent Mental Capacity Advocate (IMCA) (Section 39A of the Mental Health Act) engaged to 'provide support and representation' for Betty as she lacked capacity to make a specific decision and the family members were not in agreement as how best to progress Betty's needs. The consultant and other medical professionals doubt that Jack will be able to manage Betty's care at home and feel that her needs will be best met by 24-hour nursing care. Jack would like Betty to return home.

As the social worker involved with the family you see your role as supporting Betty to control, within her limitations, her rights and wishes for her care and, particularly, the possibility of her returning home to die. How would you approach this situation?

Mental capacity assessments were carried out three times daily to establish Betty's ability to make informed choices; assessments confirmed that capacity fluctuated but Betty was clear in her lucid moments that she wanted to return home and was aware of the risks. The DOLS required the least restrictive option to be considered. The social worker was clear and open with Betty, Jack and their children regarding the need for increased family support and the acceptance of care services input. A care package was agreed and the provision of a half-day weekly sitting service was set up to enable Jack to go out regularly. The social worker arranged a meeting at the hospice with the family, the Care Manager and IMCA to plan for discharge. Regular visits from one of the hospice clinical nurse specialists were arranged to ensure Betty's pain was monitored and managed. Betty died at home, well supported, approximately ten weeks following discharge.

Spirituality and spiritual needs

In discussing spirituality and spiritual care needs it is useful to reflect on the vision of Dame Cicely Saunders in setting up the hospice movement – the need to respond to 'total pain' and her awareness and understanding that medicine cannot relieve all suffering, particularly if spiritual issues combine in the 'pain' of dying (Kissane and Bloch 2002).

> Spiritual care is in part a way of listening to those whose lives are profoundly challenged: it is a way of attending to the spiritual assault of an illness and it provides a space in which the spiritual dimensions of human experience can be expressed, explored, and nurtured. Listening to a life from a spiritual perspective therefore requires a sensitivity and discernment towards the beliefs, values, and connections that shape the way people make sense and final meaning in their lives.
>
> (Cobb 2008: 191)

The National Institute for Health and Clinical Excellence (NICE) Guidance on Cancer Services, *Improving Supportive and Palliative Care for Adults with Cancer* (NICE 2004), sets out guidelines and expectations of service delivery of spiritual support services. The introduction notes the 'many questions that can arise relating to identity and self-worth as patients seek to find an ultimate meaning to their lives' and the re-emergence of questions at various points during disease progression. The specific recommendations relating to workforce development note the importance of health and social care staff having the 'necessary skills, knowledge and support to deliver sensitive care' (NICE 2004: 10).

Diagnosis of a life-limiting illness or disease will significantly highlight for a service user the impending loss not only of close relationships but also difficult and fractured relationships. For some service users there will be the realization and acceptance that the damage to the relationship (particularly relating to a previous abusive relationship) cannot be resolved but, nevertheless, spiritual questions and turmoil can contribute to the person experiencing 'total pain'. Working with a service user in a state of 'total pain' or with significant unresolved spiritual and emotional distress is particularly difficult and also requires good staff support systems to be in place including clinical supervision and reflection to be regularly available.

Matthews (2009: x) comments: 'At the core of social work is a working relationship between two people which has a number of spiritual overtones', and argues that 'social work is impoverished because of its lack of engagement with spirituality ... social workers need to have an awareness of both their own spirituality and the spirituality of those whom they work with' (Mathews 2009: ix). He comments on the direct relationship between spirituality and our value base, noting that social work values of dignity, respect, choice, empowerment and anti-oppressive practice 'could be seen as the spiritual basis of social work' (Mathews 2009: 6).

Reflective exercise

Reflect on the points that Matthews raises. Consider your spiritual needs, the beliefs and values you hold and the relationships and experiences that give meaning to your life. Make a note of all the things that have a spiritual significance for you and give yourself time to reflect fully on the points you have noted.

Roy (2011) asks the question: 'Does "spiritual" indicate a limit to palliative care?' He highlights the varying terms and expressions used when discussing spiritual care linked to palliative care and queries: 'Does talk about "the spiritual" draw us into some comfort zone, a zone of protection against hard, unanswered, and perhaps unanswerable questions about human existence?' It is important to reflect on the question of 'unanswerable questions about human existence' in relation to the unresolved distress that some service users will experience up to the point of dying. Witnessing a service user in continuing unresolved 'spiritual' distress or 'total' pain is particularly challenging for health and social care professionals.

Continuing this theme of the spiritual and emotional dimensions of working with loss and death, Arshinoff (2011) discusses the emotional demands for health care workers in continually caring for dying service users who will often be in distress. The emotional and spiritual demands of end-of-life care will, of course, also be experienced by social workers. She notes the spiritual quest for caregivers in finding meaning and purpose in the work they do in the face of witnessing the suffering of those they work with. The intensity and demands of the work will be exacerbated when health and social care workers are themselves experiencing personal difficulties necessitating support. The importance of supervision and support will be discussed later in the chapter. Spirituality is not by any means always linked to any formal religion as such but in many cases awareness of the religious beliefs of the individual and family is an important aspect of holistic care.

Case study

Hami is a 43-year-old Iranian male living with his wife and two of his daughters (three older children live separately). Hami has been referred to the hospice for urgent home care and psychological and social support; he has had palliative chemotherapy following initial diagnosis. Hami is Muslim and his religion and cultural issues are very important to him. He is very protective of his wife who has had long-term and, at times, severe mental health problems requiring input from the local mental health services; his wife is not able to communicate in English. Hami guards his privacy and that of his family – within their community he does not want it to be known that he is dying as he feels this will impact negatively on his family. He has stated that where he comes from illness such as cancer or mental ill health is seen as weakness or punishment. Hami and his family have suffered from discrimination. Medical investigation has also indicated that he may have been subject to torture; there is concern regarding his spiritual needs and his fears for his family following his death, particularly having brought them to England to escape the difficult conditions they had been living in. Professionals are concerned about the potential risk for Hami's wife regarding the seriousness of his condition being kept from her, and the well-being of his younger daughters who are presently managing his care when needed. There are complex financial difficulties for the family.

Hami has had two admissions to the hospice for symptom control. His wife has not been told that he is dying and he is insistent that this remains the case so as to protect her and his younger daughters. Hami had hoped to die at home but has been admitted to the hospice for end-of-life care. A social worker has been involved with supporting Hami, his wife and his teenage daughter.

The health and social care professionals involved with supporting Hami and his family needed to take time to build trust; this can be stressful in situations where pain control is difficult to manage and where there are concerns for the well-being of family members. For many months Hami had resisted palliative care services and had eventually presented at the local hospital in severe pain; he then started to engage with the hospice medical team. The social worker was eventually able to visit at home and over time Hami's wife was more at ease with visiting health and social care professionals; the use of an interpreter was crucial to clarify understanding and enable fuller representation of the needs of Hami and his family. The social worker encouraged Hami's wife to be present at the home visits. It was important to accept the wishes of Hami in terms of information given to the family, while also liaising with other services where necessary and appropriate. Good collaborative working between teams was vital to ensure professionals were working together to support Hami and his family holistically and also to support each other; ward staff found it difficult at times witnessing the concerns of Hami's daughters particularly when he was close to dying.

The importance of anticipating the needs of service users from different cultures and assessing the importance of religious and spiritual traditions was recognized and the in-patient staff and social worker worked together to clarify with the family the procedures they wished to be in place. It had not proved possible to fully explore spiritual concerns with Hami but staff felt good progress had been made in enabling Hami to accept palliative care support and for him to be cared for in the hospice, thereby removing some of the nursing care from his younger daughters.

Following Hami's death a hospice welfare adviser continued to advise the family in managing bereavement benefits. Hami's wife did not need input from the mental health team.

The importance of support, supervision and reflection

Thomson (2011: 34) explores a psychosocial perspective of workplace well-being and argues the importance of an holistic approach to combating stress in the workplace:

> A more holistic picture needs to include social and organisational factors – and the organisational factors need to encompass strategic as well as operational concerns. Without a consideration of these wider issues, we will be left with a very partial and distorted picture – and one that is dangerously misleading, in so far as it places major emphasis on the individual ... while leaving wider social and organisational processes unexplored.

This point is particularly relevant to the difficulty, for some health and social care workers, of having the time to take advantage of individual supervision and clinical supervision/reflection opportunities and highlights the organizational responsibility of ensuring that strategic and organizational pressures do not detract from allocating the time needed for staff support.

Payne (2008: 231) discusses the value of staff support and emphasizes the importance of maintaining the well-being of employees, which will also impact on 'quality of service, including psychological and social interventions for patients and service users'.

Working in palliative care will be emotionally challenging particularly in relation to the continual focus of cumulative loss for service users, their families and carers. Social workers have a working culture that includes the expectation of regular supervision and the value and importance of this relating to all areas of their work, including the opportunity for reflection and self-monitoring of the impact of demanding and challenging work with service users. Currer (2001), in discussing the relevance of theoretical understandings for practice, notes the value social work places on reflexivity and the protection it offers against burnout and over-involvement.

Working in a multidisciplinary health setting can also provide the opportunity for clinical group supervision and reflection; this is particularly valuable in highlighting the contributions of, and demands on, all professionals involved in caring for the dying and their families. The social worker in a palliative care setting can play a significant role in highlighting the value and benefit of supervision and reflection opportunities and the importance of recognizing this as crucial to effective and professional practice.

In reflecting on staff support and managing the emotional demands of working in palliative care, the challenging nature of the work needs to be balanced with the rewards and satisfaction of having the opportunity to empower, support and advocate for service users and families managing the transition of death and dying at a time when the physical and emotional demands of the dying process can be overwhelming.

Maintaining hope and resilience is vital both for service users and for self. Weinstein (2008: 166) highlights the importance for the social work practitioner of maintaining hope, particularly when working with loss. This is poignantly highlighted by Mayne (2006) at the end of his autobiography of dying:

> In these past weeks I have been pondering on the ordered rhythm of the seasons. The swifts are back, threading the air; the woods are dappled with wild blossom and the gardens full of the scent of lilac; the thrush claims his territory, early and late; the hedgerows are hung with May. Each witnesses to change, to the annual pattern of death and new life. Each summons us to a sense of wonder at nature's cantus firmus. A melody that is both hopeful and enduring.

Conclusion

This chapter has set out to provide an overview of the role of the social worker in end-of-life and palliative care, the importance of palliative care social work as a specialism and the significance of the skilled social worker in contributing to holistic end-of-life and palliative care.

The chapter has explored working with loss, multidisciplinary working, the use of narrative and spirituality and spiritual needs, aiming to provide a background to the provision of holistic care and the differing needs and responses within the case studies, while also contributing to awareness and understanding of the learning outcomes.

Finally, it is hoped that completion of the reflection tasks will have been beneficial in highlighting your understanding and self-awareness related to death and dying and how this will relate in some way to all areas of your practice as a social worker. Working with loss and death is a significant part of practice for many who work with adults, and this chapter can only provide an introduction to the complexity and depth of the engagement. However, if you want to explore this area further, there are a few core books listed below that can help to enhance your skills and understanding in this sphere of practice.

References and further reading

Arshinoff, R. (2011) When answers elude us: spiritual care as a tool for healing, in I. Renzenbrink, *Caregiver Stress and Staff Support in Illness, Dying, and Bereavement*. Oxford: Oxford University Press.

Bruner, J. S. (2002) Making stories: law, literature, life, in D. E. Gelfand, R. Raspa, S. H. Briller, and S. M. Schim (eds) *End-of-life Stories: Crossing Disciplinary Boundaries*. New York: Springer.

Cobb, M. (2008) Spiritual care, in M. Lloyd Williams (ed.) *Psychosocial Issues in Palliative Care*. Oxford: Oxford University Press.

Currer, C. (2001) *Responding to Grief*. Basingstoke: Palgrave.

DH (Department of Health) (2008) *End of Life Care Strategy for England and Wales*. London: Department of Health.

Hobhouse, J. (1993) *The Furies*. New York: Doubleday.

Hobhouse, J. (2004) *The Furies*. New York: The New York Review of Books.

Holloway, M. (2007) *Negotiating Death in Contemporary Health and Social Care*. Bristol: The Policy Press. This discusses stage theories for understanding grief including those of Kubler-Ross, Bowlby, Averill, Parkes, Worden and Rando.

Kissane, D. W. and Bloch, S. (2002) *Family Focussed Grief Therapy*. Buckingham: Open University Press.

Klass, D., Silverman, P. R. and Nickman, S. L. (eds) (1996) *Continuing Bonds: New Understandings of Grief*. London: Taylor and Francis. This provides extensive examination of the continuing bond with those who have died, in the resolution of grief.

Larkin, P. (2011) Compassion: the essence of end-of-life care, in I. Renzenbrink (ed.) *Caregiver Stress and Staff Support in Illness, Dying, and Bereavement*. Oxford: Oxford University Press.

MacLeod, R. (2008) Setting the context: what do we mean by psychosocial care in palliative care?, in M. Lioyd-Williams, *Psychosocial Issues in Palliative Care*. Oxford: Oxford University Press.

Matthews, I. (2009) *Social Work and Spirituality*. Exeter: Learning Matters.

Mayne, M. (2006) *The Enduring Melody*. London: Darton, Longman and Todd.

McGoldrick, M. (1997) *You Can Go Home Again*. London: Norton.

Mearns, D. and Thorne, B. (1988) *Person-Centred Counselling in Action*. London: Sage Publications.

NHS (National Health Service) (2010) Supporting people to live and die well: a framework for social care at the end of life. Report of the Social Care Advisory Group of the National End of Life Care Programme, available at: http://www.endoflifecareforadults.nhs/uk/assets/downloads/Social_Care_Framework [Accessed 7 January 2013].

NHS (2012) The route to success in end-of-life care: achieving quality for social work, available at: http://www.socialwelfare.bl.uk/subject-areas/services-activity/social-work-care-services [Accessed January 2013].

NICE (National Institute for Health and Clinical Excellence) (2004) *Improving Supportive and Palliative Care for Adults with Cancer*, available at: http://www.nice.org.uk/nicemedia/pdf/cgsspmanual.pdf [Accessed 10 December 2012].

Nyatanga, B. (2008) *Why Is It So Difficult to Die?*, 2nd edn. London: Quay Books.

Okitikpi, T. and Aymer, C. (2008) *The Art of Social Work Practice*. Lyme Regis: Russell Publishing Ltd.

Palliative Care Funding Review (2011) Report highlights depth of unmet need, *Inside Palliative Care*, 17: 6.

Palm, I. and Friedrichsen, M. (2008) The lived experience of closeness in partners of cancer patients in the home care setting, *International Journal of Palliative Nursing*, 14 (1): 6–13.

Payne, M. (2008) Staff support, in M. Lloyd-Williams (ed.) *Psychosocial Issues in Palliative Care*, 2nd edn. Oxford: Oxford University Press.

Reith, M. and Payne, M. (2009) *Social Work in End-of-life and Palliative Care*. Bristol: The Policy Press.

Rogers, C. R. (1967) *On Becoming a Person: A Therapist's View of Psychotherapy*. London: Constable.

Rogers, C. R. (1979) *Client Centred Therapy*. London: Constable.

Roy, D. J. (2011) Does 'spiritual' indicate a limit to palliative care?, *Journal of Palliative Care*, 27 April: 259–60.

Sevensky, R. L. (1983) The religious foundations of healthcare: a conceptual approach, in I. Renzenbrink Oxford *Caregiver Stress and Staff Support in Illness, Dying, and Bereavement*. Oxford: University Press.

Small, N., Froggatt, K. and Downs, M. (2007) *Living and Dying with Dementia: Dialogues about Palliative Care*. Oxford: Oxford University Press. This book draws on narratives of personal experience and examples of care initiatives; person-centred care is highlighted as one of the most innovative approaches to understanding the needs of people with dementia.

Thomson, N. (2011) Workplace well-being: a psychosocial perspective, in I. Renzenbrink, (ed.) *Caregiver Stress and Staff Support in Illness, Dying, and Bereavement*. Oxford: Oxford University Press.

Weinstein, J. (2008) *Working with Loss, Death and Bereavement: A Guide for Social Workers*. London: Sage Publications.

Wenham, M. (2008) *My Donkey Body*. Oxford: Monarch Books.

Worden, J. W. (1996) *Children and Grief: When a Parent Dies*. New York: Guilford.

World Health Organization (2011) *Palliative Care for Older People: Better Practices*. Geneva: WHO.

Worden, J. W. (2001) *Grief Counselling and Grief Therapy*, 3rd edn. Hove: Bruner-Routledge. This is a key text for those working with bereaved people.

12 Conclusion: The future of social work with adults

Georgina Koubel

In recent times, social work has been described variously as being at a 'crossroads' (Brindle 2012), in a state of 'transformation' (Adams *et al*. 2005) or as being at a 'watershed' (according to the final report of the Social Work Reform Board 2009, in Dickens 2011). However, as Dickens goes on to say, this is nothing new for social work. As we have seen, the evolution and modernization of social work has entailed a process of almost continuous change and development as social work seeks to encapsulate and accommodate its role through the changing context of social policy which forms and defines it.

The changes that have taken place since the development of the mixed economy with the involvement of both the state and the marketplace in the provision of welfare and social care services have, of course, had significant implications for social work with adults. In Carey's view this has led to a reduced role for practitioners.

> The consequences for social work practitioners have been many and have included adherence to numerous (and typically convoluted) administrative procedures and protocols, the rationalization of social work practice, which has led to intense deskilling and the virtual removal of therapeutic interventions and service provision.
>
> (Carey 2008: 919)

While those groups and services outlined in *Modernizing Social Services* (DH 1998) still form the majority of those who need to access social work and social services – and therefore the key areas covered in this book – the value of a book written mainly by practitioners and service users is that it looks beyond these broad categories to the narratives and stories of the people who actually use and provide such support services. Although practitioners are clearly influenced, and sometimes restricted, by prevailing legislation, policies and procedures, there are also many accounts of positive experiences informed by key social work values of respect, empowerment and person-centred engagement (Koubel and Bungay 2009) which have benefited both service users and practitioners.

One area that has become increasingly compelling is the need for social workers to be able to develop skills of critical reflection and analysis within the context of their work roles and remits. Within a fast-changing and challenging health and social care environment, there is no simple or uncontested role for social work and social care practitioners. Practitioners have to be able to account for the decisions they make within the context of competing demands around rights, risks and responsibilities (Koubel and Bungay 2012) and reflective practice is one way of ensuring that those decisions are conscious, transparent and accessible to service users as well as to managers and practitioners from other disciplines.

As Thompson and Thompson (2008) say, it is all too easy for a notion like reflective practice to become oversimplified and to be applied, if at all, in a way that is superficial and uncritical, in the sense that it does not really stand back and examine the complexities involved in practice. They argue that reflective practice is not simply a matter of stopping for a few minutes to think about what you have just done, neither is it a tick box exercise or a luxury that we can't afford. Many practitioners would contend that lack of time is the main obstacle to reflection but it seems clear that because rather than despite the limits and restrictions that put so much pressure on professionals, the need for time and space for reflection is greater than ever.

Donald Schon (1983) suggests that often practitioners carry out quite adequate levels of practice without being consciously aware of the knowledge, skills and values they are using. He calls this process *reflection-in-action* and for many experienced practitioners this is their general mode of activity. However, as you have seen in the accounts of several of the authors in this book, there is a real danger that this will lead to assumptions that what has worked in the past will always be sufficient and this can lead in turn to unthinking, unvarying practice that does not really take account of situations that do not meet the pre-formed notions or prescriptive ways of working that the practitioner may carry in his or her head. This can be particularly disempowering for service users. To address this, Schon identifies the importance of *reflection-on-action*, the space required to evaluate a piece of work, to look at the integration of theory and practice and to identify changes in knowledge, skills or values that are required to carry out more effective practice in the future.

For social work with adults to continue to progress and develop in the face of the changes that are facing it, one of the most valuable aspects of reflection is the ability for practitioners to become critically aware of the knowledge, skills and values that inform their practice. Being critically aware means not just being conscious of one's own beliefs and possibly prejudices and how these might affect practice but also being proactive in questioning the 'taken for granted' in the organizational and wider political context as it affects social work with adults. This *reflexive practice,* as it is known, offers a way for conscientious practice which consciously places the individual relationship with the service user at the heart of the social work engagement while also being aware of the political and ideological context of that engagement.

It seems to me more important than ever that the fundamental ethics and values (Banks 2006) that underpin practice with adults in social work do not get buried beneath a swathe of policies, procedures and legal documents so that the individual gets lost within the process. Reflection is a vital aspect of retaining the capacity to stand back and critically examine practice, including our own practice with adults who use services. Thompson and Thompson (2008) further suggest there is a need for *reflection-before-action* and I would suggest that this is something that many practitioners may do already but which can be brought to the surface with a model that makes this process more conscious and explicit. This is the model discussed in Koubel and Bungay (2012), which offers a framework that may be particularly relevant for those undertaking social work with adults.

PREPARED: a reflective model for integrated practice

This model is based on a notion of a number of elements which make up ethical practice; it makes a conscious and deliberate attempt to promote the views and rights of people who come into contact with health and social care services. The model highlights the need for consciously reflective, self-aware, accountable practitioners who are trying to work sensitively and effectively in complex situations. 'PREPARED' is an acronym of the essential features of what good professional practice should look like.

Professional: this requires practitioners to be aware of policies/procedures, be boundaried in relationships with service users but not distant or prescriptive; we should be proud of our own profession and the knowledge, skills and values of social work but we also need to be critically aware of our own roles and beliefs and how they might affect the interaction.

Respectful: being respectful requires that we genuinely value different perspectives, that we need to be aware of the impact of the cultures and experiences of service users, carers and colleagues; it may involve the challenging of prejudices and stereotypes to ensure that an individual's dignity and rights are not compromised.

Evidence-based: there are some discussions and divisions about what evidence-based practice really means within social work but there is no argument about the need to be up to date with relevant knowledge, research and theoretical materials and for professionals to be thinking constructively about how these can be applied in practice.

Participatory: participation and partnership, as we have seen, can be difficult to get right. However, this element of the model requires that we all need to be ethical, to engage as far as possible honestly and in partnership with service users and other participants; and to ensure that any interventions are proportional and fair and the least restrictive possible.

Alert: there is a risk of passive acceptance of policies and procedures that may not be suitable for everyone. This aspect of the model requires practitioners to be actively engaged in thinking as well as doing in practice, and to be critically aware of different accountabilities and values and their significance for positive, person-centred practice.

Reflective: all practice benefits from the ability to use reflection to weigh up and review rights, risks and responsibilities; to use supervision or support to increase self-awareness and to ensure that social work with adults never becomes routine or unconsidered.

Empowering: power and empowerment have been explored at length in this book. We need to be consciously aware of how professional power can support or disempower those who use services and consider the power dynamics inherent in any intervention.

Decisive: know when and how to be dynamic and decisive – don't just drift.

The model that is presented here is one that highlights the need for practice with adult service users to be mindful, respectful, creative and culturally sensitive (Laird 2008). Based on the accounts in this book, it highlights some of the areas raised by various contributors in thinking about relationships between service users and practitioners in the context of interprofessional working and the developing landscape of health and social work/social care. No model can encompass all the complexities of practice but having such a model can help us to be consciously aware of the constituents of good practice. This model offers an opportunity for practitioners to think constructively about their relationships with each other and with service users and all the other stakeholders who may be involved in the case of a particular individual who uses services.

The personalization agenda (Gardner 2011) has brought to the fore in a different way some of the age-old arguments about the rights and needs of service users. Questions of the 'deserving' and the 'underserving' among those who receive services are very much part of the discussion again, as if these concepts had not been effectively challenged since the days of the Poor Laws and the workhouses that were discussed in Chapter 1. There is a risk that changes to the benefit systems envisaged in current legislation are likely to penalize disabled people who have recently been able to use personal budgets to increase control over the quality of their lives. It is particularly important that those who engage in social work with adults do not get caught up in the process of stigmatizing and shaming those who use services but instead stand firm in promoting the rights of people who use social services. The balance of rights, risks and responsibilities between the individual and the state is in the process of change, and it is likely that social workers may be held to account for any decisions that make society feel uncomfortable with the consequences.

> The world outside practice, which does not recognise the complexity involved in working with the variety of adults who use services, continues to expect that somehow it should be possible to balance perfectly the relationships between rights and risks, autonomy and capacity, vulnerability and choice. While these expectations will continue to challenge the best intentions of critical and conscientious practitioners, all professionals will need to be acutely aware of their own values and attitudes, the knowledge, powers and responsibilities they hold and share, and the significance of these for promoting or inhibiting the rights and responsibilities of the people (and their carers and networks) who they encounter in their professional capacity.
>
> (Koubel and Bungay 2012: 251)

Conclusion

From the experience of editing this book, I would say that two key themes have emerged for me that I think are particularly relevant for social work and particularly social work with adults.

Similarity and difference

The first of these is the notion of 'similarity and difference'. By actually hearing the words of people in various chapters who have been in the position of being marginalized or 'othered' because of their race or their disability, it is striking that the message from each of these is of 'I am the same as you but also (because of my support needs or particular experiences of discrimination) different.' This is not necessarily an easy concept to unravel but it appears essential for us to understand the relevance for social work with adults. It seems to me to be about the recognition that, despite the diversity that makes each of us unique, there is also a common humanity that binds us. As well as valuing and appreciating the differences that contribute to a multicultural and multi-faith society we should not lose sight of the common threads that connect us with each other. In many ways this links back to our very first question about what social work really is. Is it a source of practical assistance to people so that they can manage independently of the state or is it a process of interdependence, as Louise Watch suggests, that sees us all as reliant on each other and therefore potentially working together to make society more inclusive and life-enhancing for all its citizens?

In the end, as Shakespeare says, it all comes down to the values of empowerment and anti-oppressive practice. People who use services in this book have argued strongly for the importance of recognizing the strengths they bring and the similarity of their aspirations to participate fully in society. Social work should be about promoting the broadest possible range of human opportunities for adults who use services by providing adequate, appropriate and timely support.

> Disabled people in an enabling society can also have access to this fulfilment, as parents, carers, workers, partners, artists and members of the community or simply as people who receive the love, help and support of others.
>
> (Shakespeare 2000: 79)

Choice, preferences and anti-discriminatory practice

The other message that is emphasized and explored mainly by practitioners is the difficulty society appears to find in actually tailoring services to the very different needs of particular service users. Is it acceptable to insist on the provision of individual budgets for people who have a preference for services to be provided for them rather than having, perhaps at a point where they are ill and tired, to engage with the more empowering but more demanding process of personalization?

Despite the research findings, it would be wrong to assume that this is an issue only for older people while all younger people with physical or learning disabilities would embrace the opportunity to manage their own budgets. If we are really committed to the rights and wishes of the individual, surely social work with adults should be about taking sufficient time to form relationships that can provide the basis for informed choices that suit the strengths and needs of each individual.

Teater (2010) further stresses the importance of the strengths perspective, of being aware of the importance of personal choice in the context of cultural considerations and developing collaborative relationships with adults who use services. She advises us not to make assumptions; particularly in relation to someone's cultural identity we cannot always expect to be the expert. She also highlights the importance of critical reflection, which she sees as taking a 'position of curiosity'.

> In valuing the culture of which clients are members, social workers must take the position of curiosity and participate in a dialogue with the client about how the ethnicity and culture shapes and influences the client's actions and behaviours.
>
> (Teater 2010: 81)

This links back to the idea that social work's commitment to the ideals of anti-discriminatory and anti-oppressive practice is inherently linked with the need for reflective and reflexive practice. Clifford and Burke clarify the connection between thinking reflexively, which involves trying to understand the position of the other person, and being prepared to act in ways that take their humanity and/or needs into account as well as your own.

> Anti-oppressive ethical perspectives require the interrogation of the worker's social position, behaviour, experiences and motives, in relation to the service users' perspectives and the dialogue between them.
>
> (Clifford and Burke 2009: 161)

So to come back to the original question, what is social work and what will the future for social work with adults look like? With changes in the demographics of older people and people with disabilities alongside the financial restrictions being imposed by the coalition government it is difficult to see the future shape of statutory social work with adults very clearly at all. The value of this book is that rather than presenting an idealized picture of what social work with adults should look like, it identifies and presents real-life challenges and dilemmas that affect adults using social work and social care services. However, reality does not mean acceptance of the second-rate. These real-life situations are enhanced and transformed by a strong commitment to social work values and to the ideals of empowerment, partnership and antioppressive practice. In dealing with new policy agendas in the context of globalization, financial and resource limitations and community fragmentation, practitioners not only within adult services but throughout social work are having to face the challenge of sustaining creative practice in highly regulated settings (Adams *et al.* 2005).

The question for the future shape of social work with adults takes us back to the dilemma between the ethics of care and the ethics of justice. Perhaps it is time to recognize that this is potentially a false dichotomy. It is true that without the radical and pioneering work of the disability movement and civil rights organizations the political changes and developments that have permeated society would not have been possible while the promise offered by the welfare state of care 'from the cradle to the grave' may be no longer viable. But we have by no means built the perfect world yet and in the mean time the skills and values of social work are still essential to enhance the lives of many people who use services (Trevithick 2005). Social workers are still required to assume the role of safeguarding (Scragg and Mantell 2011) individuals who may not be able to make their own decisions and there is a particular remit to ensure the rights of people who may still be disempowered, marginalized, abused and oppressed because of their position in society.

At an international social work conference in Stockholm (July 2012), there were many calls for social work to resurrect its radical base and march beside the variety of users and providers of services to demand better and more accessible services for all. In the past, one of the criticisms of radical social work has been its inability to engage constructively with the conflicts and dilemmas of practice.

Reflective practice can provide a way of managing the emotional impact of social work and a method for promoting collaborative strategies for managing both personal learning and the tensions and dichotomies that arise in the current context of practice in adult services (Knott and Scragg 2010). A commitment to reflective practice provides an opportunity for practitioners to look critically at the political context of social work while also using a model like the PREPARED model to constructively analyse the integration of social work theory and values in their day-to-day work with people who use services.

In many ways, with the move towards further restrictions in the services available to adults and the rationalization of spending in all areas of social work and social care, the need for social workers, service users and other practitioners to develop empowering, supportive partnerships where they can work together to promote real choices and opportunities and contest oppressive constructions of service users is more urgent than ever.

References and further reading

Adams, R., Dominelli, L. and Payne, M. (2005) *Social Work Futures: Crossing Boundaries, Transforming Practice.* Basingstoke: Palgrave Macmillan.

Banks, S. (2006) *Values and Ethics in Social Work*, 4th edn. Basingstoke: Palgrave Macmillan.

Brindle, D. (2012) Social work: step up to speak out, *Guardian*, 25 July.

Carey, M. (2008) Everything must go? The privatization of state social work, *British Journal of Social Work*, 38 (5): 18–35.

Clifford, D. and Burke, B. (2009) *Anti-Oppressive Ethics and Values in Social Work*. Basingstoke: Palgrave Macmillan.

DH (Department of Health) (1998) *Modernizing Social Services*, London: HMSO.

Dickens, J. (2011) Social work in England at a watershed – as always: from the Seebohm Report to the Social Work Task Force, *British Journal of Social Work*, 41 (1): 22–39.

Gardner, A. (2011) *Personalisation in Social Work*. Exeter: Learning Matters.

Knott, C. and Scragg, T. (2010) *Reflective Practice in Social Work*. Exeter: Learning Matters.

Koubel, G. and Bungay, H. (2009) *The Challenge of Person-centred Care: An Interprofessional Perspective*. Basingstoke: Palgrave Macmillan.

Koubel, G. and Bungay, H. (2012) *Rights, Risks and Responsibilities*. Basingstoke: Palgrave Macmillan.

Laird, S. (2008) *Anti-oppressive Social Work*. London: Sage Publications.

Schon, D. A. (1983) *The Reflective Practitioner: How Professionals Think in Action*. New York: Basic Books.

Scragg, T. and Mantell, A. (eds) (2011) *Safeguarding Adults in Social Work*, 2nd edn. Exeter: Learning Matters.

Shakespeare, T. (2000) *Help*. Birmingham: Venture Press.

Teater, B. (2010) *An Introduction to Applying Social Work Theories and Methods*. Maidenhead: Open University Press/McGraw Hill.

Thompson, S. and Thompson, N. (2008) *The Critically Reflective Practitioner*. Basingstoke: Palgrave Macmillan.

Trevithick, P. (2005) *Social Work Skills: A Practice Handbook*. Maidenhead: McGraw Hill/Open University Press.

Index

Social Work with Older People
Approaches to Person-Centred Practice

Barbara Hall and Terry Scragg (Eds)

9780335244201 (Paperback)
2012

eBook also available

Understanding how to practice effectively with older people is a key component of the social work degree, and an area that is growing in importance due to an increasingly ageing society.

This textbook provides readers with a basic knowledge of the legislation, policy, theory and research necessary for working in this area.

Key features:

- Focuses on the diverse and common aspects of social work with older people
- Authored by an academic / practitioner team with considerable knowledge of social work practice within the public, private and third sector
- Explores aspects of the experience of being an older person and how practitioners can work to make differences to older people's lives

www.openup.co.uk